Roots
of the Western
Tradition

A Short History
of the Ancient World

EIGHTH EDITION

C. *Warren Hollister*

Guy *MacLean Rogers*
Western Connecticut State University

Boston   Burr Ridge, IL   Dubuque, IA   Madison, WI   New York
San Francisco   St. Louis   Bangkok   Bogotá   Caracas   Kuala Lumpur
Lisbon   London   Madrid   Mexico City   Milan   Montreal   New Delhi
Santiago   Seoul   Singapore   Sydney   Taipei   Toronto

McGraw-Hill
Higher Education

Published by McGraw-Hill, a business unit of The McGraw-Hill Companies, Inc., 1221 Avenue of the Americas, New York, NY 10020. Copyright © 2008, 2005, 1996, 1991, 1982, 1977, 1966 by The McGraw-Hill Companies, Inc. All rights reserved. No part of this publication may be reproduced or distributed in any form or by any means, or stored in a database or retrieval system, without the prior written consent of The McGraw-Hill Companies, Inc., including, but not limited to, any network or other electronic storage or transmission, or broadcast for distance learning.

7 8 9 0 QVS/QVS 18 17 16 15 14

ISBN: 978-0-07-340694-7
MHID: 0-07-340694-5

Vice president and editor-in-chief: *Michael Ryan*
Publisher: *Lisa Moore*
Sponsoring editor: *Jon-David Hague*
Development editor: *Sora Kim*
Marketing manager: *Pamela Cooper*
Marketing coordinator: *Clare Cashen*
Production editor: *Anne Fuzellier*
Art director: *Jeanne M. Schreiber*
Design manager: *Margarite Reynolds*
Art manager: *Robin Mouat*
Art editor: *Emma Ghiselli*
Photo research manager: *Brian Pecko*
Illustrator: *Mapping Specialists*
Production supervisor: *Louis Swaim*
Composition: 10/12 Palatino by Newgen
Printing: Quad/Graphics
Cover image: Ancient Egyptian Hieroglyphics with Standing Woman. © Royalty-Free/Corbis

Library of Congress Cataloging-in-Publication Data

Hollister, C. Warren (Charles Warren), 1930-
   Roots of the western tradition : a short history of the ancient world / C. Warren Hollister, Guy MacLean Rogers.—8th ed.
      p. cm.
   Includes index.
   ISBN-13: 978-0-07-340694-7 (alk. paper)
   ISBN-10: 0-07-340694-5 (alk. paper)
   1. History, Ancient. I. Rogers, Guy MacLean. II. Title.
D59.H64 2007
930—dc22   2007034258

The Internet addresses listed in the text were accurate at the time of publication. The inclusion of a Web site does not indicate an endorsement by the authors or McGraw-Hill, and McGraw-Hill does not guarantee the accuracy of the information presented at these sites.

www.mhhe.com

For Honus, Ty, and Neko

About the Authors

C. WARREN HOLLISTER, late professor of History and chair of medieval studies at the University of California, Santa Barbara, received his BA from Harvard University and his MA and PhD from UCLA. A former fellow of the Medieval Academy of America, the Royal Historical Society (London), the Guggenheim Foundation, and the Medieval Academy of Ireland, he was 1984 Program Chair and Vice President for Teaching of the American Historical Association. He also served as president of the Pacific Coast Conference on British Studies, research fellow of Merton College Oxford, fellow of the Australian National University, cochair of the University of California Press Editorial Committee, and chair of the National Development Committee for the College Board Advanced Placement Test in European History. He served as president of the North American Conference on British Studies; the American Historical Association, Pacific Coast Branch; the Medieval Association of the Pacific; and the International Charles Homer Haskins Society.

Professor Hollister's books include *Monarchy, Magnates, and Institutions in the Anglo-Norman World*; *Medieval Europe: A Short History*; and *The Making of England 55 B.C. to 1399*. His books have been translated into a number of languages including Chinese, Thai, and Swedish. He also published more than forty scholarly articles on medieval history and coauthored a children's fantasy, *The Moons of Meer*. His graduate research seminars at UC Santa Barbara produced numerous published articles by his students.

Professor Hollister served on the editorial boards of virtually all the major scholarly journals in the field: *Albion, American Historical Review, Journal of British Studies, Journal of Medieval History, Medieval Prosopography*, and *Viator*. He was honored with Guggenheim, Fulbright, American Council of Learned Societies, Social Science Research Council, and American Philosophical Society fellowships and with two multiyear National Endowment for the Humanities grants.

Among Professor Hollister's other honors were the UC Santa Barbara Faculty Research Lectureship, the UC Santa Barbara Faculty Teaching Prize for 1983, the 1987 Denis Bethell Memorial Lectureship of the Medieval Academy of Ireland (Dublin), the 1988 Wilkinson Memorial Lectureship of the University of Toronto, the 1990 Landsdowne Memorial Lectureship of the University of Victoria, the Triennial Book Prize of the Conference on British Studies, the E. Harris Harbison National Award for Distinguished Teaching (Danforth Foundation, Princeton), and the Walter D. Love Memorial Prize for the best scholarly article in the field of British and Commonwealth history or literature.

GUY MacLEAN ROGERS holds a first-class honors degree in Ancient History from University College London and a PhD in Classics from Princeton University. He has been the recipient of numerous grants and fellowships in support of his research, including ones from the National Endowment for the Humanities, the Fulbright Fellowship program, and the American Philosophical Society. In 1997 he held a senior visiting fellowship at All Souls College Oxford. His first book, *The Sacred Identity of Ephesos: Foundation Myths of A Roman City*, won the 1989 Routledge Ancient History Prize. In the fall of 2004 his biography *Alexander: The Ambiguity of Greatness* was published by Random House. Greek and Russian translations appeared in 2005 and 2006. He was Chairman of the Department of History of Wellesley College from 1997 to 2001. In 2006 he was appointed the first Macricostas Chair of Hellenic and Modern Greek studies at Western Connecticut State University. He grew up and still lives in Litchfield County, Connecticut.

Contents

Part One
THE ANCIENT NEAR EAST

Part Two
ANCIENT GREECE

Part Three
ANCIENT ROME

List of Illustrations

List of Maps

List of Biographical Sketches

List of Time Lines

Preface

The text of the new, eighth edition of *Roots of the Western Tradition: A Short History of the Ancient World* takes into account the most recent scholarship on the ancient world from c. 3500 B.C. until the later Roman Empire. The chapters on the history of the ancient Near East and Greece have undergone more substantial revision than those on Rome in light of new archaeological discoveries and the availability of major new syntheses. Throughout the revision, I have tried to maintain a narrative style in keeping with the clear, direct, and lively prose of C. Warren Hollister's original text. Dr. Nancy Thompson of The Metropolitan Museum of Art in New York read through the revised text of the work many times, curing it of many faults. I alone remain responsible for any errors. Updated bibliography and links to relevant Web sites have been added to the "Suggested Readings" at the end of each part of the history.

It is a pleasure to record my thanks to Jon-David Hague of McGraw-Hill for asking me to revise and update the seventh edition of Hollister's short history of the ancient world. I also would like to express my appreciation for the assistance provided by Sora Lisa Kim of McGraw-Hill as we worked our way through the editorial and production processes. The staff of McGraw-Hill epitomized professionalism and courtesy. At the suggestion of external reviewers, a glossary of terms has been added to this edition. Terms included in the glossary appear in bold font within the text.

I am grateful as well to my History 200 students at Wellesley College and my History 198 students at Western Connecticut State University who provided valuable feedback about my revisions to the book. Finally, in keeping with the spirit of Hollister's preface to his sixth edition, I too welcome comments about the revised, eighth edition. Letters are still welcome—as are e-mail communications.

Guy MacLean Rogers
Grogers@Wellesley.edu

Introduction

Some people are rather like ants. They work together at tasks that ensure the survival and prosperity of the anthill, never wondering why. Ants have several good excuses. They are governed primarily by instinct, not by an evolving culture that must be absorbed over a period of years. Were some super-ant to develop an interest in anthill history, or in the study of comparative anthills, the result would be most discouraging. Individual anthills come and go, but anthill society does not change through time. One anthill has been much like another since the days of the First Ants.

Human beings, on the other hand, are products of sweeping cultural changes that stretch back thousands of years. Without understanding such changes we cannot understand ourselves. In our own time, the pace has become so swift that some dull-witted people see no point in studying history at all. Because the past is so different from the present, they argue, it has nothing to do with us. Anything that happened before 1985 (or 1970, 1960, or whatever date one picks) cannot possibly be worth knowing about. On this same threadbare reasoning, one needn't bother with such old-fashioned and impractical things as Shakespearian drama, nineteenth-century novels, baroque music, Gothic architecture, Renaissance painting, archaeology, or astronomy. Who cares where we are in time and space, or where we came from? The anthill beckons!

Although this book is a history of the cultural antecedents of Western civilization, it is not implied that non-Western civilizations are of less significance or less worth. There are, however, compelling reasons for American college and university students to study the Western tradition, just as they study the history of the United States. American history and Western civilization are by no means uniquely important in the course of human events. But they are important to us; they illuminate our own pasts.

Virtually all Americans are, in some sense, participants in the Western cultural tradition—a tradition so encompassing that we scarcely notice it, as a fish does not notice the ocean in which it swims. Western civilization extends back some 1,300 years or more into the European past. It rose from the ruins of a still older civilization, the Graeco-Roman, from which it derived much of its political, artistic, and intellectual framework. Western civilization also drew heavily from the Judeo-Christian tradition of the ancient Near East, which was inspired in part by the still earlier thought and practice of Mesopotamia, Egypt, and the lands between. Graeco-Roman civilization was itself a child of earlier cultures: Minoan, Etruscan, and, behind them, Egyptian and Mesopotamian. Like an immense chain, this sequence of civilizations extends backward some 6,000 years to Mesopotamia's emergence from the Stone Age and forward into an unmapped future.

This book will deal with Western civilization's cultural antecedents—the civilizations of the ancient Near East, Greece, and Rome. These early cultures contributed decisively to the rise of the West. Without them we would not exist. They are the deep roots from which our civilization has grown.

PART ONE

The Ancient Near East

THE ANCIENT NEAR EAST: AN OVERVIEW

Some of the deepest cultural roots of Western civilization are to be found in the ancient civilizations of the **Near East.** The earliest of those civilizations emerged during the fourth millennium B.C. (4000–3000) in the river valleys of Egypt and **Mesopotamia.** Civilization then spread northwestward into Asia Minor (roughly modern Turkey) and southwestward along the eastern coast of the Mediterranean Sea. There, the Israelites, whose deeply original monotheistic religion has contributed decisively to Western and world culture, established a powerful but short-lived state. In time, they and other Near Eastern peoples fell under the control of a succession of great empires—Assyrian, Chaldean, and Persian—each of which, in turn, united much, or all, of the region under a single monarch.

The Mesopotamian and Egyptian civilizations are the oldest in the world. About 4000 B.C., a highly organized society began to emerge in Mesopotamia (roughly modern Iraq), largely as a result of the diking of two neighboring rivers, the Tigris and the Euphrates, and the clearing of the great valley they formed. Within a few centuries, this diking and clearing process was repeated in Egypt. It later occurred in the Indus Valley of India and in China. But, for Western civilization, Mesopotamia and Egypt—and the Near Eastern cultures that succeeded them—hold special significance because of their influence on the direct cultural antecedents of medieval and modern Europe: the civilizations of Greece and Rome.

Near Eastern History in Comparative Perspective

	Mesopotamia	Egypt	Israel	Near East in General
All dates are B.C. and approximate.				
4000	Formation of city-states (4000 ff.)			
3000		First Dynasties (3100–2686)		
2500		Old Kingdom (2686–2181)		Ebla flourishes (2400–2250)
2250	Akkadian Empire Dynasty of Sargon (2340–2200) Empire of Ur (2119–2004)	First Intermediate Period (2181–2040) Middle Kingdom (2040–1730)		
2000	Old Babylonian Empire (2000–1530)			
1900				
1800				Emergence of Indo-Europeans (1700–1500)
1700		Second Intermediate Period: Hyksos (1730–1550)		Hittites flourish (1700–1200)
1600		New Kingdom (1550–1080)		
1500	Kassites (1530–1155)			

4

Date (BCE)	Egypt	Israel / Biblical	Mesopotamia	Near East Powers
1400	Akhenaten (1364–1347)	Bondage in Egypt biblical dates (?1450–1300)		Beginning of Iron Age (1200)
1300		Moses and Sinai period (?1300–1260)		
1200		Era of Judges (1230–1020)		
1100	Post-Empire period (1069 ff.)			
1000		United Kingdom (1020–922)		
900		Political split: Israel and Judah (922–721)		Assyrian Empire (745–612)
800		Israel falls to Assyrians (721)	Assyrian Empire (745–612)	
700	Temporary Assyrian conquest (671)		New Babylonian Empire (Chaldeans) (612–539)	Lydians (fl. 683–546)
600		Judah falls: Babylonian Captivity (587–538)		Medes (fl. 612–549); Chaldeans (fl. 612–539)
500	Persian conquest (525)	Return to Palestine (539)	Persian Empire (539–330)	Persian Empire (539–330)
400				
300	Conquest by Alexander (332)		Conquest by Alexander (330)	Conquest by Alexander (332–330)

CHAPTER 1

From Stone Age to Civilization

Prehistory and the Development of *Homo sapiens*

All dates are B.C. and approximate.

5 million	Humanoids
2.5–1.8 million	*Homo habilis*
130,000–75,000	*Homo sapiens* evolves
1.5 million–20,000	Paleolithic era
8000	Neolithic culture appears

THE OLD STONE AGE

Relative to the total time span of the human race, civilization is a latecomer. The earliest-known **humanoid** bone fragment, consisting simply of a lower jaw and two molars, is some 5 million years old. It was discovered in 1984, in fossilized form, by archaeologists at Tabran in northern Kenya. At least another 2 million years elapsed between the time of the Tabran jawbone and the emergence of the first toolmakers. In the early 1990s, a team of archaeologists discovered in an Ethiopian gully a collection of primitive stone tools dating back at least 2.5 million years—half a million years earlier than any previous finds. The tools are very crude: forty-eight small, sharp-edged slivers of volcanic stone and three fist-size cutters, probably designed to hack through the skins of animals and to butcher their carcasses. The concentration of these tools at a single site suggests a home base for a band of prowling hunters. Thus, humanoids first appeared and became toolmakers some 5 million years ago in what is now called the continent of Africa.

Although other primates such as chimpanzees (with whom humans have roughly 98 percent of their genetic material in common) use tools, of all the creatures on earth, humans alone are capable of making tools and using them purposefully. Anthropologists describe the earliest toolmakers collectively as **Homo habilis,** "the skillful man." The toolmaking breakthrough of *Homo habilis* was made possible by a relatively large brain and agile hands, cunningly contrived for the grasping of objects. But the earliest humans differed markedly from people of today in height, brain size, and general physical makeup. Gradually, across millions of years, brains grew and tools improved. People learned how to make fire and control it; they manufactured stone axes; they invented coherent speech; they sought to tame the savage, perverse forces of nature by developing religions. *Homo habilis* developed slowly, through uneven stages, into **Homo sapiens,** "the man who knows"—the prototype of all races living today. (Actually, specialists in prehistory refer to our own subspecies as *homo sapiens sapiens,* "the man who knows who knows," a cumbersome phrase that recent research has called into question. It will be avoided in this book.) Other humanoid prototypes with whom *homo sapiens* shared a common ancestor, such as Neanderthal, lost out in the grand evolutionary competition, disappearing some 28,000 years ago, after splitting off from *homo sapiens* genetically around 370,000 years ago.[*]

Long after the emergence of *Homo sapiens* some 75,000 years ago, the human economy continued to be based, as always before, on hunting, fishing, and gathering wild foods. For well over 99 percent of its existence on Earth, humanity lived in what has been called the **Paleolithic era,** or Old Stone Age. Across this vast span of time, human life remained short and desperately insecure, and cultural change occurred slowly. But change there was. Toward the end of the Paleolithic era (about 30,000 to 10,000 years ago), a *Homo sapiens* subspecies living on the continent of Europe, known as **Cro-Magnon man,** carried the art of hunting to new levels of efficiency. A Cro-Magnon site in France testifies to the killing of tens of thousands of horses, and a contemporary site in the Czech Republic contains the skeletons of a thousand hairy mammoths.

[*]At present, scientists are engaged in research to determine the complete sequence of the Neanderthal genome. The results will help us understand better when, how, and why *homo sapiens* and Neanderthal parted company and how much of our genetic makeup we owe to Neanderthal.

One of the dazzling achievements of Cro-Magnon culture was its cave paintings. In caverns such as those at Lascaux in France and Altamira in Spain, walls are ablaze with boldly realistic portrayals of animals—the woolly rhinoceros, the reindeer, the hairy mammoth—painted with assurance and skill and enlivened with bright earth-based colors. These drawings may well have had some magical intent, perhaps to aid in the hunt by depicting and thereby bewitching the hunted beasts. It has been suggested, on the basis of a more sophisticated understanding of the anthropology of hunter-gatherer societies, that the cave paintings may have served much the same purpose as dances and other rituals: to provide meaning and structure to life by creating and manipulating visual forms. The artists may well have intended to give visual expression to the interconnectedness of animal and human life. But whatever their purpose, the cave paintings occupy a unique place at the dawn of human art. The mastery of draftsmanship they display would not be paralleled for thousands of years.

The inhabitants of late Paleolithic Europe were sculptors as well. They were fond of producing stone statuettes of women, often with exaggerated breasts, buttocks, and genitals. Archaeologists have somewhat optimistically referred to these figurines as "Venuses." Perhaps these statuettes represent a fertility goddess, or perhaps simply the general idea of fertility. The Venuses have in fact inspired an exotic flowering of conflicting scholarly theories. The statuettes have been interpreted as depictions of a bird-goddess, "the layer of the universal egg"; conversely, they have been seen as expressions of the essence of "womanness." Some specialists have used them to construct elaborate theories about a culture called "Old Europe," dominated by priestesses dedicated to the veneration of the creative principle of the fertility goddess "as Source and Giver of All." But, wisely, most modern archaeologists, ever suspicious of such imaginative reconstructions, are cautious about inferring the details of religious beliefs and practices from the artifacts of ancient preliterate societies. If, for example, no written sources had survived from the Middle Ages, one might wrongly have supposed from the abundance of statues of the Virgin Mary that the religion of medieval Europe had a female priesthood and centered on the worship of a goddess.

One late-Paleolithic Venus from southwestern France holds a bison horn shaped like a crescent moon and marked with thirteen lines. Similar groups of markings, found on the tusks of hairy mammoths, on rocks, on ivory staffs, and on the bones of animals and birds, suggest the possibility that late-Paleolithic peoples had developed a lunar calendar (of thirteen months per year) in order to plan their hunting and food-gathering by anticipating changes of season. If so, the inhabitants of late–Stone Age Europe were bringing their activities under a degree of rational control unknown to all previous ages of human existence.

The appearance of the reindeer and the hairy mammoth in late-Paleolithic art bears witness to an environment far colder than today's. The Cro-Magnons inhabited Europe during the last of a drawn-out series of glacial ages, when Arctic glaciers moved slowly southward to cover large portions of Europe, Asia, and North America with deep blankets of ice.

Gradually, between about 10,000 and 8000 B.C., the last glaciation receded to the Arctic. Europe grew warmer, and the garden lands of North Africa and the Near East underwent a long drying-out period. Reindeer migrated northward, never to return (or at most, as some suppose, returning one night a year). The woolly rhinoceros and hairy mammoth became extinct, living on only in the deserted caverns of Altamira and Lascaux. Cro-Magnon culture died out, too, as new peoples settled across Europe and the Near East, with new weapons, such as bows and arrows, and a new maritime technology that included canoes, nets, and fishing lines.

THE NEOLITHIC REVOLUTION

Around 8000 B.C., in a few localities in the Near East, the initial steps were taken toward the greatest revolution humanity had yet experienced: the development of agriculture. Very likely the revolution resulted from the ingenuity of women, who gathered wild grain and discovered the uses of seed while the men were off hunting. This momentous advance ushered in what is known as the **Neolithic era,** or New Stone Age, and has aptly been termed the "Neolithic Revolution."

The emergence of farming, together with the concurrent domestication of animals for food, enabled people to cease their incessant wandering. It is clear from specialist studies that over the course of the long Neolithic Revolution there were at least some hunters who farmed, as well as some farmers who hunted. Nevertheless, gradually, after 8000 B.C., people began to settle in large, permanent communities; to build durable shelters; and to control their own food supply (including, in particular, wheat and barley, sheep, pigs, cattle, and goat cheese). At the same time, however, the shift from a wandering, foraging existence to a settled communal life created a number of new problems—from social stratification to refuse disposal and the proliferation of epidemic diseases, little known among small nomadic bands but now fostered by crowded, unsanitary living conditions and spread by the development of inter-village and long-distance trade. Moreover, farmers are more vulnerable than are foragers to extremes in climate—excessive dry or wet spells and unseasonable freezes, floods, and storms. Some scholars have suggested that Paleolithic nomads were not only less socially and economically stratified but also healthier than their Neolithic successors, but that is something of a guess.

Whatever the case, the Neolithic Revolution spread gradually through the Near East and then, slowly and unevenly, into the lands beyond. (Other peoples, in China and in Central and South America, made the transition independently.) Wherever it occurred, the advent of agriculture and animal domestication transformed human life.

The new Neolithic villages required a more complex social organization. The inhabitants had to make rational plans to till the soil, breed and slaughter their animals, defend their homes and food against raiding expeditions, and appease their moody gods. The invention of pottery during the course of the Neolithic era made it possible to store and transport liquids and created the need for a new group of specialists—potters. Indeed, village life gave rise to an increasing specialization of labor needed to perform a variety of essential tasks. And the coordination of all these tasks required supervision and centralized direction. Community leaders emerged— chiefs or "big men"—and villages came to be dominated by an elite of warriors, administrators, and priests. The warriors possessed the weapons; the administrators gave the orders; the priests appeased the gods; and the others, having no authority, obeyed.

By the middle of the fifth millennium B.C. (c. 4500), Neolithic villages were scattered over the lands of present-day Iran, Iraq, Syria, Palestine, Turkey, and Egypt. By about 3800 B.C., they had spread across Europe. The earliest major Neolithic village thus far unearthed, at **Jericho** in Palestine, the lowest city on Earth (840 feet below sea level) and perhaps its oldest permanent settlement, has been dated by radiocarbon analysis to about 8000 B.C.*

Here, on an eight-acre site, some 2,000 inhabitants lived in round houses with cone-shaped roofs. Neolithic Jericho was dominated by a columned temple in which archaeologists have found numerous figurines of baked mud representing animals, a man, a woman, and an infant boy. Pottery has been found only in later levels of the site; in 7800 B.C., the pot had yet to be invented. Some thousand years later, Jericho had become a fortified town surrounded by a moat, stone walls, and towers. By then, commerce was flourishing, and "big men" were clearly in charge of things.

Pottery abounded in the village at **Çatal Hüyük**† in southern Turkey, a twenty-five-acre site dated to the period between 6500 and 6000 B.C. The villagers, who lived in closely clustered houses, wove wool into cloth, ate more varied food (peas, nuts, vegetable oil, apples, and honey, besides the usual grain cereals), and boasted a formidable weapons technology (sharper flint spearheads and arrowheads, daggers, and lances). Indeed, it is also likely that the inhabitants of Çatal Hüyük carved out a lucrative trade with other peoples in the Near East, based upon their access to obsidian in central Anatolia. During the past generation, a number of Neolithic villages have been discovered in Iran, some of which could be even older than Jericho, as they are smaller and more primitive. A much larger site, dating to 4500 B.C., has been found at **Tepe Yahya** in south-central Iran, containing pottery, bone-handled sickles, and a remarkable fertility symbol—a green stone penis carved in the shape of a woman. In Iraq, at **Jarmo,** a village about as old as Tepe Yahya, archaeologists have discovered stone bracelets, beads, and tools in such abundance and variety as to suggest that craft specialization was by then far advanced.

These Neolithic villages disclose successive revolutionary changes in human culture. By modern standards, the changes were slow. But judged by the span of human existence across the vast Paleolithic era, the invention of agriculture sparked a chain reaction:

---

*All living organisms, vegetable and animal, absorb a known amount of the radioactive isotope carbon 14 from their environment. After death, their carbon 14 atoms disintegrate at a known rate, making it possible to determine the approximate age of the organism by measuring the amount of carbon 14 remaining in it. The radiocarbon method is reasonably accurate for dates between about 65,000 B.C. and A.D. 1000.

†*Çatal* in Turkish designates an artificial, man-made mound. The Persian word for such a mound is *tepe;* the Arabic, *tell.*

animal domestication, temples, pottery, weaving, craft specialization, fearsome new weapons, and political centralization.

Across the fifth millennium, the technology of the Neolithic villages advanced step by step. The site at Jarmo discloses twelve separate levels of settlement, and the later levels attest clearly to a more varied craftsmanship. At Jarmo and elsewhere, materials that were not available locally (such as obsidian) suggest the burgeoning of interregional commerce. And by 4000 B.C., the inhabitants of some Neolithic villages were beginning to use copper tools.

We have now reached the threshold of "civilization." The coming millennium (4000–3000 B.C.) would see the building of the world's first cities, the development of large-scale irrigation systems in Mesopotamia and Egypt, the invention of writing, the first appearance of wheeled conveyances, the birth of the state, and the smelting of tin and copper into bronze, a much stronger metal than any known before. Thenceforth, throughout most of the Near East, bronze replaced stone as the material for weapons and tools. The Stone Age drew to an end at last, and the Bronze Age commenced (although where and when bronze was used varied).

THE COMING OF CIVILIZATION

"Civilization" has been defined in various ways. The word is derived from the Latin noun *civitas* (city) on the reasonable grounds that urban life is a major component of what we know as civilization. For, although city dwellers constituted only a minority of the population in the civilizations of antiquity, they usually dominated political and cultural life. The city or urban settlement was the focal point of political authority, tax collection, commerce, religious practice, intellectual activity, literature, and art (although, of course, at least some of these activities also were carried out in the innumerable villages of the ancient world). Townspeople were thus a privileged group that had won release from the age-long burdens of gathering and producing food. Whether rich or poor, they owed their existence to the agricultural abundance of the surrounding countryside, which they siphoned off through taxes, tribute, and the profits of commerce. A critic might reflect that they had domesticated their farmworkers in much the same way that earlier peoples had domesticated their animals.

Another characteristic of the earliest civilizations was their use of metal weapons and tools. The birth of civilization is more or less concurrent with the coming of the Bronze Age. Since bronze was rare and therefore expensive, its use was limited largely to the military and priestly elites, thus contributing further to the social stratification of the emerging cities. Indeed, since stone and metal were both extremely rare in southern Mesopotamia especially, most tools had to be imported, and the cities were built largely of clay bricks.

Writing was still another mark of civilization, and it, too, tended to be monopolized by members of the urban elite. At the flourishing Mesopotamian city of **Uruk** in about 3500 B.C. (which eventually occupied an area of approximately 210 hectares, or 518 acres), temple scribes were keeping accounts in the first known examples of picture writing. With the coming of written records, humanity acquired the means of documenting its affairs, and its past, with tremendously greater precision and reliability than ever before. The dim world of campfire legend began to brighten with the oncoming dawn of recorded history.

During the fourth millennium B.C., writing, bronze metallurgy, and city life emerged concurrently—first in Mesopotamia, then in Iran and Egypt. The process was duplicated around 2500 B.C. in the Indus Valley in India, and again some 800 or 1,000 years later on the banks of the Huang Ho (Yellow River) in China. Egypt and Iran may have been influenced by the slightly earlier Mesopotamian example, and Mesopotamia may also have provided certain stimuli to the earliest civilization along the Indus River (although the issue is far from settled), but Chinese civilization appears to have owed nothing whatever to external stimuli. And the emergence of civilizations in the Americas, much later on, was obviously unaided by Afro-Asian models, despite far-fetched theories to the contrary proposing transatlantic crossings by raft or the intervention of helpful aliens from outer space who ignored the Prime Directive.

Similarly, as a result of a more meticulous application of the radiocarbon dating method, it is now clear that the inhabitants of central and western Europe can also be credited with the independent development of copper and bronze metallurgy and with the creation—without guidance from the Near East—of vast, astronomically oriented burial chambers and religious monuments such as Stonehenge in southern Britain and the remarkable Newgrange Tumulus in Ireland. Transalpine Europe cannot be described as a "civilization" until Roman times, because the earlier Europeans had neither cities nor writing. But an extraordinary archaeological excavation of a cemetery at Varna, near the Black Sea in Bulgaria, has unearthed a treasure trove of copper and gold burial goods—ornaments and tools—dating to about 4600–4200 B.C., too early to permit the possibility of a diffusion of Near Eastern metallurgical know-how.

Scholars are thus much less inclined than they once were to view the emergence of copper and bronze metallurgy, the clearing and diking of river valleys, the development of writing, and, more generally, the coming of civilization as simply a result of the diffusion of creative ideas originating in Mesopotamia. They are inclined now to view the birth of most civilizations, in both the Western and the Eastern Hemispheres, as a series of more or less independent responses by widely separated Neolithic peoples to a variety of environmental challenges.

One such challenge, common to Mesopotamia, Egypt, India, and China, was that of irrigating a river valley. The periodic flooding of the rivers—the Tigris and Euphrates, Nile, Indus, and Huang—spread silt across their valleys, making them richly and permanently fertile. But the valleys could not be settled and cultivated until the floods were brought under control and the water distributed by large-scale irrigation systems. The development and maintenance of such systems demanded a degree of coordinated human effort well beyond the capacity of Neolithic village society. The task could be accomplished only by a centralized political authority controlling large numbers of people and large stretches of land. The establishment of such authority brought with it the first city-states and the earliest civilizations.

CHAPTER 2

Mesopotamia

Mesopotamia lies in the valley formed by two neighboring rivers, the Tigris and the Euphrates. The name is derived from the Greek words *mesos* (middle) and *potamoi* (rivers) and means literally "between the rivers." The birth of civilization in this region was shaped by Mesopotamia's geography, environment, and culture during the fourth millennium B.C.

Phases of Mesopotamian Culture and Politics

All dates are B.C. and approximate.

8000–4000	Neolithic era
4000–2350	Civilization emerges; intercity wars
2400–2250	Ebla flourishes
2340–2200	Akkadian Empire: Dynasty of Sargon
2119–2004	Sumerian Empire of Ur
2000–1530	Amorite domination: Old Babylonian Empire
1700–1500	Emergence of Indo-European peoples
1530–1155	Kassites dominate Mesopotamia

THE EMERGENCE OF CIVILIZATION:
c. 4000–2350 B.C.

For thousands of years, the entire Near East had experienced steadily decreasing rainfall. Grasslands slowly became desert wastes; the valleys of the Nile and the Tigris-Euphrates, once densely overgrown swamps, gradually became habitable. As the map on page 17 shows, the Tigris-Euphrates Valley is actually a long strip of fertile lowlands with a highland region to the northeast and the Arabian Desert to the southwest. The rich lowlands of the valley form the eastern part of a large semicircular region whose western extremity runs along the eastern Mediterranean coast. This Fertile Crescent, which

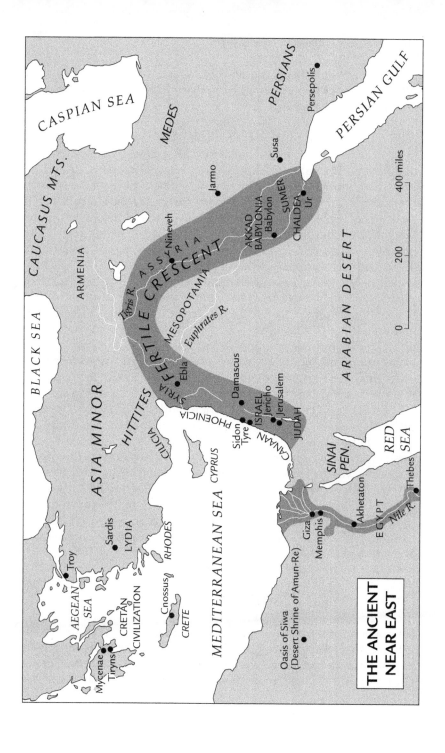

THE ANCIENT NEAR EAST

CASPIAN SEA

CAUCASUS MTS.

BLACK SEA

ASIA MINOR

MEDES

PERSIANS

Persepolis

PERSIAN GULF

ARMENIA

Jarmo

Susa

SUMER

AKKAD
BABYLONIA
Babylon

CHALDEA

Ur

Nineveh

ASSYRIA

Tigris R.

MESOPOTAMIA

Euphrates R.

FERTILE CRESCENT

CRESCENT

SYRIA

Ebla

Damascus

Jericho

ISRAEL

Jerusalem

JUDAH

CANAAN

PHOENICIA

Sidon

Tyre

HITTITES

CILICIA

CYPRUS

ARABIAN DESERT

SINAI
PEN.

RED
SEA

Sardis

LYDIA

Troy

AEGEAN
SEA

RHODES

MEDITERRANEAN SEA

Cnossus

CRETAN
CIVILIZATION

CRETE

Mycenae
Tiryns

Oasis of Siwa
(Desert Shrine of Amun-Re)

Giza

Memphis

Akhetaton

EGYPT

Nile R.

Thebes

0   200   400 miles

arches northward from the Mediterranean and the Persian Gulf, was throughout history an alluring prize for both the northern hill peoples and the southern desert peoples.

Most of the earliest Neolithic villages were established in the high country to the northeast, which had long been attracting settlers because of its fertile soil, adequate rainfall, and native grasses (wheat and barley). The valley itself presented special problems. Its soil, replenished annually by the rich silt of the flooding rivers, was vastly more fertile than that of the neighboring hills, but the swamps had to be drained, the water of the rivers had to be distributed over the dry land, and, above all, the destructive floods had to be mastered. This was more difficult to do in Mesopotamia than in Egypt, because the Tigris and Euphrates rivers rise up late in the spring (unlike the Nile, which floods in Egypt in the later summer) and can easily destroy plants. For that reason, the Mesopotamians had to devise a system of canals and storage basins to let water into the fields in the desired amounts. Once this program was initiated by organized community effort, the rich land produced a surplus, which enabled the new states to expand. No longer was everybody obliged to work the soil; other careers were now possible. The vast majority of the population remained on the land (as they would throughout the world until recent times), but a crucially important minority began to specialize in other areas, such as war, administration, manufacturing, trade, and service to the gods.

This was the process that produced civilization in the Tigris-Euphrates Valley. The evolution of civilization (organized urban life) can be understood here in part as a series of historical causes and effects (as described above), but at the core of the matter there remained an element of choice. One can analyze in retrospect the possibilities of the situation, but one cannot explain adequately why they were grasped and exploited by specific people at a specific time.

THE SUMERIANS

The people who built the earliest civilization in Mesopotamia are referred to as Sumerians. (The Sumerians lived in towns and cities in southern Mesopotamia roughly between Nippur and the Persian Gulf. It appears that peoples who did not speak or write the Sumerian language also lived among the Sumerians from the very beginning.) As far as we know at present, the Sumerians' language, which is unlike any other known to us, was the first human tongue to have been expressed in writing. Their culture became the nucleus of all later Mesopotamian civilization. Their architecture, their mode of writing, their literary and artistic styles, their social organization, and their attitude toward life and toward the gods persevered in the Valley of the Two Rivers and its neighboring lands throughout antiquity.

For the most part, the outlook of the Sumerians and their Mesopotamian successors seems to have been pessimistic. Perhaps this pessimism was ultimately related to their environment. To the ancient Mesopotamians, nature must have seemed violent and unpredictable. No matter how they tried, they could never completely tame the floods. Mesopotamia was a land of extreme contrasts. Weeks of blistering heat might be followed by torrential rains that turned field into marshland. There were furious winds and suffocating dust storms. Worse still, the fertile valley was open to incessant raids and periodic conquests by envious tribes from the northern hills or the southern desert. In short, the price of civilization in Mesopotamia was constant insecurity.

RELIGION AND CULTURE

The Sumerians projected their ever-present insecurity about their environment into their conceptions of humanity and its gods. Early peoples in general tended to regard inanimate objects as personalities with wills of their own. Mountains, trees, rivers, and even sticks and stones were alive and had volition. Awed and terrorized by nature, the Sumerians saw themselves as its servants. They were impotent before its invincible power, tragic figures subject to the whims of the gods. "Mere man—," a Sumerian observed, "his days are numbered; whatever he may do, he is but wind." The delights of heaven were not for humans; the scanty allusions to the afterlife in Mesopotamian literature portray it as a state of darkness and gloom.

Being an agricultural people, the Sumerians recognized the regularity of nature: the daily sweep of the sun and the annual procession of the seasons that governed the rhythm of planting and harvesting. Their chief deity was the sky god, **Anu,** and their most beloved was the earth goddess, **Inanna,** who symbolized fertility. The worship of the Earth Mother, which became common to many ancient civilizations, is a product of the Neolithic Revolution, when the invention of farming suddenly made the fertility of the soil all-important. But the Sumerians had other deities less benign than those of earth and sky. **Enlil,** the god of storms, symbolized destruction, wildness, and violence. Set against the orderly sequence of crops and seasons, Enlil represented the terrifying, unpredictable side of nature.

Helpless before the wrath of the elements, Sumerians saw themselves as slaves to the gods. This theme of human bondage appears vividly in the Mesopotamian *Epic of Creation,* wherein it is said, "Let man be burdened with the gods' toil, that the gods may freely breathe." The Sumerians honored their gods by building great temples in the centers of their city-states. (In fact, individual cities tended to regard themselves as the dwelling places of a particular goddess or god, such as Inanna at Uruk or Enlil at Nippur.) The temple priests controlled much of the land and labor of the inhabitants. Indeed, it was in the service of the temples and their gods that the Sumerians made many of their most fundamental and enduring contributions to civilization.

The temple buildings themselves constitute humanity's earliest efforts at monumental architecture. Most of them were built of clay bricks arranged in terraced, artificial mounds and are called "ziggurats." These constructions may have been intended to represent mountains. To the Sumerians, the mountain was the source of the earth's potency and thus constituted an intensely significant religious symbol.

The first Sumerian writing was done by temple scribes, who began to keep accounts of the considerable economic resources of their temples. Such were the mundane beginnings of human literacy. It is probably correct to say, as one writer has done, that "history begins at Sumer," for one definition of history, narrowly speaking, is the reconstruction of the past from written sources, and our first strictly historical written evidence is Sumerian. The writing consists of wedge-shaped marks inscribed on clay tablets with a reed stylus, a technique that began in the Sumerian city of Uruk and then spread through Mesopotamia and much of the Near East. The script is called **cuneiform** after the Latin word *cuneus* (wedge). The first cuneiform symbols were pictograms—that is, little pictures of the objects being described. In time, the pictograms evolved into ideograms (conven-

The Great Ziggurat at Ur
Built during the Ur III period (c. 2119–2004 B.C.). The modern word "ziggurat" is based upon an Akkadian word, *ziggurratu*. Most ancient ziggurats were constructed of a series of mud-brick platforms, piled one on top of another. (© *Michael S. Yamashita/Corbis*)

tionalized figures representing objects or abstract concepts). Scribes then gradually achieved greater flexibility by adding syllabic symbols representing various sounds. Since the cuneiform symbols were exceedingly numerous, writing was a complex art that remained for many centuries the monopoly of a small, highly trained scribal elite.

Sumerian mathematics seems also to have arisen from the necessities of keeping temple accounts. Ten was the basic numerical unit among the Sumerians, as among many other peoples, perhaps because the decimal system is based on the primitive impulse to count on one's fingers. The Sumerians also stressed units based on the numbers 6, 60, 600, 3,600, and so on, which is the source of our practice of dividing circles into 360 degrees. They understood addition and subtraction and knew how to handle fractions. They established standard units of weight and measure and perfected a lunar calendar. All these achievements were the products of hard, practical necessity and appear to have arisen first from the needs of the temple community. All the advancements in human knowledge, in short, were undertaken to better serve the gods.

The invention of writing was followed by the birth of literature. Here, too, the gods played a dominant role. The tragic and powerful *Epic of Gilgamesh* describes a Sumerian royal hero's courageous but fruitless search for immortality and includes an early version of the great flood story. Sumerian literature is characterized by a grave, solemn style that changed little from one generation to the next. Sumerian authors and poets saw less value in originality but preferred to follow earlier models and preserve a cherished tradition.

Many of these same qualities affected Sumerian sculpture. It, too, was almost exclusively religious, and much of it was devoted to the decoration of the temples. It was executed in a style that by modern standards seems somewhat static, somber, and impersonal, and despite a gradual trend toward realism, it was nearly as tradition-bound as Sumerian literature. Yet, the statuettes and relief carvings by Sumerian artists also convey a feeling of dignity and nobility. On the whole, they constitute a moving expression of the Sumerian religious outlook and take their place alongside the works of the poets and architects as the first expressions of a cultural tradition that was to dominate western Asia for thousands of years.

SOCIETY AND POLITICS

The social organization of Sumerian city-states was characterized by a male-dominated hierarchy of priests, administrator-nobles, and warriors. Beneath them were free workers and peasants, along with a growing number of slaves. Among the enslaved population was a crucially important body of female textile workers, who produced one of the cities' primary exports. The slaves—like those of subsequent ancient civilizations—were recruited largely from among prisoners of war and, to a much lesser extent, defaulting debtors. Indeed, we know that during times of economic stress, families sometimes were compelled to sell their own children, and sons even sold their own mothers into slavery. The prisoners of war were products of the incessant intercity warfare that had afflicted Mesopotamia ever since the earliest days of urban life. Since the populations of the cities did not differ notably from one another in their ethnic makeup, slavery was a product not of ethnic difference or race but of misfortune.

Figure from a Sumerian temple

Alabaster figure of standing male worshiper from the temple of the god Abu, early dynastic period (2750–2600 B.C.). Excavated at Tell Asmar in central Mesopotamia. Standing figures of this type with clasped hands and staring gaze represent worshipers. They were placed in temples to pray perpetually for the people who had commissioned them. Similar statues were often inscribed with the names of rulers. (© *The Metropolitan Museum of Art/Art Resource, NY*)

Slaves and free peasants, who far outnumbered everyone else, were obliged to work the temple lands or the lands of nobles. Some were also given the opportunity to till their own fields and to sell their own surpluses (if any), but most agrarian workers, despite the ownership of private property, remained in a state of poverty, as they would for millennia to come.

Women, too, began to assume the status characteristic of their roles in future societies. More and more, with the development of civilization, women took a place in the home. A free woman was ordinarily in immediate charge of the upbringing of her children, and she usually organized the affairs and maintenance of her residence, whether great or small, although under the overall supervision (or, rather, rule) of her husband. The husband participated in activities outside the household. Thus, Sumerian cities set the example for most future civilizations in limiting women to activities within the household while leaving public activities, in the city and beyond, to men.

Most Sumerian cities appear first to have been governed by groups of priests and nobles. The practice developed, however, of appointing a temporary king to rule during emergencies. In time, emergencies, actual or contrived, occurred more frequently until monarchy became permanent. The chief priest and the king were often the same person, for Sumerian kingship, like almost every other Sumerian institution, was primarily religious. It was the king's task to determine the gods' will by means of dreams or other portents and then to carry out that will. Even this mighty personage was merely the foremost slave of the city's chief god. The rise of monarchies stemmed largely from the growing tendency toward intercity warfare. The ultimate political unification of the region was long delayed by the fierce independence of cities bearing such poetic names as Ur, Lagash, and the aforementioned Uruk.

As the intercity struggles went on, Sumerian civilization spread northward along the Tigris-Euphrates Valley into a district called **Akkad** (roughly the area in southern Mesopotamia between modern Baghdad and Nippur.) This region was settled chiefly by Semitic-language-speaking peoples who had migrated from their original homeland in the Arabian Desert northward into Syria and then eastward into Mesopotamia. The inhabitants of Akkad built cities of their own and joined in the intercity battles. The relationships between the peoples who spoke Semitic languages and the Sumerians

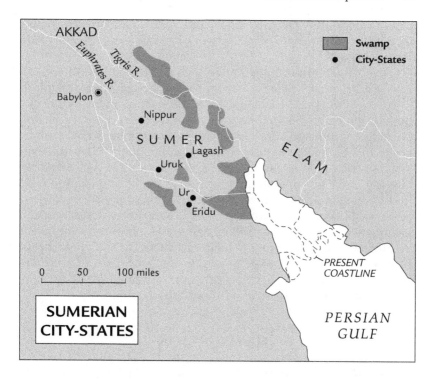

SUMERIAN
CITY-STATES

were exceedingly complex, and we must not view these peoples simply as two antagonistic blocs. The inhabitants of almost every city, Sumerian or Akkadian, included people of both language groups.

CONTACTS EAST AND WEST

As Mesopotamian civilization developed, it came into contact with city-states that were emerging far to the east and west of the Tigris-Euphrates Valley. The previously mentioned Neolithic village of Tepe Yahya in Iran, some 500 miles to the east of Mesopotamia, had evolved by about 3400 B.C. into a city-state where scribes were recording commercial transactions on clay tablets. Tepe Yahya grew much larger after about 3200 B.C., by which time other Iranian cities were also keeping written records. The scribes at Tepe Yahya, as elsewhere in Iran, inscribed their tablets in a language altogether different from that of Mesopotamia: they wrote in the earliest-known form of Old

Iranian. Tepe Yahya may well have been one of several way stations in a little-known commercial network linking Mesopotamia to the Indus Valley.

In 1975, a team of Italian archaeologists announced the discovery of a great city called **Ebla,** far to the west of Mesopotamia in northern Syria. In the "Palace of Ebla" they found thousands of clay tablets, the earliest dating back to about 2400 B.C. The tablets, only partially deciphered, are inscribed in Mesopotamian cuneiform script in a language that is not Sumerian but Semitic. The evidence suggests that Ebla (meaning, perhaps, "City of the White Stones") was the center of a flourishing kingdom in the third millennium B.C. and a potent military and commercial rival to the city-states of Mesopotamia. Ebla's trade network extended eastward past Mesopotamia into western Iran and southward and westward into Palestine and Anatolia (Asia Minor, roughly modern central Turkey). At the height of its power, around 2400–2250 B.C., Ebla appears to have controlled a considerable empire encompassing northern Syria, lower Anatolia, and, even for a time, parts of northern Mesopotamia.

UNIFICATION

While Ebla flourished, the Akkadian conqueror **Sargon I** (c. 2340–2284 B.C.) was bringing all of Mesopotamia under his dominion, creating the first empire to bind Akkad and Sumer into a single, durable unit. Sargon's descendants maintained uneasy control for several generations. During the reign of Sargon's grandson **Naram-Sin** (c. 2260–2223 B.C.), the empire reached its height. Around 2250 B.C., Naram-Sin settled the Near Eastern power struggle by leading an army into northern Syria and ravishing Ebla. And some of Sargon's successors, breaking with Mesopotamian tradition, took the step of claiming divinity for themselves. Naram-Sin, for example, claimed that the inhabitants of the city of Agade implored Ishtar, Enlil, and other gods to have him (Naram-Sin) as the god of their city Agade, and they built him a temple.

In time, invaders from the northeast destroyed Sargon's Akkadian dynasty, reducing the area under the control of the last of the kings of Agade (Shudurul, c. 2174–2159 B.C.) to the immediate vicinity of the city itself. There followed a period of political upheaval during which power was divided among local rulers in Uruk, Lagash, Kish, Agade, and Gutians in the Diyala. Around 2119 B.C., the Sumerian city of Ur rose to dominance, and its kings likewise claimed a special relationship to the gods, or even divinity itself by descent from the gods. After a century of fame and fortune, however, the empire of Ur III fell apart, the victim of grain shortages, inflation, and disruption of communication routes by pastoralists (invariably called Amorites in the documents of the government of Ur). With its collapse, Sumerian political power came to a permanent end.

During the troubled era around 2000 B.C., several new Semitic-language-speaking peoples were moving into the Tigris-Euphrates Valley. One such group, the Amorites from Syria, occupied a number of Mesopotamian cities, including the theretofore somewhat obscure community of Babylon.* As the Amorites widened their dominion, Babylon evolved into a great imperial capital. **Hammurabi** (c. 1792–1750 B.C.), the most celebrated of the Amorite kings of Babylon, conquered all of Akkad and Sumer, originally in alliance with the kings of Assyria and Larsa. He eventually extended his sway across the entire Fertile Crescent from the Mediterranean Sea to the Persian Gulf. By 1755 B.C., Hammurabi was the ruler of an empire as large as that of Ur III, and he controlled trade routes over which silver, gold, lapis lazuli, tin, copper, and horses were traded. In addition, building on a Sumerian cultural tradition that had been evolving for nearly 2,000 years, Hammurabi created a political structure of exceptional efficiency in which officials and royal servants were tied to the king through land grants, which carried with them reciprocal obligations to the king. Hammurabi's well-known law code, engraved on a pillar nearly eight feet high, provides a window into daily life in the Babylonian Empire during the period.

The code was based on a series of earlier, shorter Sumerian codes and drew heavily upon Sumerian custom. Hammurabi made no claim to personal divinity in the text but assumed the more traditional role of steward of the gods, a just king and conqueror. The society that he ruled was stratified into free citizens, royal retainers and their dependents, and slaves. Detailed mercantile regulations indicate an active, complex commercial life. Many of the laws concern marriage and inheritance. Hammurabi's collection of prescriptive

---

*The name Babylon probably means "Gate of the Gods."

laws is harsher than its Sumerian predecessors, however, perhaps suggesting a higher degree of authoritarianism than before. Capital punishment was frequent where it had once been rare, and the notion of retributive justice (the so-called *lex talionis*)—an eye for an eye—was sometimes carried to macabre extremes (from a modern perspective). For example, if a house collapses, killing its occupant, the builder is executed; if the occupant's son is killed, the builder's son must die; if a patient dies during an operation, the surgeon is executed; if the patient loses an eye, the surgeon loses his fingers, and with them, one presumes, his career.

THE EMERGENCE OF INDO-EUROPEAN PEOPLES: c. 1700–1500 B.C.

Even when the Babylonian Empire was at its height, new peoples were moving into the Fertile Crescent from the surrounding mountains and deserts. They are known collectively as Indo-Europeans, for although they were ethnically diverse, their languages were all derived from a single **Indo-European** core—the ancestor of Latin, Greek, Persian, Sanskrit, and the Romance and Germanic languages of today (including, of course, Spanish, French, and English). From the standpoint of language, these newcomers were the forebears of anyone who grew up in Europe or America speaking an Indo-European language. Between about 1700 and 1500 B.C. they, and others in their wake, disrupted the political and cultural continuity of the ancient Near East.

In 1595 B.C., the city of Babylon was sacked in a lightning raid carried out by the Hittite king Mursili I, and the First Dynasty of Babylon (to which Hammurabi belonged) came to an end. The language of the Hittites, whose capital in central Anatolia (Turkey) was named Hattusa (modern Bogazköy), was known as Nesite by the inhabitants of Hattusa and belonged to the Indo-European family of languages. By 1530 B.C., invaders, known as Kassites, who came originally from the Zagros Mountains to the northeast of Babylonia, had become the dominant power in the area and established their own dynasty centered in Babylon. As in all other major states of the Near East at the time, the Kassites used horses and chariots to conquer and intimidate their victims. The Kassite rulers of Babylon managed to dominate Mesopotamia for the next four centuries (c. 1530–1155 B.C.), not as gods or as agents of gods but simply as a landholding nobility whose kings patronized the traditional Babylonian cults and were seen by the Babylonians themselves as legitimate rulers. Before looking further at the Semitic and Indo-European kingdoms of western Asia, let us turn to the Valley of the Nile, where another great civilization was developing.

CHAPTER 3

Egypt

THE SETTING

"Egypt is the gift of the Nile." The Greek historian **Herodotus** made that observation in the fifth century B.C., but its truth had long been recognized by the Egyptians themselves. One of their most moving hymns opens with these words: "Hail to thee, O Nile, that issues from the earth and comes to keep Egypt alive!"

The Valley of the Nile winds northward like a green serpent through the barren North African desert, spreading into a vast flat delta as it approaches the Mediterranean. The narrow valley to the south and the delta to the north form two distinct regions known as Upper and Lower Egypt. (Since the two regions are named according to their location on the northward-flowing Nile, Lower Egypt will be above Upper Egypt on a modern map.) Ancient Egypt has thus been called the Kingdom of the Two Lands.

PREDYNASTIC EGYPT

The remarkable fertility of the Nile Valley, even greater than that of the Tigris-Euphrates Valley, resulted from the rich silt deposited by annual floods (which began in July, climaxed in August and September, and finally receded in October). The evolution from Neolithic culture to civilization in Egypt followed the Mesopotamian pattern: draining swamps, clearing junglelike vegetation, and digging canals, so as to exploit the black soil from which the ancient Egyptians were able to grow one crop per year. Indeed, the presence of Sumerian artifacts and artistic motifs from the beginning of this formative period suggests a Mesopotamian influence on Egypt's rise to civilization; to put it another way, a small number of ruling families, who perhaps were responsible for the consolidation of Upper Egypt into a

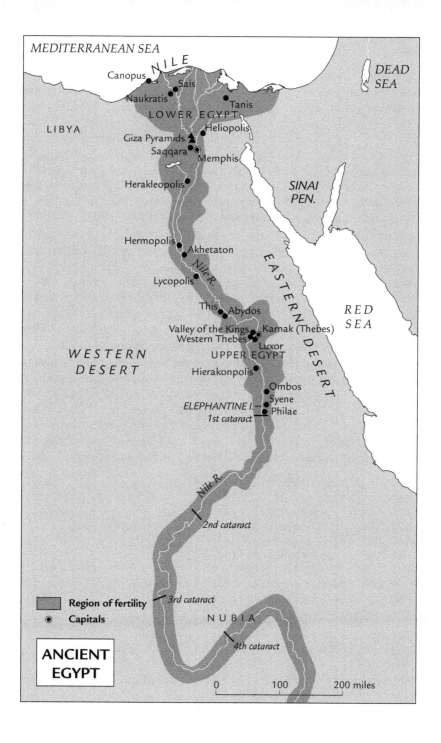

MEDITERRANEAN SEA

NILE

DEAD SEA

Canopus
Sais
Naukratis
Tanis
LOWER EGYPT
Heliopolis
Giza Pyramids
Saqqara
Memphis
Herakleopolis

LIBYA

SINAI PEN.

Hermopolis
Akhetaton
Nile R.
Lycopolis

This   Abydos
Valley of the Kings   Karnak (Thebes)
Western Thebes
Luxor
UPPER EGYPT
Hierakonpolis

RED SEA

EASTERN DESERT

WESTERN DESERT

Ombos
Syene
ELEPHANTINE I.   Philae
1st cataract

Nile R.

2nd cataract

Nile R.

3rd cataract

NUBIA

4th cataract

▨ Region of fertility
⊙ Capitals

ANCIENT EGYPT

0   100   200 miles

political unity by 3100 B.C., were wealthy enough to import decorated items with Mesopotamian and also Elamite motifs. A Mesopotamian knife, for example, turned up in an ancient Egyptian settlement near the Nile, and the early Egyptian step pyramids resemble Mesopotamian ziggurats (although the classic form of the pyramid as a royal tomb did not develop in Egypt until the period of the third dynasty, around 2686 B.C.). The fact that most of these items were found in central Egypt has suggested to some scholars that the early contacts between Mesopotamia and Egypt were made by way of the Persian Gulf and the Red Sea, rather than over land through Syria.

Before about 3100 B.C., there was at least some kind of cultural divide between Lower and Upper Egypt, as is evidenced by differences in the pottery of the inhabitants of the two areas. Around 3100 B.C., according to later Egyptian records, a half-legendary conqueror from Upper Egypt named **Narmer** (or **Menes**) is said to have unified the entire land and ruled it as the first pharaoh from his capital at Memphis. Scholars, however, question this picture of abrupt unification. More likely, before 3100 B.C., an increasingly homogeneous kingdom had developed in Upper Egypt, which gradually succeeded in incorporating the smaller communities of Lower Egypt into its sphere of political control. Menes' "unification" of Upper and Lower Egypt represented the expansion of Upper Egypt's political power into the region of Lower Egypt. Indeed, the result of that expansion was the creation of the Kingdom of the Two Lands (Lower and Upper Egypt), which was seen anachronistically by later Egyptians as the natural order.

Periods of Ancient Egyptian History

All dates are B.C. and approximate.

3100–2686	Early Dynastic Period
2686–2181	Old Kingdom
2181–2040	First Intermediate Period
2040–1730	Middle Kingdom
1730–1550	Second Intermediate Period: the Hyksos
1550–1080	New Kingdom (or Empire)

EARLY DYNASTIC EGYPT: 3100–2686 B.C.

But whether Egypt was unified into one kingdom gradually or all at once in 3100 B.C., the next few hundred years were a period of transition and consolidation during which Egypt developed characteristics later considered to be typical of it. Among these were the recognition of one king, the **pharaoh**,* as the ruler of the country, from the Nile Delta to at least Aswan; the development of a cultural homogeneity, which distinguished it from its neighbors; the characterization of those neighbors as a threat; and the emergence of Memphis as the main seat of government.

Although the early kings probably were buried in Abydos, where elaborate cults were developed, the large fields of tombs set out at Saqqara underscore the importance of Memphis. Hieroglyphic writing, which appeared rather suddenly and fully developed by 3100 B.C.,† evolved into a literary vehicle to celebrate the deeds of the kings and also to keep track of royal income and expenses. Taxes in kind on agricultural produce and animals were collected and stored in royal depots to be distributed later by the kings. The kings themselves were large landowners. They were served by royal functionaries who perhaps originally were members of the royal families. Overall, by the end of the early dynastic period, Egypt had become a state, ruled by one king in whose hands all power and wealth was concentrated. The divine nature of this powerful ruler was articulated and reinforced by the performance of elaborate rituals. Huge resources were devoted to the royal burials, including construction and maintenance of the royal tombs.

MA'AT *AND THE PHARAOH*

The early Egyptians responded to nature's favor by viewing the universe as orderly and benevolent. The key concept in Egyptian religious thought is expressed in the word *ma'at*, which can be translated variously as "truth," "right behavior," or "correct balance." The gods were not ferocious and arbitrary as in Mesopotamia, nor were the Egyptians their slaves. On the contrary, the gods cared about Egypt and favored it exceedingly. It was the gods themselves who wanted the world, particularly Egypt, kept in correct balance.

The king was responsible for maintaining ma'at and was at the same time subject to it. Indeed, the pharaoh himself was in some

---

*It was during the New Kingdom period (1550–1080 B.C.) that it became customary to refer to the Egyptian ruler as the "great house," or *per'ao* in Egyptian, from which the English word "pharaoh" derives.

†The first examples of written records from Egypt are from a tomb in Abydos.

sense a living god, an incarnation of sacred power (although he did not share in the omnipotence of other gods such as Re, the sun god), and his rule was, at least ideally, a manifestation of ma'at. All Egypt was his personal estate, and his whim was law. Egypt produced no law codes, for the law was in the pharaoh's mouth. Yet, being a god, he expressed in his words and deeds the basic harmony of the cosmos. He was the victorious champion of the Egyptians against the forces of chaos and darkness.

The god-kings of Egypt wore special robes which distinguished them from their subjects. They also were regularly depicted wearing a special kind of kilt with the tail of a bull attached at the waist. A ceremonial beard hung from the chin of the king. Most prominent was the great double crown on the head of the pharaoh, which symbolized his rule over Upper and Lower Egypt. A cobra (the so-called *uraeus,* associated with the goddess Wadjet but also with the eye of the sun god Re) was shown rearing up on his forehead, ready to protect the king.

The pharaohs were polygamous, so the eldest son of the pharaoh's principal wife normally succeeded his father as pharaoh. The coronation ceremonies of the pharaohs symbolized the creation of the universe and were reenacted each year. When the pharaohs died, equally elaborate rituals, centered around their tombs (pyramids), were staged by the Egyptians to ensure that their kings had a successful journey to join their fellow gods and goddesses.

RELIGIOUS THOUGHT

Like other ancient peoples, the Egyptians crowded their universe with gods and spirits. Their greatest god, **Re,** personified the life-giving sun. He appeared in many guises and was often merged with a local god into a kind of divine compound. During the Middle Kingdom, for instance, Re was amalgamated with the local Theban god Amun into Amun-Re. **Amun-Re** became, in middle and later Egyptian history, the most illustrious of these compound gods. During the imperial period, Amun-Re was the god of victories, and his magnificent temple at Karnak in Thebes became enormously wealthy.

Osiris, another important deity, was said to have once been a benevolent pharaoh who taught his people agriculture. His sister-wife **Isis,** symbolic of the fertile earth, was believed to have been supremely wise and adept at the arts of magic. Later legend declared that Osiris had been killed and cut to pieces by Seth, his evil, animal-headed brother. But afterward, owing to the lamentations of Isis, Osiris was miraculously resurrected and then passed on into the next world to become the king of the dead and judge of souls. This theme of death and resurrection was basic to the religious thought of many ancient cultures. A mythological expression of the death of vegetation in winter and its resurrection in spring, the concept also symbolized the death of the sun each evening and its rebirth at dawn. Indeed, the Nile itself followed this same basic sequence; the low Nile of early spring, bringing the specter of famine to the land, gave way in the summer to a new, resurgent Nile that revivified the fields. And individual Egyptians might well hope that they, too, like the sun and the river, would overcome death. The Osiris-Isis myth eventually came to symbolize this hope of individual salvation and eternal life. The story of Osiris's resurrection subsequently became the narrative base of one of the most important mystery cults of Hellenistic and Roman times: the celebration of the mysteries of Isis and Osiris.

The living pharaoh was identified with the falcon-god Horus, the son of Isis and Osiris, but he was also believed to be the son of the sun god Re. Furthermore, it was believed that another important god, **Ptah,** the god of the city of Memphis, had established the pharaoh-god as overall lord of Egypt. What seems like a somewhat confusing theological situation to us perhaps can be attributed to a desire to emphasize the primacy of Memphis and Ptah in the Egyptian order of things and to link all the important gods to Ptah.

THE OLD KINGDOM: c. 2686–2181 B.C.

The coming of age of Egyptian civilization was followed by an approximately 500-year period known as the Old Kingdom, during which Egyptian culture held together as a strong, cohesive state under the power of the pharaohs and the favor of the gods. The Old Kingdom was Egypt's classical age. At no other time was Egypt so stable. The authority and prestige of the pharaohs of this period are illustrated dramatically by the pyramids in which they were entombed. The first true pyramid was a step pyramid built of stone at Saqqara for Djoser, a famous pharaoh of Dynasty III (2686–2613 B.C.).

The largest pyramids, which have amazed visitors to Egypt from antiquity to today, were built during the Dynasty IV (c. 2613–2494 B.C.), approximately 2,000 years before the construction of the Parthenon in Athens and 2,600 years before Vespasian built the Colosseum in Rome. The Great Pyramid of Cheops (or Khufu, c. 2500 B.C.) is an immense mass of more than 6 million tons of stone, fitted together with the precision of a watchmaker—testimony not only to the skill and patience of its builders but also to their knowledge of practical mathematics. As far as we know, the great pyramids were built without the aid of tackle, pulleys, cranes, or wheeled vehicles, since the wheel had not yet come to Egypt.

On the walls of some of the royal tombs from the Dynasty V onward (c. 2494–2345 B.C.) scholars have found inscribed texts whose function was essentially magical: to aid in the resurrection of the dead pharaoh. These texts do not conform to a single prototype; rather, they show variations and ongoing speculation about the divine nature of kingship in Egypt over time. Egyptian religious thought was not static, even during Egypt's classical age.

In some cases, archaeologists also have unearthed ceremonial boats buried near these immense tombs. These boats were made for the dead pharaohs so that they could travel through the sky with the gods.

The cost in human labor of constructing and servicing these monuments must have been prodigious. Yet we need not regard the pyramids as monuments to royal vainglory, built by armies of brutalized slaves. The great pyramids of the Old Kingdom period probably were built largely by poor, but free, Egyptians who worked on these projects both because they received compensation for their labor and because of their devotion to the pharaohs. As god-king, the pharaoh was the nexus of Egyptian religious belief, and his tomb was a monument important to all Egyptians. The proper entombment of the dead pharaoh was essential, so it was believed, to the perpetuation of ma'at and the continued prosperity of the kingdom.

Illustrations on private tombs during the period show, however, that not all free labor was devoted to royal projects. Food and manufactured goods were also traded privately in local markets—a sign that private enterprise existed side by side with state projects. Not all work performed during the Old Kingdom was state supervised or compulsory.

Indeed, the traditional picture of the state during this time, as a kind of monolith dominated by the pharaoh and his relatives in positions of authority as priests and administrators, needs revision. Government service and offices certainly did evolve out of the organization of the royal house. And, in fact, the division of all the lands (villages, royal estates, and towns) of Upper and Lower Egypt into administrative units, known later to the Greeks as **nomes** (from the Greek word *nomos*, meaning "district" or "province"), by the time of the Old Kingdom did arise out of the consolidation of the pharaoh's centralization of authority during the period, and this system of administration persisted into the period of Roman domination of Egypt (c. after 30 B.C.).

At the same time, it is important to keep in mind that within the system of administration that governed the land of Egypt, there was no hereditary office or entitlement to positions by birth. According to the ideology of the state, officials attained offices as a result of service to the pharaoh and the people of Egypt. Egypt during its classical period was not a static, monolithic state. Its success, symbolized forever by its pyramids, can be attributed to its vital, flexible, and multifaceted political and religious system. Women, for instance, although barred from the formal education necessary for entry into the Egyptian bureaucracy or scribal class, were freer than women in Mesopotamia to take part in public life—to own property, to conduct businesses, to engage in lawsuits, and to participate in religious rituals. Under the absolute monarchy of their god-kings, Egyptians of both sexes were less rigidly stratified than were the inhabitants of most other early civilizations.

THE FIRST INTERMEDIATE PERIOD: *c. 2181–2040 B.C.*

The growing power of priests and nobles at the expense of the pharaoh marked the end of the Old Kingdom. The **nomarchs** (particularly of Upper Egypt), who served as the pharaohs' governors in the provinces, or nomes, became increasingly autonomous, even as many of them continued to acknowledge the royal power in Memphis. Indeed, as early as about 2180 B.C., there was considerable instability in royal control, and some nomarchs eventually became the real masters of Upper and Middle Egypt, responsible for defending their nomes and guaranteeing the food supply. The era of unrest and political fragmentation that followed (2181–2040 B.C.) is known as the First Intermediate Period. The breakdown seems to have been largely an internal phenomenon, brought about by delegation of royal rights and by the ever-increasing burden of building and maintaining the stupendous royal tombs; drought and pressure on the northeastern frontier also may have been factors. The surest signs of the breakdown of central authority during this period are the lack of royal building, the cessation of mining or quarrying expeditions, the publication of few royal inscriptions, and the creation of relatively crude art forms.

Overall, the collapse of centralized royal authority, with its concomitant social upheaval, was a devastating blow to the confidence of at least some Egyptians. Writers of the age bemoaned the loss of ma'at. Some pondered the advantages of suicide; others abandoned themselves to debauchery. One writer complained of the end of Egypt's accustomed peace: "I show you the land topsy-turvy. That which never happened has happened. Men take up weapons of war, so that the land lives in confusion."

But the reaction was neither total cynicism nor complete despair. Rather, there were also serious efforts to replace the materialism of the past with new spiritual and moral values. The issue of eternal life had formerly been associated by many with the building of huge tombs and was focused upon the pharaoh and his immediate followers. Now salvation was made to depend more on an upright life than an appropriate tomb, and the possibility of an afterlife was extended to more nobles and even commoners. Eternity was democratized.

This new cosmic egalitarianism affected Egyptian thought and society in countless ways. A text from the First Intermediate Period has the creator god say, "I made the four winds that everyone might breathe thereof . . . I made the great inundation that the poor might have rights therein like the great . . . I made everyone like his fellow." Long before the age of the socially conscious Hebrew prophets, Egypt glimpsed the doctrine of human dignity and justice extended both to the great and to the poor.

THE MIDDLE KINGDOM: c. 2040–1730 B.C.

Gradually, the Egyptian monarchy recovered something of its former position, and with this revival of centralized authority the Middle Kingdom began. By the reign of Sesostris III (1878–1841 B.C.), the power centers of the nomarchs, which had been developed at the expense of the central authority during the First Intermediate Period, were effectively curtailed.

During Dynasty XII (c. 1991–1785 B.C.), a new administrative center near Memphis, called *Itj-towy* (the Residence), was created, which helped to consolidate the Theban grip on Egypt. Also unique to this period in Egyptian history was the establishment of a co-regency by which pharaohs ruled along with their designated successors. Under the leadership of these pharaohs, Nubia was occupied from the first to the second cataract (waterfall), and Egypt was involved in trading networks that extended into the Levant and Mesopotamia. In literary works and sculpture, a physically powerful, heroic image of the pharaohs was emphasized. After the chaos of the First Intermediate Period, it was important for pharaohs to be seen as strong defenders of Egypt, especially against its external enemies, the "Asiatics" and the Nubians, as was sung in ceremonial hymns. At the same time, sculptures often depicted the pharaohs of the time as anxious, weighed down by their responsibilities.

Indeed, art and especially literature flourished during this period. In addition to the development of "loyalist literature," created to assert the legitimacy of the pharaohs, new literary forms, such as the harper's song, appeared for the first time. In a passage from one such song, the singer betrays some anxiety about the afterlife:

> Follow your heart as long as you live!
> Put myrrh on your head,
> Dress in a fine linen,
> Anoint yourself with oils fit for a god.
> Heap up your joys,
> Let not your heart sink!
> Follow your heart and your happiness,
> Do your things on earth as your heart commands!
> When there comes to you that day of mourning,
> The Weary-hearted [Osiris] hears not their mourning,
> Wailing saves no man from the pit!

Although the Middle Kingdom often has been seen as the "classical" period of ancient Egyptian civilization, when the strength and unity of Egypt were restored, it was not a period without anxieties. It was followed by an era in which the troubles of the First Intermediate Period were eclipsed by much greater threats to the tradition of Egyptian unity and even independence.

THE HYKSOS AND THE SECOND INTERMEDIATE PERIOD: c. 1730–1550 B.C.

At about the time that various speakers of Indo-European languages were disrupting Mesopotamia, a group known as the **Hyksos** (Egyptian for "king-shepherds") was settling in Egypt. Where the Hyksos came from, what their language was, and how they came to seize power in Egypt is obscure and controversial, although in contemporary Egyptian documents, such as the Kamose stele, these foreign rulers of Egypt were linked to the Levant (the eastern shores of the Mediterranean Sea).

Whatever their origins, it is clear that, after a period of progressive and extensive fragmentation of political power in Egypt after 1648 B.C., the Hyksos, from their base at Avaris (Tell el-Dab'a in the eastern delta of the Nile), at least attempted to extend their control over all of Egypt. Their ambitions probably were frustrated, however, and Nubia certainly never was incorporated into their kingdom.

While the Hyksos never may have been the rulers of all of Upper and Lower Egypt, they clearly did assume control of all of Egypt's commercial links to the Levant, the Sinai, Byblos, and the Red Sea. Lapis lazuli, silver, turquoise, incense, honey, and other luxury goods flowed into the harbor of Avaris, at least during the reign of Kamose. Excavations at the site of Avaris, conducted over the last decade or so, also have revealed beautiful frescoes that are linked artistically to the famous wall paintings found at sites on the Aegean islands of Crete and Thera. These frescoes have been dated to the reign of the pharaoh Amose (c. 1550–1520 B.C.) and were created either by Minoan artists living in Avaris or by artists influenced by Minoan artistic practices.

After the end of Hyksos domination in Egypt (c. 1550 B.C.), later Egyptian pharaohs represented the Hyksos as foreign rulers of Egypt who had violated traditional Egyptian religion (such as ma'at) and suppressed political institutions. It is now clear, however, that Hyksos rule was widely accepted by the majority of Egyptians and that the Hyksos rulers had assumed the standard titles of the pharaohs of Egypt. Indeed, evidence for real Egyptian resistance to the reign of the Hyksos is limited to the very end of the Second Intermediate Period; until then, there was accommodation, and even cooperation.

Nakht, the Paleopathology Boy

Since history as recorded by ancient writers tends to dwell almost entirely on the deeds of emperors, kings, generals, and great religious prophets, it has been extremely difficult to reconstruct the lives of common people in antiquity. But the relatively new science of paleopathology—the multidisciplinary analysis (or autopsy) of mummified corpses—has cast precious light on the nutrition and health of ancient Egyptians, rich and poor alike. Such autopsies have made clear the widespread incidence among the people of ancient Egypt of malaria, tuberculosis, severe ear infections, a variety of intestinal worms and kindred parasites, silicosis (a lung disorder caused by inhaling sand over a long span of time), and perhaps smallpox, polio, and gout.

These paleopathological autopsies also disclose severe tooth loss, common to all classes in ancient Egypt, resulting from the infiltration of windblown sand into grain storehouses and kitchens. The teeth of pharaohs and commoners alike were steadily worn down, often nearly to the gums, leading to early tooth loss and chronic tooth and gum infections that could in some cases be fatal. (Conversely, the bodies of ancient Egyptians contain only about 10 percent of the lead that is found in modern bodies, indicating a dramatic increase in lead pollution in more recent times.)

Beginning in 1974, the mummy of a young man from Upper Egypt was subjected to an autopsy of unprecedented thoroughness by a team of some forty specialists employing such sophisticated techniques as computerized X-ray scanning and electron microscopy. Written on his coffin was the young man's name, Nakht, and the fact that he had been a weaver at a great temple at Thebes. Nakht died in about 1200 B.C., during the era of the New Kingdom, roughly 150 years after the death of the pharaoh Akhenaten. People of Nakht's modest social class were rarely mummified; the expense of his entombment and coffin would have been well beyond his means and must have been funded by his temple, perhaps as a perquisite of his job.

Nakht was only about fifteen or sixteen years old when he died. He was roughly five feet eight inches tall and weighed between 100 and 120 pounds. Judging from what we know of other Egyptian workers of his era, he would have lived in a small mud-brick house and been undernourished. This last guess is confirmed by his autopsy: a careful analysis of the growth patterns of his bones discloses recurring bouts of severe illness, probably associated with malnutrition, during the final years of his short life.

Nakht's bloodstream hosted a particularly nasty tropical parasite, schistosome, the eggs of which were discovered in his kidneys and liver. The resulting disease, schistosomiasis, damaged his bladder and kidneys and caused cirrhosis of the liver. Indeed, Nakht's body was a beehive of various parasites. Tapeworm eggs were identified in his intestines, and tests of the tissue of his enlarged spleen suggest that, like many other Egyptians in antiquity, he suffered from malaria.

We know nothing of the day-to-day details of Nakht's life. He appears in no surviving written record except for the name and occupation written on his own coffin. Through his autopsy, however—conducted some 3,200 years after his death with the aid of remarkable new paleopathological techniques—we have learned that he suffered many of the afflictions common to his fellow Egyptians, great and humble.

Had Nakht lived on into early adulthood, he might very well have contracted such degenerative diseases as arteriosclerosis and arthritis. We tend today to associate these ailments with middle or old age, but they are often identified in autopsies of ancient Egyptians who died in young adulthood. And of course Nakht's teeth probably would have been ground down to a painful level in a few more years. Nakht's early death spared him the afflictions of adulthood, but his autopsy serves as a valuable reminder of the pervasive incidence of disease in even a highly civilized kingdom of the ancient Mediterranean world. The energy level of ancient Egyptian society, and of other Mediterranean societies of premodern times, must have been severely sapped by these debilitating afflictions.

THE NEW KINGDOM: c. 1550–1080 B.C.

By about 1550 B.C., the pharaoh Amose had successfully driven the Hyksos out of Egypt and indeed had pursued them into southern Palestine. Continued aggressive militarism eventually brought the Egyptians of this period, referred to by Egyptologists as the New Kingdom, into contact and conflict with the powerful states of the Mitanni during the fifteenth century B.C. and with the Hittites a century later. (In the period from c. 1500–1200, B.C., the so-called Hurrian kings of the Mitanni carved out for themselves an empire that extended from the area around Assyria and Arrapha in northern modern Iraq all the way to the Mediterranean coast, including Enar, Aleppo, and Alalah. For the "Hittites" see Chapter 4.) Campaigns into Nubia as far as Semna also were mounted by Amenophis I (c. 1527–1507 B.C.) to secure Egypt's southern border.

Although the pharaohs had always wanted to be seen as the defenders of Egypt against its foreign enemies, Egypt's military aggressiveness during the New Kingdom fundamentally changed the state once it was reunified. Egyptian kings of the New Kingdom period preferred to be represented as warriors, masters of archery fighting from chariots, who subjugated and punished Egypt's Nubian and Syrian enemies. Military officers became more prominent in the state, and they closely surrounded the pharaohs. High-ranking military officers also received grants of land from the kings and were given war captives to use as slaves. The system of granting land to veterans of the royal and imperial wars led to an intensification of land use in Egypt during the New Kingdom period. A professional standing army was established, and the Egyptians began to use fast, light, two-wheeled chariots in battles—a legacy perhaps of the Hyksos rule of Egypt.

Although the provincial shrine of Amun in Thebes was enlarged into a much greater temple (Karnák) for the cults of Amun-Re and the pharaoh, the main center of the court was moved from Thebes to Memphis. It was in Memphis that Egypt's campaigns against its neighbors were planned and from which its armies now set out. Viziers of the northern and southern parts of the country were responsible for keeping civil order and for the assessment and collection of taxes. Grain taxes and taxes on the harvests of royal estates were funneled into the royal granary, from which they were paid out to royal administrators. Some of the royal estates were worked by slaves, but other royal land was leased out to free people, from important officials of the state to poor men and women. All paid part of the produce of the land they leased back to the pharaohs. The pharaohs also dedicated booty from their wars, including slaves and treasures, to the great temples of Egypt. The pharaoh's dedication of this wealth previously had been thought to have enriched and empowered a separate priestly class in Egypt during the period, but more recent studies have reminded us that the priests of the great temples were, in fact, royal administrators whose interests were closely intertwined with those of the pharaohs themselves. Moreover, many of the great temples were explicitly dedicated to the royal cult.

At the same time that the kings' military prowess was emphasized on reliefs and in inscriptions during the period of Egypt's imperial expansion, the divine nature of the king also was reaffirmed at the celebration of annual festivals and jubilees, which marked important points in the reigns of the pharaohs. As the divine son of Amun-Re, the pharaoh also was associated with the cult of the sun itself. During this period, the cult of the sun became increasingly prominent as a symbol of the empire—to which the king was thereby linked. Queens also were invested with new potency and divinity through association with divinities such as Hathor or Sakhmet, the lion goddess. Such associations were intended to suggest the power of the royal wives. The principal wives of the New Kingdom pharaohs were usually Egyptian, although the kings often married subsidiary foreign wives (usually princesses from foreign courts).

Etched against this background of both change and continuity is the enigmatic figure of the pharaoh Akhenaten (c. 1364–1347 B.C.), who has been described variously as a heretic or a monotheist. Akhenaten perhaps rejected the many gods whom Egyptians had habitually worshiped, or perhaps he believed that all the other Egyptian deities were a manifestation of one deity, Aten, who was represented in the art of the period by a solar disc with rays extending outward and ending in hands. (See accompanying biographical sketch.)

Akhenaten

The pharaoh Akhenaten originally bore the traditional royal name Amenophis IV. It was probably to advertise his new god to the Egyptians that he changed his name (from Amenophis IV) to Akhenaten (He-who-is-beneficial-to-Aten). Removing the royal court from Thebes, with its temples and temple priesthood dedicated to Amun-Re, in the fourth year of his reign Akhenaten and his wife Nefertiti built a new capital 300 miles to the north in Middle Egypt and named it Akhetaten (Aten-on-the-horizon—the modern el-Amarna). There, they devoted themselves to the worship of Aten (the sun disc), whom Akhenaten regarded as the god of the universe, the ultimate source of ma'at, the creator of the world. Akhenaten declared in his hymn to the god Aten:

> *O sole god, beside whom there is none!*
> *You made the world as you wished, you alone.*

In this hymn and on reliefs, Aten (the sun disc) is represented as the sole king of heaven, with Akhenaten as his earthly incarnation. The close association of this one god and his earthly incarnation was emphasized artistically on reliefs that showed rays of sunshine emanating down from the sun disc, ending in hands that held the Egyptian symbol of life, the ankh, to the nose of the king and his family members.

The worship of Aten scarcely survived Akhenaten's death. Within a few years, the bold heresy had been expunged, and Osiris and Amun-Re returned in triumph. Why did Akhenaten fail? It is difficult to be certain; according to a recent hypothesis, a plague that devastated the Levant and the Hittite empire at the same time may also have affected Egypt. A large number of Akhenaten's immediate family members died early deaths. It is at least possible that these deaths within Akhenaten's family were seen by Egyptians as a kind of judgment upon his abandonment of the traditional cults of Egypt. This perhaps accounts for the more certain facts that later Akhenaten's name was not included in standard lists of pharaohs kept by the Egyptians themselves and that his reign was in effect expunged from the official record altogether where possible. Akhenaten's experiment with monotheism was not repeated by the Egyptians because it had so clearly led to disaster. Consequently Aten had no real impact on Egypt at large much after Akhenaten's reign. The theory that Akhenaten's religious ideas influenced the Hebrews who were in Egypt, thereby propelling Israel toward monotheism, thus also seems most unlikely. But whatever its weaknesses, Akhenaten's vision was of singular originality and scope. If he fell short of monotheism, he approached it more closely than anyone had before him.

In the century after Akhenaten's death, with the traditional Egyptian cults fully restored, Ramesses II's attempt to expand Egypt's borders in Syria was checked by the Hittites and their king Muwatalli at the battle of **Kadesh** on the Orontes River in Syria perhaps in May of 1274 B.C.—despite later Egyptian claims of a great victory both in an epic poem and in reliefs. Further, Libyan attacks on Egypt's western frontier probably impelled the Egyptians to conclude a peace with their Hittite rivals, who were contending with the rising power of Assyria. (Scholars have found both the Egyptian and Hittite versions of the peace treaty.) After the reign of Ramesses VI (1142–1134 B.C.), just after the disappearance of Egypt's Hittite ally in Asia Minor in 1150 B.C., Egypt lost control of its Canaanite territories. By the early eleventh century B.C., the country was effectively divided between northern and southern spheres, ruled from Thebes

Akhenaten and Nefertiti
Akhenaten and his wife Nefertiti (immediately behind him) offer libations
to the sun-disc god Aten, whose life-giving rays end in small hands. The
hands nearest to the nostrils of Akhenaten and Nefertiti hold the ankh, the
Egyptian symbol of life. The relief signifies the close connection between
Aten and Akhenaten and the royal family. Behind the white crown worn by
Akhenaten, a scarf flares out, and on his chest is written the name of Aten
in royal cartouches. Nefertiti wears the khat headdress and a long, pleated,
transparent dress. This limestone relief is from the Great Palace at el-
Amarna. (*Erich Lessing/Art Resource, NY*)

and Tanis. Attempts to reunify the country continued for another 400 years after the end of the last New Kingdom dynasty (Dynasty XX) in about 1069 B.C.

The empire survived Akhenaten's death by nearly three centuries, but it ultimately succumbed to internal disintegration and external attacks. Thereafter, Egypt was ruled for the most part by foreign dynasties or foreign peoples—Libyan, Assyrian, Persian, Greek, and Roman. During the intervals between these periods of foreign domination, the Egyptians sought to recapture their earlier creative spirit, but it always eluded them. The forms of the past were repeated endlessly, but the independent spirit of the past was beyond recovery.

Egyptian civilization had remained vigorous and essentially unified for about 2,000 years despite periods of fragmentation and loss of central control. Although Egypt lost its true independence after the end of the New Kingdom period, there is no doubt that its art and architecture, its science and medicine, and its religion deeply influenced the peoples with whom they came into contact, and even conflict, over the immense duration of its independent history, peoples including Hebrews and Persians and Greeks.

CHAPTER 4

The Diffusion of Near Eastern Civilization

THE COMING OF THE IRON AGE

In the years following 1200 B.C., the civilizations of the ancient Near East were slowly transformed by the development and spread of iron smelting. As iron came to replace bronze more and more in the making of tools and weapons, the Bronze Age ended and the Iron Age began.

Well before 1200 B.C., iron technology was known to the people of Hatti, known commonly as the Hittites. The Hittites spoke and wrote an Indo-European language (called **Nesite,** the language of the city of **Kanesh,** modern Kültepe) and had established a kingdom in central Anatolia (Turkey) centered at their fortified capital of **Hattusa** (Bogazköy) by around 1700 B.C. The Hittite empire reached the peak of its power after about 1430 B.C. While the pharaoh Akhenaten was offering devotion to the sun-disc god, the Hittites were extending their authority into Syria, as far as Lebanon and the Damascus region, at the expense of Egypt. Subsequently, Hittite kings (e.g., Mursili II) also extended Hittite dominance to the western coast of Asia Minor. And when, a century later, the pharaoh Ramesses II launched a military campaign against Hittite Syria (c. 1286 B.C.), the Hittites fought the Egyptians to a strategic stalemate and forced Ramesses to accept a treaty of "good peace and brotherhood" sealed by a dynastic marriage. Then, around 1200 B.C., Hattusa was destroyed by a massive fire. It is uncertain who wiped out the capital of the Hittite empire. What is more certain is that after the destruction of Hattusa, the Hittite empire itself dissolved, after dominating central Anatolia for more than 400 years.

Before the catastrophe that destroyed the Hittite empire, the Hittites certainly had used iron, but largely for ornamental purposes. It is clear, however, from inventory texts that the Hittites never fully developed effective techniques for producing iron tools and weapons. Once thought of as great innovators in metallurgy, the Hittites are no longer seen by scholars as inventors with respect to this technology, and they were not great disseminators of iron metallurgy either.

Indeed, it was largely after 1200 B.C., when Hattusa lay in ruins, that iron tools and weapons spread across the ancient world. Iron smelting is more complicated than bronze smelting, but once the technique was understood, iron came into widespread use. It was not only harder and more durable than bronze but far more abundant as well. The much-increased availability of metal that resulted from this "iron revolution" had a significant social impact: states came to rely for their defense on larger armies made up primarily of common people armed with iron weapons. Bronze Age aristocracies lost their monopoly on metal weapons and tools.

THE CANAANITES

The collapse of the Hittites around 1200 B.C. and the concurrent decline of the Egyptian New Kingdom presented a unique opportunity to tribes of Semitic-language speakers in Syria and Palestine, whose lands had hitherto been an imperial battleground. Indeed, the entire period from about 1200 to 750 B.C. was in some ways an interlude between imperial eras. The Hittites were crushed, and by the reign of Ramesses VI (1142–1134 B.C.), Egypt had lost control of its territories in Syria-Palestine. The great Near Eastern empires of Assyria and Persia lay off in the unknown future. In the interim, the peoples of the eastern Mediterranean shore found their place in the sun.

The dominant people in Syria-Palestine around the middle of the second millennium were known as Canaanites. (In Egyptian texts of the Amarna period, Kinahni, or Canaan, was defined as the area extending up the coast of Palestine from Gaza to the present border between Israel and Lebanon.) Because of the demands placed upon the city-states of the Canaanites by the large centralized states of Egypt and the Hittites, the Canaanite city-states concentrated their efforts on producing luxury items such as ivory-inlaid furniture or on the manufacture of textiles to be used for the payment of tribute. They also made one very important original contribution of tremendous significance: the development of the first true alphabet. Instead of hundreds of syllabic signs, the Canaanites used twenty-nine symbols representing the consonants. The alphabet was later reduced to twenty-two letters, and still later the Greeks added vowels. But even without these improvements, the Canaanite alphabet constituted an enormous simplification, and its use opened up the possibility of a vast expansion of literacy. Writing was no longer a mysterious art, and the monopoly of the old scribal class was doomed. Like the coming of iron, the invention of the alphabet extended the effects of civilization to a much larger segment of society than ever before.

The city-states of the Canaanites were subjected to violent attacks between 1300 and 1000 B.C. First came the Israelites, who had crossed the Sinai Desert from Egypt. The next invaders were the Philistines (after whom Palestine is named); some scholars have associated them with the group of "sea peoples" that invaded the New Kingdom of Egypt around 1200 B.C. The Canaanites lost most of their cities to the Israelites and Philistines but managed to maintain control of a narrow coastal strip known as Phoenicia.

The Phoenicians, as these later Canaanites were called by Greeks and Romans, had a remarkable talent for commerce. Independent Phoenician cities such as Sidon and Tyre (in modern Lebanon) sent their ships throughout the Mediterranean, carrying goods and ideas into southern Europe and North Africa. The Greek language, for example, is written in an alphabet adapted from the Phoenician (which had evolved by about 1000 B.C.), and our own alphabet is adapted from the Greek.

Merchants sailing westward from Phoenicia passed through the Strait of Gibraltar and out into the Atlantic. They may well have reached present-day Brittany and Cornwall, and they made their way southward down the west coast of Africa to Cape Verde. The greatest of the many Phoenician trading bases was Carthage in the western Mediterranean (modern Tunisia), founded by Tyre during the early first millennium B.C., and destined to acquire wealth and power far beyond the dreams of the Phoenicians themselves.

THE ISRAELITES

No other ancient Near Eastern people is as familiar to us as the Israelites. The Hebrew Bible (Old Testament), studied by scholars and believers throughout the centuries of Western civilization, is the fountainhead of Judaism, Christianity, and Islam and remains a crucial element in the heritage of billions of people today. As a historical source, it enables us to endow the dry bones of ancient Israel with flesh and life. When we use the Hebrew Bible as a historical source, however, we have to remember that this text was not intended as a straightforward factual history; rather, in its current form, it is a compilation of stories, stitched together over time from different written sources (down to the second century B.C.), detailing the interactions of a people, Israel, and their god, Yahweh, who had chosen them to work out his divine plan. Nevertheless, the Hebrew Bible provides unique and unrivaled historical insight into how one people understood its historical experience during this period.

The Hebrew Bible attests that the history of the Jews began when the patriarch Abraham entered into an agreement or covenant with a specific deity, "the God of Abraham." Abraham promised not to recognize or worship any other god, and in return he and his family were taken under the special protection of the God of Abraham. The covenant was renewed by all succeeding generations of Abraham's clan and became a basic ingredient of Jewish religious thought. Abraham probably would have conceded the existence of other deities, yet from a practical standpoint, even he was a monotheist. The existence of other gods was irrelevant to him, for it was his god alone that Abraham honored.*

Biblical evidence suggests that the first Hebrews came from Mesopotamia: the creation account, the Garden of Eden, and the Flood all seem to echo Mesopotamian traditions, and the biblical Tower of Babel may have been inspired by a ziggurat. Around the middle of the fifteenth century B.C. (according to the chronology of the Hebrew Bible), perhaps in the wake of the Kassite invasion of Mesopotamia, the Hebrews migrated to Palestine, and subsequently, so the book of Genesis relates, they were driven by famine into Egypt. The migration (Sojourn) to Egypt is said to have been led by Joseph, Abraham's great-grandson, who, after becoming the chief official of the pharaoh, was joined there by his father and eleven brothers. But the Hebrew community in Egypt was clearly not limited to Joseph and his family; it included kindred folk and probably other

---

*Scholars call a system of religious belief in which there is one preeminent god among many **henotheism.**

Semitic-language-speaking people who had filtered earlier into the Nile Valley.

It was the policy of the Egyptian New Kingdom pharaohs to enslave foreigners (the lesson of the Hyksos was not soon forgotten), or at least to use them as forced labor. While performing forced labor for the pharaohs, the Hebrews extended their Covenant of Abraham to include greater numbers of oppressed people. In the meantime, Egypt enriched itself from the profits of empire, and Akhenaten experimented with his solar religion. But the Hebrews, at the bottom of the Egyptian social order, were unaffected.

At length, perhaps around 1300 B.C., a Hebrew, trained in the Egyptian bureaucracy and bearing the Egyptian name of **Moses,** led a band of his own and other enslaved peoples to freedom. For a long generation (forty years), they wandered in the wilderness of the Sinai Desert, where they became a unified people and transformed the personal covenant into a covenant between God and the whole Hebrew nation. The God of Abraham was given the name Yahweh (traditionally, although misleadingly, translated as Jehovah, a name that, according to Hebrew doctrine, was never to be uttered). It is to this Sinai period that the Hebrew Bible ascribes the divine dictation of the Ten Commandments.

Moses had vowed to lead his people to the "promised land" of Canaan (modern Israel, Jordan, and Lebanon). But when the Hebrews emerged at last from the wilderness, Moses was dead and a new generation had arisen. According to the Hebrew Bible tradition, under the leadership of Joshua the Hebrews entered Palestine, perhaps around the mid-1200s B.C., and won a series of victories over Canaanite cities. The best known of Joshua's battles was fought at the ancient city of Jericho, whose formidable walls, we are told, came tumbling down. The struggle with the Canaanites continued for another two centuries, during which the Hebrews were deeply influenced by Canaanite culture. They adopted a Canaanite dialect and the Canaanite alphabet—an indication, perhaps, that the biblical tradition of the conquest of Canaan by the Israelites at this time may best be understood as a later (seventh-century-B.C.) attempt to differentiate Israel from other peoples in the region (after the fall of its northern kingdom) and to justify its claim to the land it held. The settlement of Cannan may have come about as a result of a more peaceful process, or perhaps even through a social revolutionary movement from within the Canaanite city-states. The latter hypothesis would help to explain, at any rate, the concern found in the Hebrew Bible that some of the Hebrews worshiped Canaanite gods, much to the chagrin of the orthodox. What is clearer is that, during these years, the Hebrews were loosely organized into tribes under local military leaders, but at length a unified monarchy emerged as a response to the increasing pressure of new invaders, the Philistines.

THE UNITED ISRAELITE KINGDOM AND ITS AFTERMATH

In about 1020 B.C., the priest Samuel anointed **Saul** as Israel's first king, perhaps in response to a Philistine victory over Israelite forces at Aphek. Saul waged war against the Philistines with some success but was outshone by his able successor, **David** (c. 1000–960 B.C.), who is said to have demonstrated his prowess even as a child by slaying the gigantic Philistine, Goliath, with a slingshot. Under David, who had been an officer in Saul's retinue and the leader of a private army, and his younger son **Solomon** (960–922 B.C.), Israel reached its political zenith in the ancient world, dominating nearly all of Syria-Palestine and extending far inland toward the Euphrates. Phoenicia retained its independence only through a policy of submissive cooperation. This was the golden age that etched itself on Israel's imagination for all time to come—the age that endless generations of Jews never despaired of recovering.

It was David's great hope to build a permanent central temple for Yahweh in Jerusalem, a strategically located Canaanite or Jebusite city that he had recently conquered, and under Solomon the temple was completed. (The Jebusites were one group of people, possibly related to the Canaanites culturally, who lived in the land conquered by Israel.) In it was enshrined the Ark of the Covenant (brought to Jerusalem by David), containing the two stones bearing the original inscriptions of the Ten Commandments. Jerusalem itself became the cosmopolitan capital of a wealthy empire; skilled laborers from Tyre came to Jerusalem to work on Solomon's building projects, and Solomon probably used his control of caravan routes to profit from the lucrative Arabian incense and spice trade. Solomon also surrounded himself with all the trappings of Near Eastern monarchy, from bureaucrats to concubines. But his subjects were obliged to pay for all this imperial glory with taxes and forced labor, and at least some of

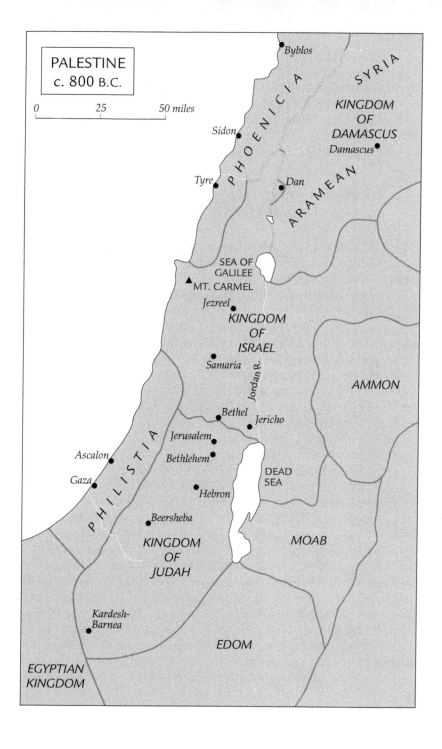

PALESTINE
c. 800 B.C.

0   25   50 miles

Byblos

SYRIA

PHOENICIA

KINGDOM
OF
DAMASCUS

Sidon

Damascus

Tyre

Dan

ARAMEAN

SEA OF
GALILEE

MT. CARMEL

Jezreel

KINGDOM
OF
ISRAEL

Samaria

Jordan R.

AMMON

Bethel

Jericho

Jerusalem

Bethlehem

Ascalon

DEAD
SEA

Gaza

PHILISTIA

Hebron

Beersheba

KINGDOM
OF
JUDAH

MOAB

Kardesh-
Barnea

EDOM

EGYPTIAN
KINGDOM

them concluded that the price was too high. Even before Solomon's death, some states (Aram Zobah, Damascus, Edom) had achieved independence, and upon his death in 922 B.C., his realm broke into two halves: a large kingdom to the north, known thenceforth as Israel, and the smaller, more unified kingdom of Judah, centered upon Jerusalem, to the south.

This split brought an end to Hebrew imperialism. And with the rise of new empires, the Hebrews lost their political independence. The first of the new empires, the Assyrian, exerted increasing military pressure against both Israel and Judah. Israel fell to the Assyrians in 721 B.C., and its king, nobles, and cavalry were scattered across the Near East, where they faded into the indigenous populations and vanished from history. They have been known ever since as the "ten lost tribes of Israel."

Judah survived the Assyrian attacks only to fall to Assyria's imperial successor, the New Babylonian Empire, in 587 B.C. The temple was destroyed and Judah's political and intellectual leaders were banished to Babylon, where they and their children endured that tragic epoch in biblical history, the Babylonian Captivity (587–538 B.C.). The bitterness of exile is captured in the opening lines of Psalm 137:

> By the rivers of Babylon,
> There we sat down, yea, we wept,
> When we remembered Zion.*

THE PROPHETS

The devastating experiences of a divided kingdom and the Babylonian Captivity evoked a profound religious response. During these years, the moral initiative passed from kings and priests to inspired individuals known as prophets, whose spiritual insights—arising out of an age of despair—deepened and ennobled the religion of the Hebrews. To the prophets, law and ritual were insufficient without sincerity of purpose and righteousness of life. The prophet Micah expressed this idea with striking brevity:

> It has been shown to you, O man, what is good
> and what the Lord requires of you:

---

*Originally, Zion was the name of the hill in Jerusalem on which Solomon's temple stood, the holy center of the Hebrew kingdom and faith. The term later acquired broader meanings: the Heavenly City or the people of Israel.

Only to do justice, and live loyally, and walk humbly
    with your God. (Micah 6:8)

The teachings of the prophets were based on two fundamental concepts: (1) the covenant between God and his Hebrew people and (2) the consequent obligation of Israelites to treat one another justly. Their vision of justice and righteousness was not applied originally with any consistency to humanity at large, but only to the Jewish community; yet even with that important qualification, it was a profound affirmation of human dignity. Unlike the ephemeral social consciousness of the Egyptian Middle Kingdom, the prophetic teachings became a fundamental component of Hebrew thought. More than that, they underlay the tradition of social justice that developed in Western civilization. The prophets' insistence that all Israelites were equal in the sight of God ultimately would expand into the doctrine of universal human equality.

In the words of the prophets, the concept of Yahweh was universalized. They explained the collapse of Solomon's empire and the Assyrian and Babylonian conquests by asserting that Yahweh had used the Hebrews' enemies to punish his chosen people for their transgressions and to prepare them for a triumphant future. If this was so, then Yahweh's power was evidently not limited to the Hebrews but embraced all peoples. Whereas Yahweh had formerly been the only God that mattered, he was now proclaimed as the only God that existed. The prophet Amos quotes the Lord as saying,

Did I not bring up Israel
    from the land of Egypt
and the Philistines from Caphtor
    and the Syrians from Kir? (Amos 9:7)

Yahweh was the Lord of all nations, yet the Hebrews remained his chosen people. History itself could be understood only in terms of Israel's encounter with God. The Hebrews were unique among the peoples of the ancient Near East in their sensitivity toward history, for to them God's relations with humanity occurred in a historical dimension, and history itself was directed by God toward certain predetermined goals. Thus it was Yahweh, not the Babylonians, who sent the Hebrews into exile, and in the fullness of time, so the prophets said, Yahweh would build their kingdom anew. A divinely appointed leader of the house of David—a Messiah—would one day be sent to consummate the divine plan by reestablishing the political glory of Israel.

LATER JEWISH HISTORY

In 539 B.C., the New Babylonian Empire gave way to the Persian Empire, and the conquerors permitted the Hebrews to return to their homeland and rebuild the Temple of Jerusalem. They could now practice their faith without interference, but they remained under Persian political control. Two centuries later, Persian rule gave way to Greek rule, and in time the Romans replaced the Greeks. During these centuries, the Hebrews collected, sifted, and expanded their sacred writings, and the Hebrew Bible (later called the Old Testament) acquired its final form.

From time to time, the Jews rebelled against their political masters, but never with lasting success. A rebellion in A.D. 66 prompted the Romans to destroy the rebuilt Second Temple in A.D. 70 (never rebuilt) and to scatter the Jews throughout the Roman Empire. There followed an exile far more prolonged than the earlier ones in Egypt and Babylon, lasting until the middle of the twentieth century. But the Jews had long before demonstrated their unique capacity to survive as a people and a faith even though they were without political unity or a modern nation-state—for they possessed what no other people of the ancient Near East had, namely, a book that was not only a source of theological beliefs and rules of moral and social conduct but also a kind of national history that was portable.

The impact of the ancient Hebrews on future civilizations has been immense. The Hebrew Bible, a tremendous literary monument in itself, has been of incalculable importance in the development of European culture and the cultures of other civilizations as well. The Hebrews' sense of history—as a dynamic, purposeful, morally significant process of human and divine interaction—went far beyond the historical concepts of other Near Eastern peoples and became a fundamental element in the historical vision of Western civilization. But at the core of everything is the idea of ethical monotheism, the vision of a single God of infinite power who expects righteous behavior from human beings but is also a God of mercy. The Hebrews confronted their universe in a new way. The myriad demons of tree, rock, and mountain dissolved before the unutterable holiness of the God of Israel.

THE NEW EMIPIRES, ASSYRIANS AND CHALDEANS: *c. 745–539 B.C.*

The last great phase of ancient Near Eastern history runs from the rise of the Assyrian Empire in the mid-eighth century B.C. to the conquest of the Persian Empire by the Macedonians under Alexander the Great from 334 to 330 B.C. During these centuries, Near Eastern imperialism reached its zenith.

The Assyrians, a people from northern Mesopotamia who spoke a Semitic language, used ruthless militarism to create an empire that not only dominated the area of the Fertile Crescent from 745 to

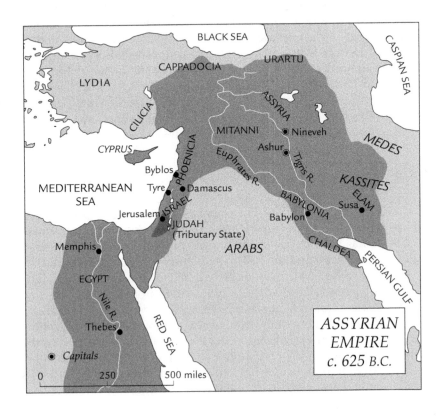

612 B.C. but also dominated territory from the Arab-Persian Gulf to Commagene in Turkey to Egypt as well. Most of the Middle East was momentarily united under a power that terrorized its subjects and crushed insurrections with fearful severity. One Assyrian king boasted of punishing a group of rebels by tearing out their tongues, mashing them alive, and feeding their corpses to pigs and vultures.

Assyrian culture was Sumerian in inspiration. Its gods were similar to those of Sumer and Akkad, although much more warlike, especially Ashur, the principal deity, who was assumed to be superior to the gods of the peoples defeated by the Assyrians. Indeed, war itself was presented to the Assyrian kings as a divine commandment of Ashur.

Assyrian militarism brought unity and a degree of peace to the long-troubled Near East. Of course it was ultimately a peace based upon force or the threat of force. (There also is documentary evidence suggesting that at least some of Assyria's smaller neighbors willingly allied themselves to Assyria to establish mutually profitable relations.) Once Assyrian leadership faltered, however, the empire collapsed after repeated attacks by two of its subject peoples. Despite fierce resistance, a coalition of Babylonians (Semitic-language speakers) and Medes from Iran (who spoke an Indo-European language) destroyed the power of Assyria for all time. The Assyrian capital of Nineveh fell in 612 B.C., and its site remains desolate to this day. The destruction of mighty Assyria was taken as an object lesson by later Greeks.

Until the rise of Persia (c. 539 B.C.), the Near East was divided among several powers. Egypt had already recovered its independence and unity under the leadership of a former Assyrian client-king, Psammetichus (664–610 B.C.). Following the decline of the kingdom of Urartu in eastern Anatolia and Phrygia (centered on Gordion), domination of western Anatolia passed to the Lydians, a people who produced what was probably the world's first real coinage and whose last king, Croesus, achieved fame as a monarch of legendary wealth. Part of the wealth of the Lydian kings was derived from the gold extracted from deposits washed down by the Pactolus River, on whose banks Sardis, the capital city, lay. The Lydians, along with other peoples in the Near East, were continuously threatened during this period by raiding nomads called "Cimmerians" and "Scythians" in later Greek sources. Assyria itself, together with the northern and eastern provinces of its former empire, became subject to the Medes. The southern and western provinces fell to the Babylonians, who established a New Babylonian Empire.

The Babylonians rebuilt Babylon with unprecedented splendor in glazed, colored tiles of deep blue, decorated with molded reliefs of bulls and dragons. This was the age of the Hebrews' Babylonian Captivity. It was also the age of the "hanging gardens of Babylon," attributed to Nebuchadnezzar II (604–562 B.C.), and the climax of Mesopotamian astrology. In their efforts to foretell the future and discern the will of the gods, Chaldaean wise men among the Babylonians made painstaking observations of the stars and planets from observatories atop the towers of their fascinating city. They also made fundamental advances in mathematics, developing the concepts of square roots and cube roots, linear and quadratic equations, and a system very close to modern algebra. Although monarchy was the traditional form of government in the New Babylonian Empire, there also was a strong sense of corporate identity among city dwellers in Babylonia, and a concept of "citizen" also developed. This last, brief Babylonian renaissance came to an end when the city fell to the Persians in 539 B.C.

The Persians, like the Medes to whom they were closely related, spoke an Indo-European language (Old Persian). They settled on the Iranian plateau. (The traditional homeland of the Persians corresponds with the modern Iranian province of Fars, at the southeastern end of the Zagros Mountain range.) The traditional domination of the Persians by the Medes (who lived in the Zagros region proper, around Ecbatana or modern Hamadan) was reversed in 550 B.C. when the Persian leader **Cyrus II** (called "the Great") defeated the Median King Astyages, seized the Median royal city of Ecbatana, and thenceforth ruled both peoples. During the subsequent decade, Cyrus conducted an astonishing series of military campaigns that won him a wide empire stretching from India through Mesopotamia, Lydia, and Syria-Palestine. With the conquest and absorption of Egypt shortly after Cyrus's death by his son Cambyses, who ruled from 530–522 B.C., the Persians unified almost all of the Middle and Near East into a single empire.

The Persian Empire represents the synthesis of Near Eastern political and cultural traditions under a government that achieved stability not solely through military terror but through greater tolerance and flexible administration. The Jews were allowed to return to their homeland and rebuild their temple, perhaps as part of a policy

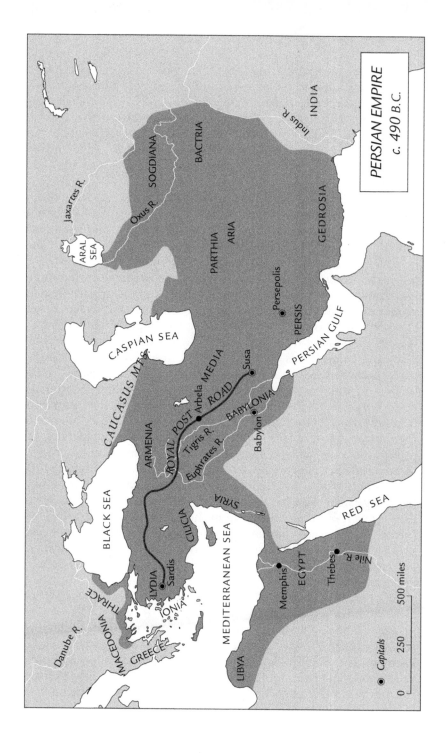

PERSIAN EMPIRE
c. 490 B.C.

of resettling and rebuilding provincial centers. In general though, the Persians allowed the peoples of their empire a generous degree of religious and cultural autonomy as long as they paid their taxes and did not rebel against Persian rule. These taxes were paid in kind, in the form of agricultural produce and also in precious metals, usually silver. On the whole, the Persians preferred to work through local institutions to advance their own interests. This was one of the secrets of their success.

At its height under **Darius I** (called "the Great," 521–486 B.C.), the imperial government, with its center at the great fortress-palace at Persepolis (Fars), consisted of an absolute, theoretically hereditary monarchy (although the Persian kings were free to choose their successors from among the Achaemenid royal family circle) assisted by a central group of hereditary nobles and represented in the imperial provinces by Iranian governors called "satraps." (Some peoples nominally under Persian imperial control, such as the Arabs and the Scythians, however, were linked to the imperial authority by a flexible measure of regulated control, which was of mutual benefit.) The king himself, his family members, the nobility, and favored subjects owned estates throughout the empire; the presence of the owners of these estates strengthened imperial control of the vast empire. Although the monarchy permitted the various provinces to retain many of their individual customs, it kept close watch over them through a network of imperial inspectors who saw to it that the satraps remained both honest and loyal. At the same time, the system of imperial control depended heavily upon cooperation between the satraps and local elites. Commerce was stimulated by an extensive, heavily guarded network of roads throughout the empire and by the introduction of imperial coinage in the Lydian tradition. The Greek historian Herodotus commended the efficiency of the Persian postal service in these familiar words: "Neither snow nor rain nor heat nor gloom of night stays these couriers from the swift completion of their appointed rounds."

Overall, the culture of the Persian Empire was a summation rather than a departure. In most respects, it was a development of age-old Mesopotamian concepts, although the use of tall stone columns (page 63) gave Persian architecture a delicate elegance all its own. The Persian "king of kings," for all his imperial pomp, refrained from claiming divinity and was satisfied merely to stress his divine appointment. The great god **Ahuramazda** (which means

Palace at Persepolis
The ruins of the royal audience hall (*apadana*) of the palace at Persepolis,
built between 520 and 460 B.C. by the Persian kings Darius I and Xerxes I,
were part of a sprawling complex of many adjoining buildings. (© *Paul
Almasy/Corbis*)

"wise lord" in Persian) had set the Persian king over the varied lands
and peoples of the earth and given Persia supremacy over them.

It was in the religious sphere that the Persians eventually
showed their greatest originality. They, no less than the Jews, broke
sharply with Near Eastern religious tradition. The almost legendary
Persian prophet **Zoroaster** (or **Zarathustra**) proclaimed a highly in-
tellectualized doctrine of ethical monotheism centering on the god
Ahuramazda. In the centuries after Zoroaster's death, Zoroastrianism

incorporated older Iranian gods as lesser deities and elevated the evil god Ahriman to a position almost equal to that of Ahuramazda. Zoroastrianism thus evolved into an intensely dualistic faith that stressed the universal struggle between good and evil. Ahuramazda became the god of light, goodness, mind, and spirit; Ahriman represented darkness, evil, and matter. The material world and the human body came to be viewed as evil; the spiritual world and the human soul were seen as good. Zoroastrianism alone among ancient Near Eastern religions transcended both the state and the people that gave it birth and became a universal faith. It remained dominant in Iran and Mesopotamia until the Islamic conquests of the seventh century A.D. and exerted a strong influence on Jewish, Hellenistic, Roman, and medieval religious thought.

The last century of Persian rule saw a failure of imperial leadership, although it is now clear that Darius III, the last of the Achaemenid kings, mounted a very effective defense of his empire against Alexander the Great and the Macedonians. Alexander's victories over Darius and the Persians were not a foregone conclusion, and it is often forgotten that Alexander and the Macedonians had to fight for twelve long years to stamp out Persian resistance to Macedonian rule. Unfortunately for Darius and the Persians, however, neither they nor anyone else in the ancient Near East had ever encountered a military leader quite like the young Macedonian king.

The defeat of the last great Near Eastern empire did not spell the end of the history of the peoples of the Near East, and by the time Alexander defeated the Persians, the peoples and empires of the ancient Near East had already deeply influenced Greek culture. Ancient Greece was indebted to the Near East for its alphabet, much of its mythology and architecture, and the beginnings of its technology and science. The Greeks nevertheless developed this intellectual and cultural legacy in ways unimagined by their predecessors. One Greek writer emphasized the point with charming immodesty when he said, "Whatever the Greeks take over from foreigners, they transform it by making it something finer." Yet behind Greece and Rome lies the rich experience of the ancient Near East, without which these later civilizations would be inconceivable.

SUGGESTED READINGS

Prehistory

G. Barker, *The Agricultural Revolution in Prehistory* (2006). A global view of the evidence for the transition(s) from foraging to the domestication of animals.

M. Cohen, *Health and the Rise of Civilization* (1989). This meticulous study argues that the Neolithic Revolution and the emergence of civilization brought a decline in nutrition and health.

B. Fagan, *World History: A Brief Introduction* (1996). A short, approachable introduction.

D. Johanson and J. Shreeve, *Lucy's Child: The Discovery of a Human Ancestor* (1989). The best general account.

R. Lewin, *Human Evolution: An Illustrated Introduction* (4th ed., 1999). A valuable recent account of the origins of humanity, drawing on East African evidence.

J. Mellaart, *The Neolithic of the Near East* (1975). Discusses archaeological investigations of Neolithic villages.

S. Milisauskas, *European Prehistory: A Survey* (2002). Comprehensive and up-to-date.

C. Scarre, *Exploring Prehistoric Europe* (1998). Especially valuable for discussions of megalithic monuments.

A. Sherratt, *Economy and Society in Prehistoric Europe: Changing Perspectives* (1997). Brings an acute theoretical perspective to all the most important questions.

The Ancient Near East

J. Aruz with R. Wallenfels, *Art of the First Cities: The Third Millennium B.C. from the Mediterranean to the Indus* (2003). A splendid catalogue tied to a phenomenal museum exhibition.

I. M. Diakonoff, ed., *Early Antiquity*, trans. Alexander Kirjanov (1991). An intriguing, up-to-date survey of ancient Near Eastern civilizations.

A. Kuhrt, *The Ancient Near East c. 3000–330 B.C.* (1995), 2 vols. Far and away the best two-volume survey available in English. A prize-winning, monumental work of scholarship to which revisions of this edition are heavily indebted.

M. Roaf, *Cultural Atlas of Mesopotamia and the Ancient Near East* (1990). Excellent maps and illustrations.

J. Sasson, ed. *Civilizations of the Ancient Near East* (1995), 4 vols. A collection of up-to-date contributions on the history, archaeology, languages, etc., of the ancient Near East.

M. Van De Mieroop, *A History of the Ancient Near East ca. 3000–323 B.C.* (2004). The best general one-volume synthesis available, with excellent lists of Near Eastern kings. Probably the place to start for those interested in going into a little more depth.

Mesopotamia

G. Algaze, *The Uruk World System: The Dynamics of Expansion of Early Mesopotamian Civilization* (1993). This valuable study of Mesopotamian politics and economics concludes that vigorous cross-cultural commerce gave rise to imperial expansion.

J. Bottéro, *Everyday Life in Ancient Mesopotamia* (1992). Discusses cooking, eating, drinking, sexuality, medicine, magic, and other topics related to the day-to-day lives of the ancient Mesopotamians.

J. Bottéro, *Mesopotamia: Writing, Reasoning and the Gods* (1992). An essential study by the dean of French Assyriology.

S. Kramer, *History Begins at Sumer* (3rd ed., 1981). Gracefully written and adept in its use of Sumerian writings.

A. Oppenheim, *Ancient Mesopotamia* (1977). The best intellectual history.

M. Van De Mieroop, *The Ancient Mesopotamian City* (1999). An accessible study of the world's first real cities.

Egypt

C. Aldred, *Akhenaten: King of Egypt* (1988). A sensible account.

C. Aldred, *The Egyptians* (rev. ed., with color plates, 1987). A good general account.

C. Desroches-Noblecourt, *Tutankhamen* (1963). Stunning illustrations recreate the world of the New Kingdom pharaoh.

N. Grimal, *A History of Ancient Egypt*, trans. Ian Shaw (1992). A lucidly presented political and economic history that makes adroit use of archaeological evidence.

B. Kemp, *Ancient Egypt: Anatomy of a Civilization* (1989). Highly original and idiosyncratic.

A. Nibbi, *The Sea Peoples and Egypt* (1975). A fascinating, controversial work of historical revisionism that makes expert use of archaeological evidence.

D. Redford, *Akhenaten: The Heretic King* (1984). Authoritative and vividly written, the best study of the subject.

D. Redford, *Egypt, Canaan, and Israel in Ancient Times* (1992). Admirable scholarship, artfully presented.

D. Redford, ed., *The Oxford Encyclopedia of Ancient Egypt* (2001), 3 vols. A treasury of up-to-date information.

I. Shaw, ed., *The Oxford Illustrated History of Ancient Egypt* (2002). Lively essays and excellent illustrations.

W. Simpson, trans., *The Literature of Ancient Egypt: An Anthology of Stories, Instructions, and Poetry* (1973).

E. Strouhal, *Life in Ancient Egypt* (1992). An up-to-date account.

The Diffusion of Near Eastern Civilization

J. Bottéro, C. Herrenschmidt, and J.-P. Vernant, *Ancestor of the West: Writing, Reasoning and Religion in Mesopotamia, Elam, and Greece* (2000). A brief overview by three noted experts.

P. Briant, *From Cyrus to Alexander: A History of the Persian Empire* (2002). Far and away the best general history available in English. See also, www.museum-achemenet.college-de-france.fr for a virtual interactive Achaemenid museum online, presenting an inventory of the Persian Empire's heritage.

J. Bright, *A History of Israel* (3rd ed., 1981). A valuable survey running to the mid-second century B.C.

T. Bryce, *The Kingdom of the Hittites* (1998). Fundamental.

O. Gurney, *The Hittites* (1990). Brief but comprehensive.

J. Hooker, ed., *Reading the Past: Ancient Writings from Cuneiform to the Alphabet* (1991).

M. Liverani, *International Relations in the Ancient Near East, 1600–1100 B.C.* (2001). The best study of its kind by a very astute and witty historian.

A. Mazar, *Archaeology in the Land of the Bible: 10,000–586 B.C.E.* (1990). Comprehensive and indispensable.

J. Naveh, *The Early History of the Alphabet* (1982).

N. Postgate, *The First Empires* (1977), 2 vols. These volumes, from the Making of the Past series, provide lucid, detailed accounts of the great Near Eastern empires.

N. K. Sandars, *The Sea Peoples: Warriors of the Ancient Mediterranean, 1250–1150 B.C.* (rev. ed., 1985). Stresses the ambiguity of the evidence and the danger of overinterpreting it.

H. Shanks, ed., Ancient Israel: From *Abraham to the Roman Destruction of the Temple* (1999). An important collection of essays by experts well versed in the latest archaeological finds. As editor of *Biblical Archaeology Review* magazine, Shanks also maintains a lively Web site on issues concerning biblical and Near Eastern history at www.biblicalarchaeology.org.

PART TWO

Ancient Greece

ANCIENT GREECE: AN OVERVIEW

Homer's *Odyssey,* one of the supreme Greek epic poems, tells of the perils and adventures of the Greek king Odysseus as he sailed home after the Greek conquest of Troy. As a tale of a hero's triumph over the terrors of the ocean, the Odyssey reflects a central quality of the Greek experience, for the Greeks of the historical period were a seafaring people. Sailing out into the Aegean Sea from their barren, mountainous homeland, they planted colonies far and wide and eventually dominated the commerce of the eastern Mediterranean.

This domination was at its height during the fifth century B.C., when the great Greek cultural and political center of Athens ruled an extensive empire of formerly independent states on the isles of the Aegean and along its shores. Enriched by tribute payments from their subject states, the Athenians created one of the supreme civic cultures in human history. But even at its cultural and military height, Athens was unable to dominate Greece or bring an end to the wars that had always been waged between one Greek city-state (polis) and another. By the end of the fifth century, Athens had been forced to surrender its empire and its freedom to an anti-Athenian alliance led by the rival Greek city-state of Sparta.

Not until the 330s B.C. did the Greek city-states achieve unification, and even then it was not through their own efforts. They were conquered by the armies of the mountainous frontier kingdom of Macedon, whose most celebrated monarch, Alexander the Great, led an army recruited from throughout most of Greece on a series of dazzling campaigns that brought the Persian Empire and the entire Near East under Graeco-Macedonian control.

However, upon Alexander's early death in 323 B.C., his empire broke up into warring fragments, all of which eventually submitted to the authority of a much more cohesive empire far to the west, that of the Romans. Greek history did not end, however, when the successor kingdoms of Alexander eventually fell under Roman domination. Rather, a new chapter in Greek history was written under Roman rule. Indeed, arguably, the apogee of the Greek city-state was achieved during the second century A.D. when the Greeks were ruled by Rome.

Significant Events of Greek History

All dates are B.C.

c. 2000–1470	Minoan civilization flourishes (Palatial period)
c. 1450–1200	Mycenaean civilization flourishes (Palatial period)
c. 1200	Trojan War
c. 1200–1100	Emergence of Dorian Greeks
c. 1120–800	Dark Age
776	Celebration of first Olympic Games
c. 750–550	Era of colonization
c. 650	Rise of tyrants
c. 594	Solon's reforms in Athens
c. 582–507	Pythagoras
561–510	Pisistratid tyranny in Athens
508–507	Cleisthenes' reforms in Athens
490	Defeat of Persians at Marathon
480	Thermopylae
478	Formation of Delian League
c. 469–429	Era of Pericles
454	Delian treasury moved to Athens
432	Parthenon completed
431–404	Peloponnesian War
c. 469–399	Socrates
c. 429–347	Plato
384–322	Aristotle
359–336	Reign of Philip II of Macedon
338	Battle of Chaeronea; Macedonian mastery of Greece
336–323	Reign of Alexander the Great
323	Hellenistic Age begins; wars of Alexander's successors
146	Roman destruction of Corinth
31	Battle of Actium
30	Roman conquest of Egypt

CHAPTER 5

Crete, Mycenae, and the Dark Age

EARLY GREECE: LEGEND AND REALITY

The two great Homeric epics, the *Iliad* and the *Odyssey*, probably originated as oral poems in the eighth century B.C. (The *Iliad* seems to have preceded the *Odyssey* by some fifty years.) Both poems tell of the conclusion and aftermath of a half-legendary, long-ago war between the Greeks and the Trojans—a struggle that ended with the Greek conquest of **Troy.** These epics marked the dawn of Greek literature when they were written down, yet they hark back to a far older civilization.

Not much more than a century ago, the Homeric epics and the Trojan War were seen merely as inspired fancy. The picture that emerges in Homer's poems of a highly developed civilization on the Greek mainland dominated by King Agamemnon of **Mycenae** was thought to be a folk myth and nothing more. But during the 1870s and 1880s, Heinrich Schliemann, a retired German business-man and amateur archaeologist, confounded the scholarly world by excavating Troy (Hisarlik in modern Turkey), Mycenae, and other sites referred to in the *Iliad* and the *Odyssey,* thereby giving reality to a supposedly imaginary civilization that had flourished some eight centuries before the golden age of Athens.* Early in the twentieth century, Sir Arthur Evans's excavations at **Knossos** on the

---

*At Troy, however, subsequent and more scientific excavation of the site has shown that Schliemann's identification of Troy II as the level corresponding to the period when Homer's Trojan War was fought is incorrect. The remains of Troy II, including the so-called Priam's Treasure, which Schliemann smuggled out of Turkey to Germany, date to the period from 2500–2300 B.C. Scholars who believe that there was a Trojan War similar to the one described by Homer associate that war now with archaeological levels of the city dated to a much later period, Troy VIIa or VIIb, 1260–1050 B.C.

island of Crete produced evidence of a civilization resembling that of Mycenae on the Greek mainland, but even older and more splendid. In 1952, Michael Ventris deciphered the script used at Knossos and several mainland sites, which is known as **Linear B.** The work of Schliemann, Evans, Ventris, and other students of early Aegean culture has opened a new world to us. But the study of this first European civilization remains fluid and exciting as old theories are constantly being upended by new discoveries.

MINOAN CIVILIZATION

Early Aegean civilization, known conventionally as Minoan (after Minos, a legendary king of Crete) or Mycenaean (after an ancient fortress-town on the Greek mainland), endured in later Greek literature like a half-remembered dream. Minoan civilization emerged in the fourth millennium B.C. (c. 3500 B.C.) on the island of Crete. The Minoans derived their technological and artistic skills from Mesopotamia, Egypt, Asia Minor, and a slightly earlier culture centered on islands in the Aegean Sea known as the Cyclades, which produced an impressive legacy of decorative art in lead and silver and marble funeral statues.

The Minoans developed these artistic legacies in novel and creative directions. Excavations on Crete have unearthed ruins of great rambling palaces, their walls decorated with vivacious paintings, their rooms containing exquisite statuettes and delicate polychromatic pottery fashioned with consummate skill and taste. Minoan art is light and flowing: plants, animals, marine life, and youths playing games, all were portrayed with stylistic flair and stunning naturalism during the neo-Palatial period (to c. 1470 B.C.).

The lively spirit of the Minoans is nowhere better illustrated than in their love of games. Minoan art has left us scenes of boxing matches, acrobatics, and bull-leaping. The last, which may have had a religious significance, involved both male and female athletes grasping a bull by the horns and leaping over its body. A group of curious scholars went so far as to ask an American cowboy how this might have been done; he told them flatly that it could not be done at all. Yet bull-leaping scenes abound in Minoan art, and we can only conclude that it was done somehow—perhaps through the joint efforts of superbly trained athletes and an unusually obliging bull.

Throne room at Knossos
Arthur Evans's reconstruction of the throne room from the palace of the
Minoan king Minos at Knossos, Crete (c. 1600 B.C.) shows the bulbous,
downward-tapering wooden columns and fresco-painted walls that typi-
fied Minoan architecture. (© *Wolfgang Kaehler/Corbis*)

Minoan religion has been the subject of much fascinating guesswork, but in the absence of decipherable religious texts we can be
certain of nothing. A Minoan statuette of a stylishly dressed, bare-
breasted young woman holding snakes might represent a fertility
goddess of the sort that abounded in prehistoric Europe, or it might
not. Overall, however, Minoan civilization seems to have developed
as a centralized urban theocratic society similar to those of contemporary eastern states. Round tombs known as *tholoi* characterized
communal religious activity during the third millennium B.C. During the Palatial period, the Minoan palaces themselves probably
were major foci of religious ritual. The famous depictions of double
axes found at Minoan palace sanctuaries probably represented the
primary instrument of sacrifice and the symbol of new life to come
from the blood of the sacrificial victim.

Surprisingly, the palaces and towns of the Minoan golden age
had no appreciable fortifications, yet scenes of warfare in some
recently discovered Minoan frescoes would seem to rule out the

Bull-leaping fresco at Knossos
The walls of the great palace at Knossos were painted with frescoes of
great fluidity and vigor, like this scene of acrobats leaping over the back of
a bull. Bulls seem to have played an important part in Minoan religion;
whether this activity was part of a religious ritual or an athletic competition
is unknown. (© *Erich Lessing/Art Resource, NY*)

notion that the Minoans were pacifists. More likely, the whole island
of Crete was united under the kings of Knossos, and the Minoan
fleet provided sufficient protection against enemies from without.

The Minoans owed their success to their isolation and their
ships, but the lure of the sea also resulted in cultural dynamism.
Long before the Phoenicians ventured into the Mediterranean, Minoan seafarers were trading with Asia Minor, Syria, North Africa,
the Aegean islands, and even Spain. They imported tin and copper for the superb Minoan bronzeware that in turn became a
chief item of export, along with delicate pottery fashioned by
Minoan artisans.

Minoan agriculture, based on a large, semi-free peasantry, was
devoted chiefly to the production of wine, olive oil, and grain (wheat
and barley)—the so-called Mediterranean triad—which became

Minoan statuette
Several similar female figurines, clad in open-bodiced, flounced skirts and wearing high headdresses, some holding snakes, have been found in Crete. It is unclear whether they represent a mother goddess or priestesses.
(© *Gail Mooney/Corbis*)

dominant in the Aegean area after about 3000 B.C. and would also be the chief agricultural commodities of classical Greece. The Minoan economy was exceptionally prosperous during the golden age of Crete, enabling the aristocracy to live luxuriously. By about 1500 B.C., the economy had reached a level of complexity that required the keeping of extensive records. These records were kept on clay tablets in a script that has not yet been deciphered and that Sir Arthur Evans called **Linear A.**

Aristocratic women seem to have enjoyed a relatively high status in Minoan civilization. They were not confined to the private sphere of hearth and home, as they had been in Mesopotamian society, but are depicted in frescoes participating in public ceremonies and attending public functions alongside men. In the statuettes and frescoes of the age, they are frequently dressed in hooped skirts with wasp waists, tight-fitting bodices that leave the breasts exposed, and marvelously complex hairstyles. A mother goddess and other female deities, whose shrines have been found in some twenty-five caves throughout the island, clearly played a major role in Minoan religion.

THE MYCENAEAN GREEKS

It is uncertain whether the first Greek-speaking peoples arrived in southern Greece around 2100 B.C., 1900 B.C., or perhaps several centuries later, according to the most recent research. It is far more certain that their language, called Proto-Greek by linguists, derived from a common Indo-European language ancestor. Certain other Indo-European languages of the ancient world, including Latin and Persian, also were descended from that common ancestor language.

From about 1580 B.C. onward, the settlements of the early Greek speakers were increasingly influenced by Minoan civilization, although they seem to have retained their political independence. Fortress-cities such as Mycenae and Tiryns in the Peloponnesus dominated the surrounding country, and in time—if Homer's later testimony can be trusted—all the princes of southern Greece recognized the overlordship of the warrior kings of Mycenae.

The Mycenaean Greeks learned much from the Minoans; their culture differed from that of Crete chiefly in its emphasis on fortifications. They adapted the Minoan script Linear A to their own very different language. The result was Linear B, which used a Minoan

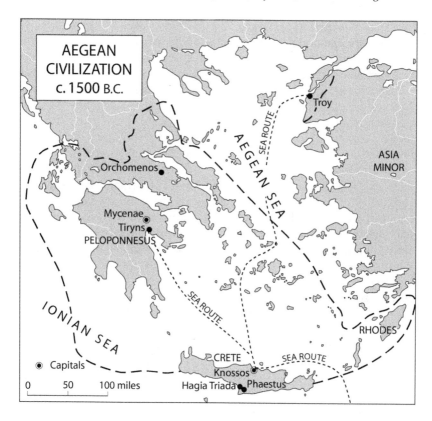

syllabary to express Greek words. Their art, architecture, and customs, however, were all strongly influenced by the Minoan; they even took up bull-leaping. And Mycenaean women began adopting Minoan dress, hairstyles, and cosmetics.

Before long, Mycenaean sailors were challenging Cretan supremacy in the Aegean. In about 1475 B.C., a band of Greeks seems to have seized power in Knossos itself, for thereafter the records of Knossos were kept in the Greek Linear B (which is found nowhere else on Crete). In about 1400 B.C., Minoan civilization was severely disturbed when a devastating invasion of the island, probably by other Mycenaean Greeks, left the towns, villas, and palaces in ruins. The great palaces were never rebuilt on their previous scale, although there is evidence that Knossos was inhabited for several generations thereafter.

With the disintegration of the Minoan state, Mycenaean ships became increasingly active in the trade of the eastern Mediterranean. Between about 1450 and 1200 B.C., the Mycenaeans grew rich on their commerce and flourished exceedingly, dominating the southern Aegean and the coast of Asia Minor from Miletos to Knidos, where Hittite texts reveal that the Mycenaean Greeks (particularly the king of a place called Ahhiyawa—perhaps Mycenae itself) came into conflict with Hittites and their allies. It is at the end of this period, perhaps around 1200 B.C., that King Agamemnon of Mycenae was believed by later Greeks to have led the Greeks against Troy. (Some scholars believe that the Trojan War described by Homer is a kind of reminiscence of the conflicts between Mycenaean Greeks and the Hittites for control of the coasts of Asia Minor, which, at the time of the war, was inhabited by another Indo-European-language-speaking people, the Luwians, allies of the Hittites to the east during the late Bronze Age.) But even at the time of the Trojan War, the political stability of Mycenaean Greece was being disturbed, not only by natural disasters such as earthquakes but also by internal stresses and the emergence of the Dorian Greeks and related tribes.

Traditionally, scholars have assumed that the Dorians invaded from the north, but more recent investigations suggest that they may have already been settled in Greece as a subject people before their rise to power. Whatever the case, the Dorian Greeks were little affected by Minoan-Mycenaean culture, and they helped to destroy it through military violence. Linear B tablets found in Mycenaean cities of about 1120 B.C. record frantic but ineffective preparations for defense. One after another, the Mycenaean cities were sacked and burned, and the civilization that had begun in Crete and later spread to the Greek mainland faded into legend.

THE GREEK DARK AGE: c. 1120–800 B.C.

The disintegration of Mycenaean culture was roughly concurrent with the collapse of the Hittite empire and the decline of the Egyptian New Kingdom. The far-flung maritime activities of the Phoenicians in the following epoch were made possible not only by the troubles of the Near Eastern empires but also by the disruption of Mycenaean commerce.

Between Mycenaean and classical Greece lies a chasm of several centuries known as the Dark Age of **Hellenic** history.*

As far as we know, the Greeks lapsed into illiteracy, and when they began to write once again they did so not in the old Minoan syllabary but in an alphabet adapted from the Phoenicians. In the meantime, as we know from archaeological evidence, most of the Peloponnesus had fallen under the control of the new Dorian Greeks, and the leadership of that area, once exercised by Mycenae, passed to the Dorian city of Sparta. Athens, as yet a humdrum town, became a haven for Mycenaean refugees. A mixed group of Mycenaean Greek refugees known as Ionians (who later traced their descent from Athens and kept the festival of the Apaturia) fled across the Aegean Sea and settled along the western coast of Asia Minor and on the islands offshore. Thenceforth, that region was known as Ionia and became an integral part of Greek civilization (see map on page 89).

In the chaotic conditions of Dark Age Greece, political authority crumbled. The Greeks were divided into tribes that, in turn, were subdivided into clans. Each clan included a number of related families that had their own distinctive religious cult and held their lands and wealth in common. The sovereign powers once exercised by cities descended to the level of the elders of the tribes and clans.

HOMER

With the appearance of the Homeric epics in Ionia in the eighth century B.C., the darkness began to lift. Both the *Iliad* and the *Odyssey* are the products of a long oral tradition carried on by the minstrels of Mycenaean and post-Mycenaean times, who related their songs of heroic deeds at the banquets of the nobility. Whether the epics in their final form were the work of one man or several is in dispute. A number of scholars doubt that the *Iliad* and the *Odyssey*, which appear to have been written about five decades apart, could have had a common author.

---

*"Hellenic" refers to the "descendants of Hellen," the son or brother of Deucalion. It was the Romans who called the Hellenes "Greeks," mistaking one group of Hellenes for all Greeks.

Both epics are filled with vivid accounts of battle and adventure, but at heart both are concerned with the ultimate problems of human life. The *Iliad,* for example, depicts the tragic consequences of the quarrel between two sensitive, hot-tempered Greek leaders, Agamemnon and Achilles, toward the end of the Trojan War, with which the *Iliad* opens. "Divine Muse, sing of the ruinous wrath of Achilles, Peleus' son, which brought ten thousand sorrows to the Greeks, sent the souls of many brave heroes down to the world of the dead, and left their bodies to be eaten by dogs and birds: and the will of **Zeus** was fulfilled. Begin where they first quarreled, Agamemnon the King of Men, and great Achilles."*

Despite Homer's allusion to the will of Zeus, his characters are by no means puppets of the gods, even though divine intervention occurs repeatedly in his narrative of almost 16,000 lines. Rather, they are intensely—often violently—human, and they are doomed to suffer the consequences of their own deeds. In this respect, as in many others, Homer foreshadows the Greek tragic dramatists of the fifth century B.C.

Achilles' dazzling career, with its harvest of ten thousand sorrows, prefigures the career of Greece itself. The gods were said to have offered Achilles two alternatives: a long, tedious life or glory and an early death. His choice—to sail to Troy along with the vast Greek armada of 1,186 ships, rowed by members of 164 kingdoms or communities that sent men to Troy—symbolizes the meteoric course of Hellenic history.

Homer was the first literate European poet, and his influence on Greek civilization cannot be overestimated. The *Iliad* and the *Odyssey* were studied by every Greek schoolchild and cherished by Greek writers, artists, and leaders as an inexhaustible source of inspiration. Alexander the Great, for instance, carried a copy of the *Iliad,* which had been annotated for him by the great philosopher Aristotle, all the way to India on his military campaigns!

These epic poems were typically Greek in their rigorous and economical organization around a single theme, their lucidity, their moments of tenderness that never slip into sentimentality—in short, their brilliantly successful synthesis of heart and mind.

---

*Translated by H. D. F. Kitto, in Kitto, *The Greeks,* rev. ed. (Harmondsworth, England: Penguin Books, 1957), p. 45.

THE HOMERIC GODS

The gods of Mount Olympus, who play such a significant role in the Homeric poems, had diverse origins. Poseidon, the sea god, was Minoan; Zeus, the hurler of thunderbolts and ruler of Olympus, was a god of the Dorian Greeks; **Aphrodite,** the goddess of love, perhaps was an astral deity from Babylonia; and **Apollo** and a number of others were local deities long before they joined the divine pantheon on Olympus. By Homer's time, these diverse gods had been arranged into a hierarchy of related deities common to all Greeks. The Olympic gods were **anthropomorphic**—that is, they were human in form and personality, capable of rage, lust, jealousy, and all the other traits of the warrior-hero (and the rest of us as well)—but they also possessed immortality and other superhuman attributes. The universality of the Olympic cult served as an important unifying force that compensated in part for the characteristic localism of Greek politics. Yet each clan and each district also honored its own special gods, many of whom, like **Athena,** the patron goddess of Athens, were included in the Olympic pantheon. The worship of these local gods was associated with feelings of family devotion or regional and civic pride. The gods were concerned chiefly (although not exclusively) with the well-being of social groups rather than with the prosperity or salvation of the individual.

Ancient fertility deities rivaled the Olympians in popularity. **Demeter,** the goddess of grain, and **Dionysus,** the god of wine, were almost ignored in the Homeric epics but seem to have been at least as important to most Greeks as were the proud deities of Olympus. Through initiations into their mysteries, Demeter and Dionysus offered their followers the hope of personal contact with the divine and salvation—at least during life. Eleusis, a small town near Athens, became the chief center for the worship of Demeter (whose name means "earth mother"); the annual rites celebrated there, the Eleusinian mysteries, dramatized the ancient myth of death and resurrection. For the Athenians, these were the most solemn of all religious observances: the yearly return of life-giving crops depended on the favor of Demeter.

The Greeks honored Dionysus (also called Bacchus), the god of wine, with wild celebrations during which female worshipers known as Bacchants would dress in fawn skins and crowns of ivy, abandon their families, and dance through the night by torchlight to the music of flutes and drums, shouting the ritual cry "Euoi!"

Finally, and particularly among the poor, animism (the belief that material objects have souls) persisted in all its numberless and exotic forms. The world of the Greek peasants, like that of their Near Eastern neighbors, was crowded with gods.

CHAPTER 6

The Rise of Classical Greece

By Homer's time, Greek culture was developing throughout the area around the Aegean Sea—in Ionia along the coast of Asia Minor, on the Aegean islands, in Athens and its surrounding district of Attica, in the Peloponnesus, and in other regions of mainland Greece (see map, on page 89).

But the Greek-speaking peoples did not coalesce into a single pan-Hellenic state. Political unity was discouraged by the roughness of the Ionian coast, the insularity of the islands, and the mountains and inlets that divided the Greek peninsula itself into a number of semi-isolated districts. The existence of the myriad city-states of ancient Greece cannot, however, be explained entirely by the environment. There are numerous examples of small independent states separated by no geographical barriers whatever. Several autonomous districts, for example, might coexist on a single island. The Greek polis seems to have arisen rather as a result of a great rise in population, prosperity, and civilization itself during the period from c. 900–700 B.C. Whatever the reason, classical Greek culture without the independent city-state is inconceivable.

THE POLIS

We have used the term "city-state" to describe what the Greeks knew as the polis (pl., poleis). Actually, the Greek word *polis* is untranslatable, and "city-state" fails to convey its full meaning. Originally it was used simply to describe a fortified place. It eventually came to mean a self-governing society, a political community of adult male citizens who lived with their families along with free noncitizens and slaves in a (normally) fortified city and its agricultural hinterland. The Greek idea that a polis was essentially based upon a community of citizens living in a city was reflected in the fact that city-states were known not as geographical entities, such as Sparta or Athens, but as ethnic entities. Thus Athens was known as the polis of the Athenians and was referred to as such in official documents or decrees of the polis. English words such as "political," "politics," and "policy" come from the Greek *polis;* to the Greeks, politics without the polis would be a contradiction in terms. Aristotle is often quoted as saying, "Man is a political animal"; what he really said was that man was a creature who was suited to live in a polis.* Indeed, during the classical era there were something like 1,000 Greek poleis, which ranged in size from approximately 10 to 3,000 square kilometers and had populations from under 1,000 to roughly 300,000 inhabitants. During the Roman Empire, as many as 30 million Greek-speaking peoples may have lived in poleis.

The polis was the Greeks' answer to the perennial conflict between the individual and the state, and perhaps no other human institution has succeeded in reconciling these two concepts so well, at least for the adult males who were its only fully participatory members. The Greeks expressed their intense individualism through the polis, not in spite of it. The polis was sufficiently small that its members could behave and relate as individuals; the chief political virtue was participation, not obedience (at least for its male citizens). Accordingly, the polis became the vessel of Greek creativity. A unified pan-Hellenic state might have eliminated the intercity warfare that tormented classical Greece. It might have brought peace, stability, and power, but at the expense of the very institution that made classical Greece distinctive in human history.

Still, the system of independent, warring poleis was a remarkably inefficient basis for Greek political organization. The poleis were able to evolve and flourish only because they developed largely in a political vacuum. Since no external power was much interested in Greece, the chief threat to the Greeks of the Dark Age was the violence of their own people. As a matter of security, the inhabitants of a small district would often erect, atop a central hill, a citadel that they

---

*Aristotle is exaggerating slightly. Some political units in Greece were not dominated by a single city but consisted of villages or towns spread across a large area, with populations larger than an autonomous polis, which surrendered some political powers, such as control of warfare, to a common assembly and were known as *ethne* (sing., *ethnos*).

called an *acropolis* (high town). The acropolis was the chief religious center of the district and its natural assembly place in time of war. With the quickening of local commerce, an agora, or marketplace, usually developed at the foot of the acropolis, and many of the farmers whose fields were nearby (in the agricultural hinterland known as the *chora* or *ge*) built houses around the market, for reasons of sociability and defense.

At about the time that the polis was emerging (perhaps first on Cyprus under Phoenician influence or on Sicily or south Italy, or in the eastern part of Greece), descendants of original tribal elders probably were evolving into a hereditary aristocracy. An occasional polis might be ruled by a king (known among the Greeks as a *basileus*), but, generally speaking, monarchy was diminishing; often it was reduced to a merely ceremonial office. By about 700 B.C. or shortly thereafter, most Greek kings had been overthrown or shorn of all but their religious functions, leaving the aristocracy in full control. The aristocrats had meanwhile appropriated the lion's share of the lands that clan members had formerly held in common. Slowly, the polis was replacing the clan as the object of primary allegiance and the focus of political activity, but the aristocracy rode out the change, growing in wealth and power.

Below the aristocracy was a class of farmers who had managed to acquire fragments of the old clan common lands or had developed new farms on virgin soil. They had no genuine voice in public affairs, and their economic condition was always precarious. The Greek soil is the most barren in Europe, and while the large-scale cultivation of vine and olive usually brought prosperity and power to the aristocrats, the small farmers tended to sink from free status into some kind of dependency or outright slavery. Their condition was portrayed vividly in the eighth century B.C. by the poet **Hesiod,** a farmer himself. In his *Works and Days,* Hesiod describes a world that had declined from a primitive golden age to the present "age of iron," characterized by a corrupt nobility. For the common farmer, life was "bad in winter, cruel in summer—never good." Yet Hesiod insisted that righteousness would triumph in the end. In the meantime, the farmer must work all the harder. "In the sweat of your face shall you eat bread." Out of an age in which the farmer's lot was declining, Hesiod proclaimed his faith in the ultimate victory of justice and the dignity of toil.

COLONIZATION: c. 750–550 B.C.

In the course of the eighth century B.C., when Hesiod wrote his *Works and Days,* the Greek world underwent a major increase in population. The exact extent of this population boom and the reasons for it are unknown. It may have been stimulated by a shift to more intensive farming, but this is by no means certain. Whatever its causes, the effects of the population surge were potentially devastating to the small farmer and to the even lower classes of the landless and homeless. In response to this problem, the Greeks began sending out colonists far and wide across the eastern and central Mediterranean.

By about 750 B.C., many Greeks had once again taken to the sea—as pirates in search of booty or as merchants and traders in search of copper and iron (rare in Greece) and the profits of trade. In this adventurous age, a single Greek crew might raid and plunder one port and sell the loot as peaceful merchants in the next. Greek seafarers found many fertile districts ripe for colonization, and during the next two centuries (750–550 B.C.), a vast movement of colonial expansion transformed not only Greece itself but the whole Mediterranean world. Indeed, some scholars have argued that this great expansion itself was what gave rise to the "polis-culture" of classical Greece, if not to the classically developed idea of the polis as an independent, autonomous political community.

A number of Greek poleis, great and small, sent bands of colonists across the seas to found new communities on distant shores (either trading stations known as *emporia* or new city foundations called *apoikiai*). In time, some of these colonies sent out colonists of their own to establish still more settlements. The typical colonial polis, although bound to its mother city by ties of kinship, sentiment, and commerce and by a common patriotic cult, was politically independent; because its citizens often went to the new colony with equal political rights, the colonization movement helped to make Greek society more egalitarian. At the same time, we cannot speak of colonial empires in this period; even the word "colony" is a little misleading.

The motives behind the colonial movement are to be found in the economic and social troubles afflicting the Greek homeland, which were aggravated by the population surge. Colonization meant new opportunities for those with little or no land. It provided the aristocracy with a useful safety valve against the pressures of rising

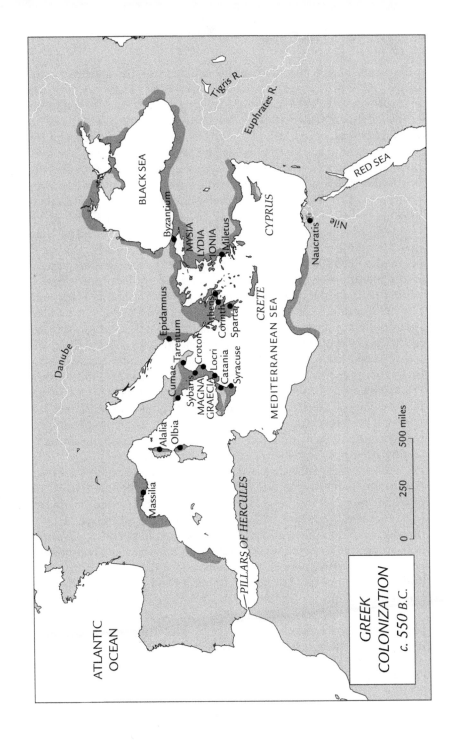

GREEK COLONIZATION
c. 550 B.C.

population and accumulating discontent. And there were always a few adventurous or disaffected aristocrats ready to lead the enterprise—or to be sent out, after losing out in disputes with their fellow aristocrats. In the stark environment of the pioneer colony, hard work was more likely to bring reward than in the Greece of Hesiod. Here were all the opportunities for rapid social and economic advancement that are commonly associated with a frontier society.

In the course of two centuries, the Greek polis spread out along the coasts of the Mediterranean and Black Seas. The Ionian polis of Miletus alone founded some eighty colonies. So many Greek settlements were established in southern Italy and Sicily that the whole area became known as *Magna Graecia* (Great Greece). The small colonial polis of Byzantium, dominating the trade route between the Black Sea and the Mediterranean, became, a millennium later, the capital of the Eastern Roman Empire (under the name Constantinople). Throughout the Middle Ages, it remained one of the greatest metropolitan centers on Earth and even now, as the modern Istanbul, is the largest city in Europe. The Greek colony of Neapolis (New Polis) in southern Italy is now known as Napoli or Naples; Nikaia, on today's French Riviera, became the modern Nice; Massilia became Marseilles; and Syracuse, in Sicily, remains to this day one of the island's chief cities. Through the poleis of Magna Graecia, Greek culture was transmitted to the Romans, but this was merely one important episode in the diffusion of Greek civilization along the shores of southern Europe, North Africa, and western Asia.

The colonial experience was profoundly significant in the evolution of the Greek way of life. The flourishing commerce that developed between the far-flung settlements brought renewed prosperity to Greece itself. The homeland became an important source of wine, olive oil, and manufactured goods for the colonies. The needs of the new settlements stimulated the growth of industrial and commercial classes (smiths and potters, stevedores, and sailors) and transformed many poleis from quiet agrarian communities into bustling mercantile centers. Coinage, which had been invented not long before in western Anatolia, was now introduced into the Greek world, where it dramatically stimulated commerce by providing a welcome alternative to the cumbersome process of bartering goods. A new elite of merchants and manufacturers began to elbow its way into the councils of government alongside the old noble families.

THE TYRANTS

The century from about 650 to 550 B.C. was an age of fundamental economic and political change. It was in this age that the Ionian poet Pythermus wrote the golden line that alone of his works has survived: "There's nothing else that matters—only money." The ever-increasing abundance of metal enabled people of only moderate wealth to purchase the heavy iron armor necessary for the warfare of the day. As a result, the mounted aristocratic armies of earlier times began to give way in the early seventh century B.C. to citizens' armies of well-drilled, mailed foot soldiers, called "hoplites," whose tight formation, known as the **phalanx,** came to dominate warfare in the eastern Mediterranean.* Before long, the classes who fought for the polis began to demand a voice in its affairs.

Meanwhile, the colonial movement was waning. By about 550 B.C., the best colonial sites were occupied, and the rise of new powers such as Carthage in the west and Lydia and Persia in the east prevented further expansion. As the safety valve slowly closed, the old pressures of economic and social discontent returned. One after another, the poleis of Greece and Ionia were torn by civil strife. In many instances, these conflicts resulted in the overthrow of aristocratic control by tyrants who, with the support of discontented members of the polis, often claimed to govern in the interests of the common people. Among the best known of the early tyrants were **Pheidon** of Argos and **Cypselus** and **Periander** of Corinth.

To the Greeks, a tyrant was not necessarily an evil ruler but simply one who rose to power without hereditary or legal claim.† Typically, the tyrants did not smash the machinery of government but merely controlled it. Tyrants usually were upstarts from within the aristocracies who were attuned to the temper of their age. They used the new coined money to hire armies of mercenaries and to manipulate social discontent to their own advantage. Since they

---

*The hoplites took their name from the protective armor they wore in battle, particularly the characteristic shield (*hoplon*). Each infantryman carried a slightly concave, circular shield made of wood or leather and sometimes covered with a thin layer of bronze, which was held by an elbow grip, combined with a baldric (an ornamental belt) slung over the left shoulder.

†The word "tyrant" (Greek, *tyrannos*) apparently was a Lydian word borrowed by the Greeks to describe their extra-constitutional rulers.

owed their power to the masses, they sought to retain mass support by canceling or scaling down debts, sponsoring impressive public-works projects, redistributing the lands of aristocrats, and reforming taxation.

But in most Greek communities, tyranny proved ephemeral, usually lasting for about two generations. Some tyrants were overthrown by the older privileged classes. Others succumbed to those supporters among the poorer members of the polis who, as they became increasingly self-confident, sought to assume direct control of political affairs.

SPARTA

Sparta and Athens, the two dominant poleis of the fifth century B.C., stood at opposite ends of the Greek political spectrum. Neither played an important role in the colonization movement, for both adopted the alternative course of territorial expansion in their own districts. Athens evolved through the stages of monarchy, aristocracy, tyranny, and democracy, but Sparta developed a peculiarly mixed political system that discouraged commerce, cultural inventiveness, and the amenities of life for the sake of rigid discipline and military efficiency.

During the eighth and seventh centuries B.C., Sparta underwent the same political and social processes as did other Greek states, and it played a vigorous role in the development of Greek culture. Yet, from the beginning, the Spartan artistic aesthetic was sober, and military concerns were central to Spartan life. The severity of its art and its Dorian architecture contrasted sharply with the charming elegance of Ionia and the cultural dynamism of Attica. Politically, Sparta had always been conservative. When the aristocracy rose to power, the monarchy was not abolished but merely weakened. With the rise of the poorer citizens, certain democratic features were incorporated into the Spartan constitution, yet the monarchy and aristocracy endured. Sparta could adapt cautiously to new conditions but found it difficult to abandon anything from its past.

Toward the end of the eighth century B.C., when other Greek states were beginning to relieve their social unrest and land hunger through colonization, Sparta instead conquered the fertile neighboring district of Messenia, appropriating large portions of the conquered land for its own citizens. (The territory of Lakedaimon and Messenia combined was approximately 8,400 square kilometers, making Sparta one of the largest city-states in Greece.) They reduced many Messenians, who were ethnically Greek, to a state of semi-slavery to the Spartan state, as opposed to slavery to individual owners. The Messenians' status was identical to that of the Spartans' slaves back in their homeland, the Laconians, some of whom may have lost their freedom during the original Dorian conquests. The Spartans' slaves, now including the Messenians, were known as **helots**. The main responsibility of the Messenian helots was to provide their Spartan masters with a fixed amount of produce from the land they worked.

A Spartan poet likened them to "asses worn down by intolerable loads," and a modern historian of ancient Greece has described them as "little better off than farm animals." As fellow Greeks, they were ethnically and linguistically identical to their Spartan masters, whom they outnumbered. And they did not accept their servitude with quiet resignation. In the late seventh century B.C., the Spartans crushed a helot revolt after a desperate struggle. It became clear that the helots could be held down only by strong military force and constant watchfulness. Consequently, Sparta transformed itself into a garrison state whose citizens became a standing army. Culture declined to the level of the barracks; the good life became the life of basic training.

Sparta became a tense, humorless society dedicated to the perpetuation of the status quo by force. Fear of helot rebellion grew into a collective obsession, as some 8,000 Spartan citizens assumed the task of keeping the proud and restless Greek helots in a state of permanent repression. Sandwiched between the citizens and the helots was a group of free noncitizens excluded from political life, the *perioikoi* (those who lived around), who nevertheless did military service alongside the Spartans, engaged in commercial activities forbidden to the citizens themselves, and were therefore indispensable to the life of the city. The Spartan state divided its lands into numerous lots, one for each citizen, and the helots who worked these lots relieved the citizens of all economic responsibility, freeing them for a life of military training and service to the state. Spartan citizen women were excluded from formal politics, but they were freer than their counterparts in most other Greek cities. They were permitted to own land, manage farms, and engage in business. They, along with the perioikoi and the helots, shielded the male citizenry from all nonmilitary distractions.

THE CONSTITUTION OF LYCURGUS

Writers of antiquity ascribed the Spartan constitution to a legendary lawgiver named Lycurgus. In fact, although it drew from earlier Spartan traditions, the constitution operated with such rigorous logical consistency as to suggest the hand of a single author. Sparta had two kings (drawn from two royal houses), whose powers had been greatly reduced by the sixth century B.C. One or the other served as supreme commander on every military campaign, but at home their authority was overshadowed by that of three political bodies: (1) an aristocratic council of elders (the *Gerousia*), consisting of thirty men at least sixty years old, elected for life; (2) an executive board of five **ephors** elected annually from the whole citizenry; and (3) an assembly of citizens, known as "equals" (*homoioi*), that included every eligible Spartan male over thirty. Thus, Sparta was technically a democracy, although a limited one. All citizens could participate in the assembly, but citizenship was denied to many freemen, to all women, and of course to the helots. The assembly had the function of approving or disapproving important questions of state, but it did so by acclamation rather than ballot, and its members were not permitted to debate the issues. Accordingly, the assembly was by no means an arena of rough-and-tumble political conflict.

The lives of Sparta's citizens were tended and guided by the state from cradle to grave, always for the purpose of producing strong, courageous, highly disciplined soldiers. The introduction of styles, luxuries, and ideas from without was strongly discouraged and tightly controlled. At a time when coinage was stimulating economic life elsewhere, Sparta used simple iron bars as its medium of exchange. Spartan citizens seldom left their homeland except on military campaigns, and outsiders were discouraged from visiting. Small or malformed infants were abandoned to die of exposure by state order. (Abandonment of unwanted children was common in the ancient world, but it usually stemmed from the father's decision, not the state's.) At the age of seven, the Spartan boy was turned over to the state and spent his next twenty-two years in a program of education (the *agoge*) in military skills, physical training, the endurance of hardships, and unquestioning devotion to the polis.

A boy was typically guided through this training program by a young adult citizen, who might also choose him as his lover. Often a powerful emotional bond would develop between the two. Once the protégé reached adulthood, he and his tutor would usually fight in the Spartan army side by side, as a team. Often, indeed, the citizen-tutor helped his protégé choose a wife. In Sparta as throughout ancient Greece, erotic love between men, or between men and boys, was by no means incompatible with marriage and procreation; the prevailing lifestyle for men was what we might call bisexual, although in ancient Greek there were no such terms or categories equivalent to modern categories such as "heterosexual," "homosexual," or "bisexual."

At twenty, assuming that he shaped up, the young Spartan entered the citizen army and lived his next ten years in a barracks. He might marry, but he could visit his wife only if he was sufficiently resourceful to elude the barracks guards (this seems to have been regarded as a test of skill). At thirty, if all went well, he became a full-fledged citizen. He could now live at home, but he ate his meals at a public mess (*syssitia*) to which he was obliged to contribute the products of his assigned fields. (These were the fields worked for the state by the helots.) The fare at these public messes was Spartan in the extreme. One visitor, after eating a typical meal, remarked, "Now I understand why the Spartans do not fear death."

The Spartan citizen had almost no individual existence; body and soul, he was dedicated to the state. If the helot's life was hard, so was the citizen's. Life in Sparta would seem to be a violent negation of Greek individualism, yet many Greeks were unashamed admirers of the Spartan regime. To them, Sparta represented the ultimate in self-denial and commitment to a logical idea. The Greeks admired the well-ordered life (*eunomia*), and nowhere was life more ordered than in Sparta. To some ancient Greeks at any rate, there was a crucial difference between the helot and the Spartan citizen: helots endured hardships because they had to, citizens because they *chose* to. And the Spartans always remembered that the object of their regime was the maintenance of the status quo—not aggressive imperialism. Their superbly drilled hoplite armies were the best in Greece, yet they employed their military advantage with restraint. To the accusation of artistic sterility, a Spartan might reply that Sparta, with all its institutions directed toward a single ideal, was itself a work of art.

ATHENS

Athens was already a significant population center during the Mycenaean Age, but not until much later did it assume a leading role in Greek politics and culture. By about 900 B.C., all the small communities of Attica were unified politically into the larger Athenian community; looking back later, the Athenians called this combination *synoikismos,* and they attributed the political unification of Attica to the early king Theseus. The later Athenians also maintained that the inhabitants of Attica itself always had been the same, or **autochthones**—literally sprung from the land itself!

The unification of Attica meant that the polis of Athens comprised a singularly extensive area, and consequently the Athenians suffered less severely from land hunger than did many of their neighbors. (The territory of Attica eventually comprised approximately 2,500 square kilometers.) Athens therefore sent out no colonists, yet, being a town only four miles from the coast, it was influenced by the revival of Greek commerce.

According to Athenian tradition, the power of the early kings was replaced by the institution of annual archons (Greek *archontes*) in 683/2 B.C. The archons were the chief officers of the state and clearly belonged to the wealthy aristocracy of Athens.

SOLON AND PISISTRATUS

In 594 B.C., the Athenians granted extraordinary powers to an aristocratic poet-statesman named **Solon** to reform the laws of their polis. Solon's reforms left the preponderance of political power in the hands of the wealthy but nevertheless created the preconditions for the development of later Athenian democracy by widening eligibility for holding political office. His laws also abolished enslavement for default of debts and freed all debtors who had been enslaved. Moreover, the lowest classes of free Athenian males were now admitted into the popular assembly (whose powers were as yet distinctly limited), and a system of popular courts was established whose judges were chosen by lot from among the all-male citizenry without regard to wealth. For the Athenian, selection by lot was simply a means of putting the choice into the hands of the gods. Its consequence was to raise to important offices men who were their own masters and owed nothing to wealthy and influential political backers. On the whole, selection by lot worked well in Athens and gradually became a characteristic feature of Athenian democracy.

Solon's laws were seen by many among the privileged classes as dangerously radical, but the lower classes demanded still more reforms. The consequence of this continued popular unrest was the rise of tyranny in Athens. Between 561 and 527 B.C., a colorful and popular tyrant named **Pisistratus** dominated the Athenian government (see accompanying biographical sketch). He was succeeded by two sons who carried on their father's policies of lavish building and jobs for the poor, but with diminishing success. The Pisistratid dynasty was driven from power in 510 B.C. by exiled nobles who returned with Spartan military support.

Pisistratus and Sons

Unlike many tyrants, Pisistratus was nobly born. He was a tyrant nevertheless, according to the ancient Greek definition of the word, because he seized power unconstitutionally. Twice he was expelled by rival aristocrats, but in 546 B.C. he returned from exile with an army, seized control of Athens for a third time, and stayed in power until his death in 527. He achieved the elusive goal of all despots: he died peacefully—in power and in bed.

Pisistratus was succeeded by his sons. His younger son, Hipparchus, was slain in a love quarrel in 514 B.C., and Hippias, the elder son, was overthrown and banished in 510 B.C. by an Athenian aristocratic faction backed by Spartan troops. Pisistratus's luckless sons lacked their father's political skill, yet the general policies of all three Pisistratid tyrants were much the same. Although their dynasty came to power and remained in power without constitutional sanction, the Pisistratids otherwise retained most of Solon's laws. A number of aristocratic clans supported their regime with varying degrees of enthusiasm, but the power of the Pisistratids ultimately rested on popular support.

Pisistratus actively courted the poorer free people of Athens through a variety of measures. He granted them portions of the estates of exiled aristocratic rivals, thereby placing Athenian agriculture on a more stable and democratic basis. He established Athenian mercantile outposts along the waterway linking the Aegean and Black Seas and thus took the first crucial steps toward a commercial empire. He and his sons followed a cautious and restrained foreign policy and gave Athens peace, prosperity, and a degree of social and political harmony that it had long needed. By no later than 525 B.C., the dynasty had begun to coin the Athenian "owls"—silver coins with the head of Athena on one side and an owl symbolizing her wisdom on the other—that were to become famous throughout the ancient world.

The Pisistratids were also great patrons of the arts, especially Hipparchus. With their encouragement, poets such as Anacreon and Simonides and artists from throughout the Greek world flocked to Athens. During the Pisistratids' rule, the Enneakrounos fountain-house and the Stoa Basileios were built as part of the development of the Agora, the marketplace, Athens's civic center at the foot of the Acropolis. Besides the aristocratic gods and goddesses of Olympus, especially Apollo, Pisistratus and his sons encouraged popular, non-Olympic cults such as those for the Eleusinian mysteries and the wine god Dionysus. It had become a tradition at the annual festival in the god's honor—the Dionysia—to include a dramatic performance by a chorus speaking in unison. In about 534 B.C., Pisistratus awarded a prize to the first tragic playwright who separated an actor from his chorus (adding a prologue and speech to what had been a choral performance), thereby taking a giant step toward the great Greek dramas of the following century. The playwright's name, Thespis, gave rise to our own word "thespian," which means an actor, or, more specifically, an actor in a tragedy.

Until shortly before its overthrow in 510 B.C., the Pisistratid tyranny was not oppressive. Moreover, Pisistratus and his sons made Athens a major artistic, religious, and commercial center. Most important for future developments, however, Pisistratus and his sons provided the Athenians with a crucial period of relative civil peace and prosperity. During that period (561–510 B.C.), since the tyrants did not abolish Solon's political reforms and obeyed the laws themselves, more and more Athenians got used to taking part in everyday politics. Somewhat ironically, it was the tyrants of Athens who made it possible for at least some of the poorer citizens of Athens to gain experience in government. Without that experience, it is unlikely that Athenian democracy would have developed.

THE CONSTITUTION OF CLEISTHENES

Many aristocrats, however, were willing to accept diminished estates and popular rule in exchange for political stability. In the closing decade of the sixth century B.C., under the leadership of an aristocrat named **Cleisthenes,** Athens adopted a new constitution that became the political basis of the Athenian democracy during the fifth century B.C. Until the time of the new constitution, loyalty to clan and tribe had remained strong, and the wealthy dominated the clans and tribes. Cleisthenes' most important achievement was the reorganization of the citizen body. As a result of his reforms, each citizen was assigned membership in one of approximately 139 local units called **demes** (most of which we would consider villages). Clusters of demes were then combined into groups of three *trittyes* (population centers), one each from the areas of the coast, the plain of Attica, and the city of Athens itself. The trittyes were then assigned to ten new tribes.

Citizenship, military service, and political participation in the government were based thereafter upon membership in the demes, trittyes, and new tribes. Overall, the effect of the new system was to break down loyalties to locally based clans and areas and to encourage ordinary Athenian citizens from all over Attica to work together politically.

Cleisthenes may also have been responsible for introducing the principle of **ostracism,** which provided a further safeguard against violent factionalism. Each year, any Athenian citizen might propose the name of a person whom he considered a threat to the well-being of the polis. If as many as 6,000 votes were cast, the Assembly (*ekklesia*) banished from Athens for ten years whichever candidate received the most votes. The ostracized person kept his citizenship and property but was excluded from Athenian politics for the next decade.

Matters of public policy were decided by the Assembly, whose membership included all Athenian citizens, from landless laborers to aristocrats. As in Sparta and elsewhere in Greece, citizenship was limited to males, but in Athens it came to include every native-born freeman of eighteen years and over. (Citizenship was subsequently restricted to men whose parents were both Athenians.) The total citizenry of Athens in the mid-fifth century B.C. has been estimated at about 55,000 men. Together with their wives, kinswomen, and children, they would have numbered about 130,000. There were also some 70,000 free resident aliens, called **metics** (including women and children), who were often wealthy from the profits of commerce but lacked political rights. And there were perhaps 100,000 slaves, many of them Greeks from outside Athens and Attica. When we speak of Athenian democracy, we must always remember that perhaps a quarter of the Athenian population was enslaved and that slaves, women, and metics had no voice in politics (as in George Washington's America). Scholars have thus disagreed sharply as to the degree to which Athens was democratic. Can the term "democracy" be ascribed to a society in which less than 20 percent of the population could vote and participate in government? On the other hand, political participation by those who were free in Athens far exceeded that of any previous society in the ancient world, where slavery was endemic and the fully articulated concept of citizenship was unknown. Moreover, citizenship was far less exclusive in Athens than in Sparta, and with respect to the citizenry itself, Athens was more thoroughly democratic than any modern state. The citizens did not elect the legislators; they *were* the legislators.

Indeed, for the transaction of the day-to-day business of government, Cleisthenes provided a smaller body—the Council of Five Hundred—for which every male Athenian citizen over thirty was eligible. The Council (*boule*) was made up of fifty men from each tribe, chosen annually by lot from a list of tribal nominees. Each fifty-man tribal group served for one-tenth of a year. Their order of rotation was determined by a crude machine, which archaeologists have unearthed. It worked much like our modern bubblegum machines: a stone representing each of the ten tribes was put in the machine, and one stone was released each month, thus preventing any tribe except the last from knowing in advance when its term would begin. Random selection pervaded the Athenian constitution. Every day a different chairman for the fifty-man panel was chosen by lot. Most of the various magistrates and civil servants also came to be selected by lot, for limited terms, and they were strictly responsible to the Council of Five Hundred and the Assembly. This was a citizen's government in every sense of the word—a government of amateurs rather than professional bureaucrats. Selection by lot of representatives and chairmen was an expression of the Athenians' confidence in the ability of the average citizen to perform governmental tasks capably.

Such a system was not designed to provide the long-range personal leadership that many political theorists have seen as essential to the well-being of the state. The Assembly was too unwieldy, the Council too circumscribed by rotation and lot. Consequently, direction of Athenian affairs came to be exercised by citizens who had acquired great prestige and influence but did not necessarily occupy any official political position. Such a person was known as the *prostates* of the demos, or "leader of the people." His influence lasted only as long as his popularity.

Pericles, the most celebrated leader of fifth-century-B.C. Athens, was such a man. Officially, he was simply a member of the Athenian

Pericles
Although Pericles (c. 495–429 B.C.) belonged to one of the most aristocratic clans in Athens (the Alcmaeonidae), he became a popular democratic leader who was responsible for introducing pay for jurors. He also advocated an aggressive foreign policy, and during his period of political dominance in the 440s and 430s B.C., the great building program that transformed the Athenian Acropolis (including the construction of the Parthenon, which is still visible today) took place in Athens. Pericles died of the plague in 429 B.C. at the beginning of the great Peloponnesian War. (© *Scala/Art Resource, NY)*

board of generals, to which he was reelected year after year. His real authority as leader of the people hinged on his personal popularity and his prestige as an aristocrat of the most noble lineage who was also a person of keen intelligence, iron integrity, and democratic views. And the fact that Athenian citizens accepted and endorsed his leadership for some thirty years illustrates the remarkable equilibrium between aristocratic statesmanship and popular sovereignty achieved in the golden age. Even Pericles, however, was subject to the scrutiny of the Athenian Assembly, on which he depended for support. He could exercise his authority only by persuasion or political manipulation, never by force.

The success of the Greek polis in achieving harmony between the individual and society was nowhere more complete than in Athens, the scene of man's first significant encounter with democracy (though not woman's). The great Athenian historian Thucydides celebrated this achievement in words he attributed to Pericles, in a speech intended to rouse the spirits of Athenians during their war with Sparta:

> Our constitution is called a democracy because it is in the hands not of the few but of the many. But our laws secure equal justice for all in their private disputes, not as a matter of privilege but as a reward of merit. . . . Alone of all states we regard a man who holds aloof from public life not as harmless but as useless. We deliberate in person all matters of policy, holding not that words and deeds go ill together but that acts are foredoomed to failure when undertaken undiscussed. . . . In short I say that Athens is the school of Hellas, and that her citizens yield to none, man for man, in independence of spirit, many-sidedness of attainment, and self-reliance in body and mind.*

---

*From Pericles' "Funeral Oration," in Thucydides, *History of the Peloponnesian War,* book 2, chapters 35–46. I am following the translation of Sir Alfred Zimmern with slight modifications.

CHAPTER 7

The Zenith
and Transformation
of Classical Greece

During the sixth century B.C., while Solon, Pisistratus, and Cleisthenes were transforming Athens into a prosperous democracy, the cultural center of the Hellenic world was Ionia. There, on the shores of Asia Minor, the Greeks came into direct contact with the cultures of the ancient Near East. The results of this contact were fruitful indeed, for the Ionian Greeks adapted Near Eastern art, architecture, literature, and learning to their own distinctive outlook. They created a brilliant, elegant culture, more gracious and luxurious than any that existed in Greece itself. It was in this setting that Greek philosophy, science, and lyric poetry were born. Ionian poleis underwent much the same political and economic developments as those of Greece, and by the sixth century B.C., the poorer citizens were attempting to diminish the control of aristocrats. In the Ionian city of Miletus, aristocrats and commoners went to the extreme of burning each other alive.

These social conflicts were drastically affected by the intervention of outside powers. During the 560s and 550s B.C., the coastal cities of Ionia fell one by one under the control of the Lydians, and when Cyrus II (the Great) conquered Lydia in 546 B.C., they passed into the Persian Empire. In 499 B.C., the Ionian cities rebelled against Persia and persuaded the Athenians to send twenty ships to aid them. But the Athenian aid proved insufficient, and by 494 the Persians had crushed the insurrection, punctuating their victory by sacking Miletus. Ionia's gamble for independence had failed, and Darius I of Persia was now bent on revenge against Athens. The Persian Wars, Herodotus observed, were precipitated by the sending of twenty ships.

THE PERSIAN WARS: 490–479 B.C.

In 490 B.C., Darius sent an army across the Aegean, perhaps to punish the Athenians for their participation in the Ionian revolt but also to secure his rule over existing Greek subjects. As was so often the case, the Greeks, even in the face of this calamity, found it impossible to unite. The Spartans held aloof in the Peloponnesus, claiming that they could not send their army until the moon was full, and other city-states preferred to sit tight and await further developments. Consequently, Athens (along with its allies from Plataea) was obliged to face the Persians almost alone. At **Marathon** in Attica, the two armies met, and the Athenian hoplites, fighting shoulder to shoulder for the preservation of their homes and their polis, won a brilliant victory. A total of 6,400 Persians fell at Marathon, whereas only 192 Greeks lost their lives.

Marathon was not won by Athenian heroism alone. Although outnumbered (perhaps two to one), the Athenians were better armed (the Persians were said to have used wicker shields), and the Persian army lacked its customary cavalry. (The Athenians may have attacked when they learned that the horses of the Persian cavalry were off grazing.) Nevertheless, the Athenian victory was a dazzling achievement. It won Greece an invaluable postponement of the Persian threat, and it generated in Athens a powerful sense of pride and self-confidence. The great king of the world's largest empire had been defeated by a small army of free Athenian citizens. For men such as these, so it seemed, nothing was impossible. The epitaph attributed to the great Athenian dramatist Aeschylus included no mention of his surpassing literary achievements but only the proud statement that he had fought at Marathon.

The buoyant optimism that filled Athens in the wake of Marathon was tempered by the sobering thought that the Persians were likely to return in far greater numbers. Darius spent his last years planning a devastating new attack against Greece, but when the second invasion came, in 480 B.C., it was led by his successor, **Xerxes.** A Persian army of perhaps about 180,000 fighting men, stupendous by the standards of the age, moved by land around the northern Aegean shore, supported by a powerful armada.

Xerxes had paved his way to Greece by forming alliances with opportunistic Greek cities such as Argos and Thebes (the Greek Thebes, not the Egyptian one). In the meantime, Athens had been preparing (somewhat fortuitously) for the onslaught under the enterprising leadership of **Themistocles,** a statesman of great strategic imagination. He persuaded the Athenians to use a surplus from their silver mines in Attica to enlarge their fleet from 70 to 200 warships, probably for use against Athens's maritime rival, the island of Aegina. Later, those new ships played a crucial role in the defeat of the Persians.

Sparta had by now awakened to the danger of a Persian conquest but was equally alarmed at the possibility of Athens winning additional prestige from another single-handed victory. During the sixth century B.C., Sparta had established a regional defensive alliance known as the Peloponnesian League. By the end of the century, nearly every state in the Peloponnesus had joined the League, including the wealthy commercial polis of Corinth. Each League member had one vote, but Sparta alone had the privilege of summoning and presiding over the League's assembly and was usually able to dominate it. Now, in the shadow of Xerxes' invasion, representatives of the Peloponnesian states met at Corinth with delegates from Athens and a number of other poleis. Here, they agreed to form a much larger organization—the Pan-Hellenic League—to coordinate their common defense.

As Xerxes moved southward through northern Greece, a small army of Spartans and other Greeks led by the Spartan king Leonidas placed itself across the Persian path at **Thermopylae,** a narrow pass between sea and mountains through which Xerxes' host had to move before breaking to the south. When the two armies met, the Persians found that their immense numerical superiority was of little use on so restricted a battlefield and that, man for man, they were no match for the Greek hoplites. But in the end, a Greek turncoat led a contingent of the Persian army along a poorly defended path through the mountains to the rear of the Greek position. Completely surrounded, the Greeks continued to fight and died to the last man in defense of the field.

Although the battle of Thermopylae was a defeat for the Spartans, it became a long-remembered symbol of their courage and resolution. The inscription that was later placed over their graves is a model of Spartan brevity and understatement:

> Tell them the news in Sparta, passer by,
> That here, obedient to their words, we lie.*

---

*Yet, paradoxically, the probable author of this epigram, Simonides, was not a Spartan. Poets do not abound in a barracks state.

Much delayed, Xerxes' army now moved on Athens. The Athenians, at Themistocles' bidding, evacuated Attica and took refuge elsewhere, some in the Peloponnesus, others on the island of Salamis, just off the coast of Attica. The refugees on the island had to look on helplessly as the Persians plundered Athens and burned the temples on the Acropolis. But Themistocles' strategy was vindicated when the Greek and Persian fleets fought a decisive naval engagement in the Bay of **Salamis** (September 480 B.C.). The huge Persian armada did not have sufficient room to maneuver, and the smaller but heavier Greek fleet, with the new Athenian navy as its core, pulled alongside the Persian ships and overwhelmed them with marines.

Xerxes, who witnessed the disaster from a rocky headland, commanded his army to withdraw to northern Greece for the winter. He himself departed for Asia, never to return. In the following spring (479 B.C.), a pan-Hellenic army under Spartan command routed the Persians at **Plataea** on the northern frontier of Attica, and the Greeks won a final victory over the tattered remnants of the Persian army and fleet at Cape Mycale in Ionia. One after another, the Ionian cities broke loose from Persian control. Hellas had preserved its independence and was free to work out its own destiny. In an ironic postscript, Themistocles fell from power shortly after his triumph at Salamis. Banished from Athens, he ended his days in the service of the king of Persia.

THE ATHENIAN EMPIRE

To some historians, the moment of truth for classical Greece was not Marathon, Salamis, or Plataea but rather the brief period immediately afterward when the possibility of establishing the Pan-Hellenic League on a permanent basis was allowed to slip by. Yet it has always been easier to unite against a common foe than to maintain a wartime confederation in the absence of military necessity. Common fear is a stronger cement than common hope. Considering the intense involvement of the typical Greek citizen in his polis, it seems doubtful that Greek federalism was ever a genuine option—at least on a permanent basis.

Nevertheless, the Greek world in 479 B.C., lacking our hindsight, could not be certain that the Persian invasions were truly over. Sparta, always fearful of a helot revolt at home, relinquished leadership of the alliance and withdrew, along with the other cities of the Peloponnesian League. Athens, however, was unwilling to lower its guard. A large fleet had to be kept in readiness, and such a fleet could not be maintained by Athens alone. Consequently, in 478–477 B.C., a new anti-Persian alliance emerged under Athenian leadership; it included most of the maritime poleis on the coasts and islands of the Aegean from Attica to Ionia. (Altogether, the alliance consisted of more than 330 poleis.)

The alliance is known today as the **Delian League** because its headquarters and treasury were on the island of Delos, an ancient religious center in the Aegean Sea. At first the allies were free to decide who should contribute ships and who should contribute money to the new alliance: Athens and a few other cities contributed ships to the Delian fleet; the remaining members contributed money. All were entitled to a voice in the affairs of the Delian League, but Athens, with its superior wealth and power, gradually assumed a dominant position.

Slowly, the Delian League evolved into an Athenian Empire. In 454 B.C., after a defeat in Egypt, the League's treasury was transferred from Delos to Athens, where its funds were diverted to the welfare and adornment of Athens itself. The Athenians justified this financial sleight of hand with the argument that their fleet remained always vigilant and ready to protect League members from Persian aggression, but their explanation was received unsympathetically in some quarters. A party of touring Ionians visiting Athens might well admire the magnificent new temples being erected on the Acropolis, but their admiration would be chilled by the reflection that their own cities were contributing (at least indirectly) to the building fund.

Some members tried to withdraw from the League, both before and after the transfer of the treasury. But they quickly discovered that Athens regarded secession as illegal and was ready to enforce the continued membership of disillusioned poleis through military action. With the development of this policy in the 460s B.C. and the relocation of the treasury in 454 B.C., the transformation from Delian League to Athenian Empire was complete.

The half-century between Salamis and the outbreak of the Peloponnesian War was the Athenian golden age (480–431 B.C.). The empire rose and flourished, bringing Athens unimagined wealth, not only from imperial assessments but also from the splendid commercial opportunities afforded by Athenian domination of the Aegean.

Athens was now the commercial hub of the eastern Mediterranean world and the great power in Greece, while Sparta and its Peloponnesian allies basically remained aloof.

THE GOLDEN AGE OF ATHENS

The economic and imperialistic foundations of Athens's golden age are interesting to us chiefly as a backdrop for the cultural explosion that has echoed through the centuries of Mediterranean and European civilizations. Through a rare and elusive conjunction of circumstances, a group of some 55,000 politically conscious Athenian citizens created in the decades after Salamis (480 B.C.) a unique, many-sided culture of superb taste and excellence. The culture of the golden age of Athens was anticipated in the sixth century B.C. and even earlier, and the period of creativity continued into the fourth century B.C. and beyond. But the zenith of Greek culture was reached in imperial Athens during the time of Pericles, in the middle decades of the fifth century B.C. The next two chapters will examine this extraordinary cultural flowering more closely.

Despite its dazzling achievements, the golden age of Athens was no utopia. The architecture and sculpture of the Acropolis, the tragic dramas, and the probing philosophical speculation were produced against a background of petty politics, commercial greed, and large-scale slavery. Athenian women could not attend or vote in the Athenian Assembly, and, although women in Sparta and other Dorian cities of the time could own property, in Athens they could not.

The age of Pericles was also marked by growing imperial arrogance. Pericles, whose popularity remained largely unchallenged from 461 B.C. to his death in 429 B.C., provided much-needed direction to democratic Athens, but he maintained the support of the Athenian assembly by advocating an ever-expanding empire.

Pericles' policy of extending Athenian dominion across the Greek world aroused the fear and hostility of Sparta and its Peloponnesian League. Corinth, the second greatest power in the League and Athens's chief commercial rival, was especially alarmed at Pericles' imperialism. In 431 B.C., these accumulating tensions resulted in a war between the Peloponnesian League and the Athenian Empire—a protracted, agonizing struggle that ultimately destroyed the Athenian Empire and shook the Greek political structure to its foundations.

THE PELOPONNESIAN WAR: 431–404 B.C.

For the most part, the Peloponnesian War was a matter of a whale fighting an elephant. Athens was invincible by sea, Sparta by land. When the Spartans marched into Attica year after year to devastate the fields, the population withdrew behind the protection of Athens's ramparts, which included a long and virtually impenetrable wall extending several miles overland to the Athenian port of Piraeus. With Athens linked to its port and its fleet, and therefore to the commercial wealth of the eastern Mediterranean, the Athenians could live indefinitely on imported foodstuffs.

Democratic Athens and regimented Sparta represented two contrary political systems, and each tended to reproduce its own political structure in the states dependent on it. Sparta encouraged oligarchy (rule by the few) throughout the Peloponnesus, whereas Athens was inclined to support democratic factions within the cities of its empire. Yet the Peloponnesian War was not only an ideological conflict; it was also a simple power struggle. As described by the great Athenian general and historian Thucydides in his account of the war, Athens dreamed of bringing all Hellas under its sway, and Sparta and its allies were determined to end the threat of Athenian imperialism. Athens was coming to be regarded as a despot among the states of its own empire, but as long as Athenian ships patrolled the Aegean, rebellion was minimized. Paradoxically, the "mother of democracies" was driven to ever more dictatorial expedients to hold its empire together.

In 430 and 429 B.C., Athens, crowded with refugees, was struck by a plague that wiped out perhaps a quarter of its population, including Pericles himself. The loss of this far-sighted statesman, combined with the terrible shock of the plague, eventually led to a deterioration in the quality of Athenian government, according to Thucydides. Leadership passed into the hands of even more radical imperialists, and the democracy acquired many of the worst characteristics of mob rule. A general who failed to win some battle through no fault of his own might be sent into exile. (Such was the experience of Thucydides himself.) When the Athenians captured the island of Melos, a neutral in the struggle, they slaughtered all its men and enslaved its women and children.

Pericles observed on the eve of the war that he was more afraid of Athens's mistakes than of Sparta's designs. His fear was prescient,

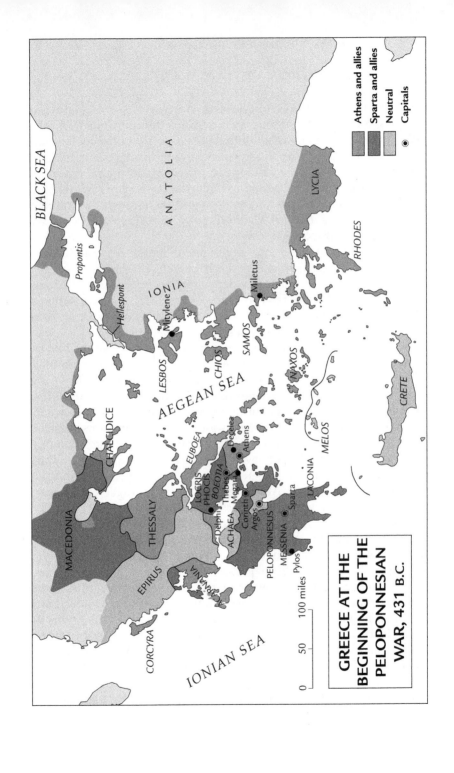

GREECE AT THE
BEGINNING OF THE
PELOPONNESIAN
WAR, 431 B.C.

for as the war progressed, Athenian strategy became increasingly reckless. The better part of the Athenian fleet was lost when two ill-managed expeditions against Syracuse-far to the west in Sicily—ended in disaster. As Athens's grip on the Aegean loosened, its subject cities began to rebel, and at length a Peloponnesian fleet, financed in part by Persian gold, destroyed what was left of the Athenian navy and thus cut off Athens's food supply altogether.

In 404 B.C., the Athenians surrendered-their wealth lost, their spirit broken, and their empire in ruins. Long thereafter, Athens remained the intellectual and cultural center of the Greek world, even making something of an economic and political comeback during the fourth century B.C., but its years of imperial supremacy were over.

THE FOURTH CENTURY B.C. AND THE MACEDONIAN CONQUEST

The period between the end of the Peloponnesian War in 404 B.C. and the Macedonian victory over an alliance of Greek city-states in 338 B.C. was an age of chaos and anticlimax during which the polis system was financially drained and progressively demoralized by intercity warfare. Athens's surrender left Sparta the dominant power in the Greek world, but only for a time. The victorious Spartan fleet had been built and maintained largely with Persian money, and Sparta paid its debt by allowing Persia to reoccupy Ionia. For a time, Spartans followed a policy of establishing oligarchic regimes throughout the former Athenian empire—indeed, in Athens itself—but they quickly proved incapable of giving direction to Hellas. The Spartans were much too conservative to be successful imperialists. Moreover, the pool of full Spartan citizens declined drastically during the fourth century B.C., and the Spartans also had to worry about the problem of the helots.

In Athens and many other states, the oligarchies were soon overthrown, and Greece passed into a bewildering period of military strife and shifting hegemonies. For a brief period, Thebes rose to supremacy, led by brilliant and charismatic generals who developed new hoplite tactics. Athens began to form a new Aegean league but was foiled by Persian intervention. In the middle decades of the fourth century B.C., power tended to shift among Sparta, Athens, and Thebes, while the Greek colony of Syracuse dominated Sicily and southern Italy. Envoys from Persia, always well supplied with money, saw to it that no one state became too powerful. A Greece divided and wracked by warfare could be no threat to the Persian Empire. Ironically, Persia's diplomacy opened the way for an event that it had been determined to avoid at all costs: the unification of Greece.

The debilitating intercity wars left Greece unprepared for the intervention of an emerging power on its northern frontier. Macedon (or Macedonia) had been ruled by a dynasty called the Temenidae since the middle of the seventh century B.C., but the Temenidae had not been able to consolidate their hold on Macedon, an area far richer in natural resources and products than most Greek city-states, including horses, cattle, crops, wine, gold, silver, and timber, because of conflicts with the barbarian kingdoms by which Macedon was surrounded. Partially for that reason, during the sixth and fifth centuries B.C. Macedon did not develop the institutions characteristic of most Greek city-states (such as courts of law and regular assemblies). Rather, into the fourth century B.C., Macedon remained a warrior kingdom, evoking the days of Homer's heroes. In 359 B.C., a talented opportunist named **Philip II,** whose brother, the king Perdiccas, had been killed in a disastrous battle against the Illyrians, ascended to the throne of Macedon as regent for his young nephew. Philip tamed and unified the Macedonian tribes, secured his northern frontiers, and then began a patient and artful campaign to bring all Greece under his control.

Having spent three years of his boyhood as a hostage in Thebes, Philip of Macedon had acquired a full appreciation of both Greek culture and Greek political instability. He hired the great philosopher Aristotle as tutor for his son, **Alexander III.** He exploited the ever-increasing Greek distaste for war by fighting, bluffing, and cajoling his way into the south. He accompanied his conquests with repeated declarations of his peaceful intentions, and when at last Athens and Thebes resolved their ancient rivalry and joined forces against him, it was too late. At **Chaeronea** in 338 B.C., Philip won the critical battle—eighteen-year-old Alexander led the decisive infantry charge—and Greece lay at his mercy.

Philip allowed the Greek states to handle their own internal affairs, but he organized them into a league whose policies he controlled. With the subordination of Greek city-states to the will of King Philip, the age of the completely autonomous Greek city-state, free to make its own foreign policy without outside interference, came to a close. The accession of Philip's illustrious son Alexander launched a new era, known as the Hellenistic Age, that would witness the emergence of vast new kingdoms stretching across the Near East, ruled by Greek dynasties. Greek culture would spread far and wide, and Greek life would be transformed into something drastically different from what it had been before.

CHANGE AND THE POLIS

With the emergence of these Hellenistic kingdoms, the political orientation of the ancient Greeks shifted. The polis, which had developed as the characteristic form of Greek communal life during the Archaic period (along with the *ethnos,* or tribal organization), gave way to the *metropolis,* or federations of city-states, and self-governing citizens devolved into subjects.

The essential characteristic of the polis was the participation of its (male) citizens in the political and cultural life of the community. Citizens were expected to take care of their private business and at the same time attend the assembly, participate in decisions of state, serve in the administration, and fight in the army or navy whenever necessary. Statesmen such as Pericles were at once administrators, orators, and generals. The polis was a community of well-rounded citizens, with many interests and capabilities—in short, a guild of gifted amateurs. Much of what the individual polis managed to accomplish can be attributed to the extreme identification felt by the members of the guild, the citizens, with the polis itself.

In the sixth and early fifth centuries B.C., when Greek life had been comparatively simple, it was possible for one citizen of a polis to play many roles. But as the fifth century progressed, the advantages of specialization grew. Military tactics became more complex. Administrative procedures grew increasingly refined. Oratory became the subject of specialized study. As the various intellectual disciplines developed, it became more and more difficult to master them. The age of the amateur gave way to the age of the professional. The polis of the fourth century B.C. was filled with professional administrators, orators, scholars, bankers, sailors, and merchants whose demanding careers left them time for little else. Citizens were increasingly absorbed in their private affairs, and political life, once the very embodiment of Greek civic patriotism, lost some of its fascination. It was no longer possible for the polis to function as a face-to-face community. Citizen-soldiers gave way increasingly to mercenaries, partly because civic patriotism was running dry but also because fighting was now a full-time career. The precarious equilibrium between competence and versatility—between individual and community—that had been achieved in the golden age was only momentary, for the intense creativity of the fifth century B.C. led to the specialization of the fourth. As the celebrated classical scholar H. D. F. Kitto once observed, "Progress broke the polis"; yet progress was a fundamental ingredient of the way of life that the polis created.

The classical Greek polis was the seedbed of an idea central to much of the Western political tradition: namely, that man was an animal suited by nature to live in a small, self-governing community of fellow citizens (as Aristotle famously claimed). But it was precisely because the polis never evolved into an organization fully capable of expanding its community of fellow citizens beyond its largely inherited membership that it did not win out over other forms of social and political organization in the Graeco-Roman world. The exclusivity of the polis was the source of both its greatest strength and its greatest weakness.

CHAPTER 8

Literature and Philosophy in Greece

The intellectual achievement of the Greeks has been of immense importance to Western civilization. The civilizations of the ancient Near East did significant pioneer work in mathematics, engineering, and practical science, and the Hebrews developed a profound ethical system based on the revelation of their one, all-powerful creator-god. The Greeks, in contrast, first took the step of rigorously examining humanity and the cosmos with the tool of logic. It was Greek philosophers who went beyond the mythical and poetic approach to cosmology and began to look at the universe as a purely natural rather than a supernatural phenomenon, based on discoverable principles of cause and effect rather than on divine will. And it was they who first attempted to base morality and. the good life solely on reason.

Thus Greeks were the first philosophers, the first logicians, the first theoretical scientists. Babylonians had studied the stars to discern the future; Egyptians had mastered geometry to build tombs and chemistry to create mummies. Greeks had much to learn from their Near Eastern predecessors, but they turned their investigation toward a new end: a completely rational understanding of humanity and the universe.

This is not to say that the Greeks were irreligious. Their dramas, civic festivals, and Olympic Games were all religious celebrations. Their art and architecture were devoted largely to honoring the gods. Their generals sometimes altered strategy on the basis of a divine portent. But at least some of them attempted to untangle the natural from the supernatural. The Greeks had no powerful official priesthood to enforce correct doctrine. To them, as to other ancient peoples, the cosmos was awesome. But at least some Greeks possessed the open-mindedness and audacity to use their intellects.

Significant Events of Greek Cultural History

All dates are B.C.

c. 650	Archilochus: elegiac poet from Parof
c. 600	Sappho of Lesbos: the first great lyric poet, establishes her circle of female friends on Lesbos
c. 585	Thales: the first important Greek scientist and philosopher, proposes that water is the primary element
c. 582–507	Pythagoras: mathematician, mystic, and founder of a quasi-religious brotherhood
c. 550	Anaximander proposes that humans are descended from an embryo in the sea
c. 525–456	Aeschylus: the first great tragic dramatist
c. 496–406	Sophocles: tragic dramatist, author of *Antigone*
c. 485–406	Euripides: tragic dramatist who portrays his characters with unparalleled realism and psychological insight
c. 484–420s	Herodotus: the first major Greek historian
c. 469–399	Hippocrates: the first major Greek physician
c. 469–399	Socrates: who devotes his philosopher career to the proposition that an unexamined life is scarcely worth living
c. 460–400	Thucydides: the first critical historical scholar, historian of the war between the Athenians and the Peloponnesians
c. 450–386	Aristophanes: the greatest Greek comic playwright
432	Completion of the Parthenon on the Athenian Acropolis
c. 429–347	Plato: student and reinterpreter of Socrates who revolutionizes philosophy
384–322	Aristotle: universal scholar and student of Plato who further revolutionizes philosophy

IONIA: THE LYRIC POETS

Open-mindedness and audacity were nourished by the free and turbulent atmosphere of the polis. Greek rationalism was a product of Greek individualism, and among the first manifestations of this new spirit of self-awareness and irreverence for tradition was the development of lyric poetry in Ionia in the seventh and sixth centuries B.C.

Greek lyric poetry was a literary achievement of the highest importance, yet its significance transcends the field of *belles lettres.* The works of lyric poets such as **Archilochus,** from the island of Paros, in the mid-seventh century B.C. and **Sappho** of Lesbos in the mid- to late sixth century B.C. disclose a self-consciousness and

Sappho
In antiquity, Sappho was considered the Tenth Muse, and her poetry was collected into nine books. Of those nine books, unfortunately, only one complete poem and several substantial fragments, among approximately 189 fragments, survive. (© *Alinari/Art Resource, NY*)

intensity of experience far exceeding anything recorded in literature before. At a time when Spartan mothers reportedly were sending their sons to war with the stern admonition, "Return with your shield—or on it," the free-spirited Ionian Archilochus was expressing a more individualistic viewpoint:

> Some lucky Thracian has my shield,
> For, being somewhat flurried,
> I dropped it by a wayside bush

As from the field I hurried.
Thank God, I made it clean away.
To blazes with the shield!
I'll get another just as good
When next I take the field.

Here, Archilochus is clearly concerned about living to fight another day. Elsewhere in his poetry, he expresses no qualms about compromising the honor of young women. In sum, Archilochus emerges as a vivid, engaging, individual (if slightly roguish) personality.

The most intensely personal of the lyric poets, however, was Sappho, an educated (although probably illiterate) poetess who may have been involved in contemporary aristocratic power struggles on Lesbos. Most of her surviving poems were composed for solo performances, and many have as their subject love between women or girls. Such love may have taken on a n institutionalized form at the time, as erotic relations among young men also did in some poleis at the same time—although Sappho's own sexual preferences are a matter of controversy. Whatever Sappho's own inclinations were, never, before her poetry, had human feelings of desire been expressed with such perception and sensitivity:

Love has unbound my limbs and set me shaking
A monster bitter-sweet and my unmaking.

THE IONIAN PHILOSOPHERS

The same surge of individualism that produced lyric poetry gave rise to humanity's first effort toward a rational understanding of the physical universe. So far as we know, the first natural philosopher and theoretical scientist (or cosmologist) in Western history was an Ionian, **Thales** of Miletus, who predicted a solar eclipse in 585 B.C. and set forth the proposition that water was the beginning, or first principle, of all things. This hypothesis, crude though it seems in retrospect, constitutes a deeply significant effort to impose a principle of intellectual unity on the diversity of experience. The world was to be understood as a single physical substance. Presumably, solid objects were made of compressed water, air of rarefied water, and—one supposes—empty space of dehydrated water. Thales' "Water Hypothesis" was not upheld by his successors, but the crucial point is that Thales *had* successors. Others followed his example and continued the effort to explain the universe through natural rather than supernatural principles. Intellectual history had taken a bold new turn.

The Ionian philosophers after Thales continued to speculate about the primal substance of the universe. One suggested that air was the basic element; another, fire. The Ionian **Anaximander,** perhaps a student of Thales', was the first to make a map of the inhabited world and set forth a primitive theory of evolution, declaring that people were descended from a kind of embryo, which floated in the sea. But these intellectual pioneers, their originality notwithstanding, disclose a basic weakness that characterized Greek thought throughout the classical age. They exhibited the all-too-human tendency to rush into sweeping generalizations on the basis of grossly inadequate factual foundations. Beguiled by the potentialities of rational inquiry, they failed to appreciate how painfully difficult it is to arrive at sound conclusions. Consequently, the hypotheses of the Ionians are of the nature of inspired guesses. Anaximander's theory of evolution, for example, was quickly forgotten because, unlike Darwin's, it had no significant supporting data.

THE PYTHAGOREAN SCHOOL

Pythagoras (c. 582–507 B.C.) represents a different intellectual trend. A native of the island of Samos in Ionia, he migrated to the city of Croton in southern Italy, where he founded a sect or society that was half scientific, half mystical. He drew heavily from the mystery cults of Dionysus and Demeter and was influenced especially by Orphism, a salvation cult that was becoming popular in the sixth century B.C. The cult of **Orpheus** stressed guilt and atonement, a variety of ascetic practices, and an afterlife of suffering or bliss depending on the purity of one's soul. This and similar cults appealed to those who found inadequate solace in the heroic but worldly gods of Olympus.

Pythagoras and his followers advocated the doctrine of transmigration of souls and the concept of a quasi-monastic communal life. Fundamental to all this was their profoundly significant notion that the basic element in nature was neither water, air, nor fire, but number. The Pythagoreans studied the intervals between musical tones and worked out basic laws of harmony. Having demonstrated the relationship between music and mathematics, they next applied these principles to the whole universe. They asserted that the cosmos obeyed the laws of harmony and, indeed, that the planets in their courses produced musical tones that combined into a cosmic rhapsody: the music of the spheres. Implicit in this bewildering mixture of insight and fancy is the pregnant concept that nature is best understood mathematically.

The mathematical thought of the Pythagoreans was clouded by a dogmatic reverence for the number ten, which they saw as magical. Consequently, they have inspired a great deal of numerological nonsense down to our own day. But they also played a crucial role in the development of mathematics and mathematical science. They produced the Pythagorean theorem and the multiplication table, and their notions contributed to the development of modern science in the sixteenth and seventeenth centuries. The Greeks were at their best in mathematics, for here they could reason deductively—applying self-evident concepts to specific cases—and their apparent distaste for the slow, patient accumulation of data was no hindrance.

ATOMS, MEDICINE, AND HISTORY

In the course of the fifth century B.C., Greek thinkers raised and explored a great many of the central problems that have occupied philosophers (and thoughtful human beings) ever since: whether the universe is in a state of flux or eternally changeless; whether it is composed of one substance or many; whether or not the nature of the universe can be grasped by the reasoning mind. About 440 B.C., **Democritus** of Abdera in Thrace set forth a doctrine of materialism that anticipated several of the views of modern science. He maintained that the universe consists of countless atoms in random configurations and that it has no center and no periphery but is much the same in one place as another. In short, the universe is infinite and the earth is in no way unique. Like Anaximander's theory of evolution, the atomism of Democritus was essentially a philosophical assertion rather than a scientific hypothesis based on empirical evidence. And because infinity was not a concept congenial to most Greeks, atomism long remained a minority view. But in early modern times, Democritus's notion of an infinite universe contributed to the development of a new philosophical outlook and to the rise of modern astronomy.

Thucydides
The Greeks feared
excessive civic self-
promotion and sought
to distill the essence of
a human being in his
portrait, so they erected
statues of their great
men posthumously and
only in generalized
form. Thus this portrait
of Thucydides is
probably an idealized
likeness. (© *Erich
Lessing/Art Resource,
NY)*

In medicine and history, however, the Greeks of the fifth century
B.C. were able to resist the lure of premature generalization and con-
centrate on the tiresome but essential task of accumulating accurate
data. In the field of medicine, **Hippocrates** of Cos, roughly a contemporary of Socrates (c. 469–399 B.C.), and his followers recorded case
histories with scrupulous care and avoided facile and hasty conclusions. Their painstaking clinical studies and their rejection of supernatural causation launched medicine on its modern course.

A similar reverence for the verifiable fact was demonstrated by
Greek historians of the period. History, in the modern sense of an
inquiry into past events (based on the ancient Greek verb *historein,*
"to inquire"), begins with Herodotus, a non-Athenian from Halicarnassus in Caria, who migrated to Athens and became one of its
unabashed admirers. Herodotus was a person of boundless curiosity
and, in the course of his extensive travels through Greece and the
Near East, accumulated a vast store of data for his brilliant and en-
tertaining history of the Persian Wars (described earlier). Herodotus

made some effort to separate fact from fable as he attempted to explain what caused the Greeks and the Persians to go to war with each other, but he was far surpassed in this regard by Thucydides, a disgraced Athenian general who wrote his account of the Peloponnesian War with unprecedented objectivity and an acute sense of historical criticism (see accompanying biographical sketch).

Thucydides

Born around 460 B.C. to an aristocratic family with property and political influence in a mining district of Thrace, Thucydides played an active role in Athenian politics during the closing years of the age of Pericles, whom he much admired. He served as a general in the Peloponnesian War until 424 B.C., when he was exiled for failing to lead his troops to the relief of a city, Amphipolis, which was under attack by the Spartans. During the years that followed, Thucydides traveled widely to gather evidence for his great history of the Peloponnesian War. His history was not an effort at self-justification, however, but an even-handed, brilliantly analytical study of politics and warfare during the first twenty years of the war. (Unfortunately, the final part of his history is incomplete; Thucydides died around 400 B.C.)

As he tells us near the beginning of his history, Thucydides took great pains to accurately report what happened during the Peloponnesian War. "Of the events of the war," he wrote, "I have described nothing but what I either saw myself or learned from others whom I questioned most carefully and specifically. The task was laborious, because eyewitnesses of the same events gave different accounts of them, as they remembered or were interested in the actions of one side or the other."

Thucydides approached history in a new way. The writers of the Hebrew Bible viewed it as the unfolding of a divine plan; some of Thucydides' own Greek predecessors had believed that historical events could be foretold by oracles and omens and could be affected by the intervention of deities. To Thucydides, however, human events had no supernatural dimension. They were the outgrowth of political action on the part of statesmen and popular assemblies, whose plans were often thwarted by mistaken assumptions or simply by chance. Thucydides had no real interest in social or economic history; rather, his approach was political and psychological. His chief interest lay in the motivations underlying political action, and a central theme of his work is the deleterious effect of prolonged warfare on political prudence. As he put it: "In peace and prosperity, poleis and individuals have better sentiments because they do not find themselves suddenly confronted with imperious necessities. But war takes away the easy supply of daily wants, and so proves a rough master that brings most men's characters to a level with their fortunes."

Thus, as the Peloponnesian War dragged on, "Reckless audacity came to be considered the courage of a loyal ally; prudent hesitation, specious cowardice; moderation was held to be a cloak for unmanliness."

At the center of Thucydides' conception of history was the polis. Like no one before him, he subjected the political conflicts in the Greek poleis to keen, unsentimental analysis. To Thucydides, the polis was an endlessly fascinating arena of contending political views and interests, and since he tended to see political issues as the central problems of existence, he ascribed to the polis a dominating role in the dynamics of history.

THE SOPHISTS

In philosophy, history, and science, reason was winning its victories at the expense of the supernatural. The anthropomorphic gods of Olympus were especially susceptible to rational criticism. Few people acquainted with Ionian philosophy or the new traditions of scientific history and medicine, for example, could seriously believe that Zeus hurled thunderbolts or that Poseidon caused earthquakes. Some came to see Zeus as a transcendent god of the universe; others rejected him altogether.

But one who doubts that Zeus tosses thunderbolts might also doubt that Athena protects Athens. And the rejection of Athena and other civic deities clearly was harmful to the traditional ethos of the polis. Religious skepticism was gradually undermining civic patriotism. Once again, we are confronted with the dynamic and paradoxical nature of the Greek experience: the polis produced inquiring minds, but in time some of the inquirers helped to undermine many of the most fundamental traditions of the polis.

In the fifth century B.C., the arch skeptics of Athens were the Sophists, a diverse group of itinerant professors of higher education and professional teachers drawn from every corner of the Greek world by the wealth of the imperial city. Much of our information about the Sophists comes from the writings of Plato, who disliked them heartily and portrayed them as intellectual prostitutes and tricksters. In reality, most of them were dedicated to the life of reason and the sound argument.

Unlike the Ionian natural philosophers, the Sophists of this time were interested chiefly in human behavior rather than the cosmos. They investigated ethics, politics, history, and psychology and have been called the first social scientists. In applying reason to these areas and in teaching their students to do the same, they aroused the wrath of intellectual conservatives and doubtless encouraged an irreverent attitude toward tradition. Many of the Sophists taught their pupils techniques of debating and getting ahead while questioning the traditional doctrines of religion, patriotism, and dedication to the welfare of the community. To Protagoras is attributed the claim that he knew how to make the weaker argument defeat the stronger. Plato describes one of them as advocating the maxim that "Might makes right." Collectively, the Sophists stimulated an attitude of doubt, relativism, and ambitious individualism, thereby contributing (according to their critics) to the dissolution of loyalty of the polis.

SOCRATES (c. 469–399 B.C.)

Socrates was at once a participant in the Sophistic movement and an opponent of it, according to his admirer Plato. During the troubled years of the Peloponnesian War, Socrates wandered the streets of Athens urging his followers to test their beliefs and preconceptions with the tool of reason. "An unexamined life," he observed, "is scarcely worth living."

Like the Sophists, Socrates was largely interested in human rather than cosmic matters, but unlike many of them he was dissatisfied with merely tearing down traditional beliefs, and he never received any money from the members of his circle. He set the stage by posing seemingly innocent questions that invariably entangled his listeners in a hopeless maze of contradictions. Then, after demolishing their opinions, he substituted closely reasoned conclusions of his own on the subject of ethics and the good life. Wisdom, he seems to have believed, was synonymous with virtue (Greek, *arete*), and it was not possible for a person to know the better and then to do the worse. Impelled by this conviction, he continued to attack the cherished opinions of those who thought they knew what virtue was—to play the role of gadfly, as he put it. At the same time, Socrates (as

Socrates
Although probably created posthumously, this portrait of the great thinker captures his satyric appearance and beetled brow. (© *Scala/ Art Resource*)

represented in the dialogues composed by Plato) consistently denied that he had the knowledge of wisdom that was necessary to live the good life. Unlike the Athenians with whom he conversed, however, he at least knew he was ignorant of this knowledge, whereas they (wrongly) believed they knew wherein wisdom lay and thus were ignorant of their ignorance. It was for this reason, that he knew he knew nothing worthwhile, that the Delphic Oracle had proclaimed that there was no one wiser than Socrates.

Gadflies have seldom been universally popular, especially gadflies who have made it their business to expose the ignorance of their fellow citizens. The Athenians, put on edge by their defeat in the Peloponnesian War, which was hastened by the treachery of one of Socrates' pupils, could at last bear his interrogations no longer. In 399 B.C., five years after their surrender to Sparta, a group of prosecutors brought Socrates to trial for not reverencing the gods of the polis, but introducing new gods, and also for corrupting the young. Behind the first charge seems to have lain Socrates' claim that he heard the voice of some kind of divine "little spirit" (*daimonion*), which came to him at times and stopped him from taking certain actions. No one else in Athens could see or hear the voice of this divine spirit. In a democratic polis such as Athens, the sole access Socrates had to his private, divine spirit was perhaps seen as a challenge to the idea that the assembly of citizens had the responsibility and authority to manage relations with the gods and goddesses who controlled the destiny of the city. Socrates' private spirit represented a direct challenge to the structure of authority of the polis itself.

Behind the prosecutors' second charge (corrupting the youth of the city) perhaps lay the argument that Socrates continued to urge young Athenians to question all of their own beliefs, including beliefs about the justification for their democratic form of government, even after the Athenians had managed to get rid of the oligarchy installed in the city at the end of the Peloponnesian War; to restore their democratic form of government; and then to pass an amnesty exempting all but a few citizens for their antidemocratic activities during the periods of oligarchic government (in 411 and 404 B.C.). By the terms of the amnesty, Socrates could not be prosecuted for influencing such antidemocratic figures as Alcibiades or Critias, but he could be prosecuted for teaching antidemocratic ideas to young men after the amnesty. Thus, from the point of view of his prosecutors, Socrates was seen as antidemocratic.

The Athenian jury in his case found Socrates guilty by a narrow majority. In accordance with Athenian law, he had the right to propose his own punishment. He suggested that the Athenians punish him by giving him free meals at public expense for the rest of his life. By refusing to take the business seriously, he was in effect condemning himself to death. Declining an opportunity to escape into exile, he was executed by poison (drinking hemlock). He expired with the cheerful observation that now at last he had the opportunity of discovering for himself the truth about the afterlife.

PLATO (c. 429–347 B.C.)

Socrates would not have done well on an American university faculty, for although he was a splendid teacher, he did not publish.* We know about the questions he asked others largely through the

*Jesus would have been denied tenure on the same grounds.

gracefully written dialogues of his student, **Plato,** an Athenian nobleman and one of history's supreme intellects.

In his *Republic,* Plato outlined the perfect polis—the first utopia in literary history. Here, ironically, the philosopher rejected the democracy that he knew and described an ideal state more Spartan than Athenian. Farmers, workers, and merchants were without political rights. A military-executive elite of experts, the Guardians, trained with Spartan rigor, defended and administered the state under the direction of philosopher-kings, the wisest and most virtuous products of a state training program that consumed the better part of their lives. Culture was not encouraged in the *Republic.* Dangerous and novel ideas were forbidden, poets were banished, and all music was prohibited except the martial, patriotic type. In Plato's ideal state, justice for the individual consisted of the individual identifying his own self-interest with that of the state.

What are we to make of a utopia that would ban Mozart, a polis that could never have produced a Plato? We must remember that from Plato's point of view, democratic Athens was in decline. He could not admire the polis that had executed his master, nor was he blind to the selfish individualism and civic irresponsibility that afflicted Greece in the fourth century B.C. Plato had the wit to recognize that through the intensity of its cultural creativity, and the freedom and breadth of its intellectual curiosity, the polis was burning itself out. Achilles had chosen a short but glorious life; Plato preferred longevity even at the cost of mediocrity, and he designed his Republic to achieve that goal. There would be no Sophists to erode civic virtue, no poets to exalt the individual over the community (or abandon their shields as they fled from battle). Plato's cavalier treatment of the mercantile classes represents a deliberate rejection of the lures of empire. Like a figure on a Grecian urn, his ideal polis would be frozen and rigid—and enduring.

There remains the paradox that this intellectually static commonwealth was to be ruled by philosophers. We tend to think of philosophy as a singularly disputatious subject, but Plato viewed truth as absolute and unchanging. He assumed that all true philosophers would be in agreement essentially—that all future thinkers would be Platonists.

This assumption has proved to be resoundingly wrong, yet Plato's conception of reality has nevertheless exerted an enormous influence on the development of thought. His purpose was to reconcile his belief in a perfect, unchanging universe with the diversity and impermanence of the visible world. He stated that the objects we perceive through our senses are merely pale, imperfect reflections of ideal models, or archetypes, that exist in a world invisible to us. For example, we observe numerous individual cats—some black, some marmalade colored, some fat, some skinny. All are imperfect particularizations of an ideal cat existing in the Platonic heaven. Again, in the world of the senses, we find many examples of duality: lovers, twins, pairs, bookends, and so on. But they merely exemplify, more or less inadequately, the idea of "two," which in its pure state is invisible and intangible. We cannot see "two"; we can only see two things. But—and this is all-important—we can conceive of "twoness" or abstract duality. Likewise, with sufficient effort, we can conceive of "catness," "dogness," and "rabbitness"—of the archetypal cat, dog, or rabbit. If we could not, so Plato believed, we would have no basis for grouping individual cats, dogs, or rabbits into a single category.

In short, the world of phenomena is not the real world. The phenomenal world is variegated and dynamic; the real world, the world of archetypes, is clear-cut and static. We can discover this real world through introspection, for knowledge of the archetypes is present in our minds from birth, dimly remembered from a previous existence. (Plato believed in a before-life as well as in an afterlife. Our souls are immortal and are endlessly reborn into different bodies through transmigration.) So the philosopher studies reality not by observing but by thinking.

Plato illustrated this doctrine with a vivid metaphor. Imagine a cave whose inhabitants are chained in such a position that they can never turn toward the sunlit opening but can see only shadows projected against an interior wall. Imagine further that one of the inhabitants (the philosopher) breaks his chains, emerges from the cave, and sees the real world for the first time. He will have no wish to return to his former shadow world, but he will do so nevertheless out of a sense of obligation to enlighten the others. Similarly, the philosopher-kings rule the Republic unwillingly through a sense of duty. They would prefer to contemplate reality undisturbed. Yet, they alone can rule wisely, for they alone have seen the truth.

Plato's doctrine of ideas has always been alluring to people who seek order, unity, stability, and virtue in a universe that appears fickle and chaotic. Plato declared that the greatest of the archetypes is the idea of the Good, and this notion has had great appeal to people of religious temperament ever since. His theory of knowledge, which emphasizes contemplation over observation, is obviously hostile to the method of experimental science, yet his archetypal world is largely compatible with the world of the mathematician, the world of pure numbers. Plato drew heavily from the Pythagorean tradition— "God is a mathematician," he once observed—and Platonic thought, like Pythagorean thought, has contributed immensely to the development of mathematical science. As for philosophy, it developed over the next 2,000 years in the shadow of two giants. One of them is Plato; the other is Aristotle, Plato's greatest pupil.

ARISTOTLE (384–322 B.C.)

Plato founded a school in Athens called the **Academy** (the source of our word "academic"). To this school came the young **Aristotle,** the son of a Greek physician in the service of the king of Macedon. Aristotle remained at the Academy for nearly two decades. Then, after serving at the Macedonian court as tutor to Alexander the Great, he returned to Athens, founded a school of his own (the so-called **Lyceum**), and wrote most of his books. Later, he was condemned by the Athenians for "impiety" and escaped into exile, explaining as he fled that he wished to prevent the Athenians from sinning twice against philosophy. He died shortly thereafter, in 322 B.C., one year after the death of Alexander. Thus, Aristotle's life spanned the final years of the classical age of Greece and the onset of the Hellenistic Age.

Aristotle was a universal scholar, a polymath. He wrote definitively on a great variety of topics including biology, politics, literature, ethics, logic, physics, and metaphysics. He brought Plato's theory of ideas down to earth by asserting that the archetype exists in the particular—that one can best study the archetypal cat by observing and classifying individual cats. He thus gave scientific observation a much higher priority than had Plato. Like Hippocrates and Thucydides, but on a much broader scale, Aristotle advocated the painstaking collection and analysis of data. Although his political studies included the designing of an ideal commonwealth, he also investigated and classified the political systems of many existing poleis and demonstrated that several different types were conducive to the good life. In the field of ethics, he advocated moderation in all behavior, arguing that emotions and actions (anger and love, eating and drinking) are themselves neither good nor evil and should be neither suppressed nor carried to excess: virtue is the avoidance of extremes, the "golden mean."

Aristotle's ground-breaking biological studies employed methods of observation and classification similar to those he applied in his other works. He set forth the concepts of genus and species that, with modifications, are still used. His work on physics has been less durable because it was based on an erroneous concept of motion, a fundamental belief in purpose as the organizing factor in the material universe, and an emphasis on qualitative rather than quantitative differences. For example, he believed that the heavenly bodies are more perfect than earthly objects. Mathematics had no genuine role in his system; in general, modern science draws its experimental method from the Aristotelian tradition and its mathematical analysis from the Pythagorean-Platonic tradition.

Aristotle's physics and metaphysics were based on the concept of a single deity who was the motive power behind the universe—the unmoved mover and the uncaused cause to which all motion and all causation must ultimately be referred. Hence, Aristotelian thought was able to serve as a philosophical framework for later Islamic and Christian thought. Aristotle's immense significance in intellectual history arises from his having done some of the best thinking up to his time in so many significant intellectual disciplines. It was he who first set forth a systematic logic, who first produced a rigorous, detailed physics, who literally founded the science of biology. Although he was a pioneer in observational method, he has been criticized for basing conclusions on insufficient evidence. Even Aristotle was not immune to the tendency toward premature conclusions, yet he collected data as no Greek before him had done. His achievement, considered in its totality, is unique in the history of thought.

Plato and Aristotle represent the apex of Greek philosophy. Both were religious men. And both were dedicated also to the life of reason. Building on a rational heritage that had only begun in the sixth century B.C., both produced philosophical systems of unparalleled sophistication and depth. Their thought climaxed the intellectual revolution that brought such glory and turmoil to Greece.

CHAPTER 9

The Culture
of the Golden Age

History rarely has seen anything quite like the outburst of cultural creativity that took place in Athens in the fifth century B.C. Virtually every surviving work of art, from the greatest temple to the simplest ornament, was created with taste and assurance. Emotions ran strong and deep, but they were controlled by a sure sense of form that never permitted ostentation and never degenerated into formalism. The art of the period was an incarnation of the Greek maxim "Nothing in excess."

Classical Greek culture reflected the liberty and dynamism of the polis. Compared to the societies of the Near East, the world of the polis was intense, fluid, and dynamic. Political systems, philosophical concepts, and artistic styles evolved at a furious pace. Aristocracies declined, tyrannies flourished, and democracies emerged in an atmosphere of social change and acute political awareness. At least some of the citizens of the Greek poleis believed that they were a people apart and that what separated them most fundamentally from their predecessors and contemporaries was their freedom. Herodotus describes Greeks as speaking to a Persian official in these words: "A slave's life you understand, but never having tasted liberty, you cannot tell whether it is sweet or not. Had you known what freedom is, you would have bidden us fight for it." One of the major themes of Herodotus's investigation into the causes of the war between the Greeks and the Persians was the struggle between slavery and freedom.

It is not difficult to understand how Greek citizens, whose freedom (that is, their constitutional right to govern themselves) exceeded that of previous peoples, produced such a dynamic culture. It is harder to explain the harmony and restraint of Greek classicism, for political life in the Greek poleis also was lived with great intensity.

Herodotus tells us that the barbaric Scythians lamented the Greek impulse toward frenzy, and a speaker in Thucydides observes that the Athenians "were born into the world to take no rest themselves and to give none to others."

Perhaps the Greeks of the classical period stressed the importance of moderation and restraint in art precisely because these qualities were needed by an intense people. A degree of cooperation and self-control was also essential to the communal life of the polis, and civic devotion acted as a brake on rampant individualism. During its greatest years, the polis stimulated individual creativity but directed it toward the welfare of the community. Individualism and civic responsibility achieved a momentary and precarious balance.

The achievement of this equilibrium in the fifth century B.C. was a precious but fleeting episode in the evolution of the polis from the aristocratic conservatism of the previous age to the unbridled individualism of the next century and thereafter. This process is illustrated in the development of Greek art from the delicate, static elegance of the "archaic style," through the serious, balanced classical style of the fifth century B.C., to the increasing individualism and naturalism of the late-classical fourth century B.C. and the post-classical Hellenistic Age. Sculptures of the fifth century B.C. were depictions of idealized human beings, one might almost say Platonic archetypes. A century later, sculptors tended to abandon the archetype for the specific and concrete. In short, as Greek life was evolving from civic allegiance to individualism, from traditionalism to self-expression, from aristocracy to democracy, there was a moment when these opposites were balanced. That moment was frozen and immortalized in some of the finest works of architecture, sculpture, and dramatic literature the world has known.

The golden age of Greece was the golden age of Athens, for the wealth of empire and the ambitious building program of Pericles drew talent from throughout the Greek world. Periclean Athens had a long artistic tradition behind it, as well as a buoyant self-assurance that was born at Marathon, confirmed at Salamis, and heightened by a successful career in imperialism. But the Athenian golden age was expensive for the rest of Greece in both money and talent. Indeed, the Greek polis system at its cultural zenith had already evolved considerably from the original ideal of the independent, self-contained state. Athens was not merely a polis; it was the heart of an empire. And although civic spirit vitalized Athenian culture, imperial trade

Maiden (Korē) in Dorian garment, the peplos
The idealized, youthful figure (c. 530 B.C.) embodies the archaic style (the period c. 600–480 B.C.). Statues of both young men and young women were dedicated to the gods or erected in cemeteries to commemorate the dead.
(© Nimatallah/Art Resource, NY)

**The Discobolus
(Discus thrower)**
A Roman marble copy
of a bronze original
by the Greek sculptor
Myron (fifth century
B.C.) in the style of the
golden age. Myron (ac-
tive c. 470–440 B.C.) was
one of the leaders of
the period of artistic
experimentation in the
early classical period
and was especially well
known for his bronze
sculptures. This statue
is a study of the ar-
rested moment between
the backswing of the
athlete and his momen-
tum forward to release
the discus. (© *Alinari/
Art Resource, NY*)

and tribute helped to pay the bills. The culture of the golden age was
unquestionably a polis culture, but it was the culture of a polis that
was losing its innocence.

In Periclean Athens, individualism was still strongly oriented
toward the polis. One of the basic differences between the daily life
of the Athenian citizen of this time and that of the modern American
is the Athenian's emphasis on public over private affairs. The private
lives of even the most affluent Athenian citizens were rigorously
simple: their clothing was plain, their homes were modest, their furniture was rudimentary. With the intensification of individualism in
the fourth century B.C., private homes became more luxurious, but
during the golden age the Athenian's private life was, by our standards, almost as Spartan as the Spartan's.

The austerity of private life was counterbalanced, however, by the brilliant diversity of public life. Under Pericles, imperial Athens lavished its wealth and genius on its own adornment. The great works of art and architecture were dedicated to the polis and its gods. Life was enriched by the pageantry of civic religious festivals, by spirited conversation in the agora, by exercise in elaborate civic gymnasiums complete with baths and dressing rooms, and, of course, by participation in political affairs. The Greeks socialized the amenities of life. The pursuit of excellence in body and mind, so typical of Greek culture, was carried on in a communal atmosphere. The good life was not the life of the individual but the life of the citizen.

But although citizens constituted an enormously greater portion of the population in Periclean Athens compared to cities of the ancient Near East, most inhabitants of Athens were not full citizens in our sense of the word. Women, slaves, children, and metics were all excluded from at least some of the privileges of citizenship. And even though many metics prospered in business, many slaves were well treated, and some women played important roles in very public religious festivals, only adult male citizens could participate fully in almost all aspects of the life of the polis. (Some religious festivals were restricted to women.) Aristotle sought to provide a rational justification for this arrangement by proving to his own satisfaction that slaves and women were inferior beings.

The golden age of Pericles thus rested on economic foundations not only of imperial tribute but of slavery as well. As elsewhere in the Near East, most slaves in Athens were former prisoners of war or their descendants. Others had been purchased from slave traders into whose hands they had fallen as victims of bandit or pirate raids (as in the case of Diogenes; see page 160). Still others were simply noncitizens whose taxes had become excessively delinquent. Slaves might be consigned to agricultural labor, or they might serve as industrial workers, artisans, mine workers (whose treatment could be pitiless), or personal servants. Whatever their vocation, they were under the absolute authority of their masters, who were free to beat them, chain them, or sexually abuse them. In reality, many masters appear to have treated their slaves decently, and household slaves usually led tolerable lives. But, lacking all legal rights, slaves were entirely dependent on their masters' dispositions and whims. It must always be remembered that slavery was a basic, structural component of all ancient economies; Athens was not unique in this

Aspasia
A Roman copy of a Greek original (fifth century B.C.). Not a true portrait, this Aspasia was given an idealized face. The fashionable hairstyle is a Roman addition. (© *Alinari/Art Resource, NY*)

regard. In fact, there were substantial numbers of slaves in every single society of the ancient world, although slavery in the ancient world (unlike in the modern world) was never based upon race or racial discrimination. Nevertheless, Periclean Athens, with its large numbers of slaves (which historians have been unable to quantify accurately) and disenfranchised women, was no egalitarian paradise.

The lives of Athenian women, even the wives of citizens, were restricted largely, but not exclusively, to the home. A wife usually had heavy domestic duties but few social responsibilities and was legally under her husband's control. As noted, except for religious festivals and ceremonies, which were at the center of the communal life of the polis, public life in Athens was largely a male realm. Like other Greek men, many Athenian citizens enjoyed homosexual companionship outside the home, and sometimes heterosexual companionship as well. The parties and festive gatherings of the wealthier citizens included no wives but were enlivened by the presence of *hetairai* (female companions), high-class prostitutes of good education and free status. The hetairai were usually non-Athenians, often from Ionia, and were celebrated for their wit and charm. Notable among them was an Ionian woman named Aspasia, who owned her own bordello, enjoyed intellectual conversations with Socrates, and became Pericles' mistress (see accompanying biographical sketch). Her name, appropriately, means "welcome."

For wives, the age of Pericles was far from golden. Their lot is expressed eloquently in one of the tragedies of Euripides:

> A man, when he's bored with being at home
> Can go out and escape depression
> By turning to some friend, or whatever.
> But we wives have one soul to look to.
> They say we lead a safe life at home
> While they do battle with the spear.
> What imbeciles! I'd rather stand to arms
> Three times than bear one child.*

Aspasia

In the male-dominated society of classical Greece, two of the most important careers open to women were those of priestess and prostitute, and these two careers could be closely intertwined. The most famous of all prostitutes (hetairai) in classical Greece was Aspasia, born around 470 B.C. to the wife of a citizen of the prosperous Ionian city of Miletus. Since Greek towns normally forbade free women to become prostitutes, it has been conjectured that Aspasia's parents dedicated her as a child to a temple of Aphrodite, goddess of love, to be trained to become a temple prostitute. Such a parental decision must be seen in the context of an age that would have regarded it as an act of piety, and in which unwanted infants—females in particular—might lawfully be abandoned by their parents to die of exposure.

Temple prostitution was viewed as an honorable profession, indeed, a holy one, but the prostitutes were nevertheless slaves of their temples. At some point early in her career, Aspasia gained her freedom, perhaps as a gift from an admirer, and established her own practice. A young woman of beauty and keen intelligence, she soon

---

Medea, in Frank J. Frost, trans., *Greek Society,* 4th ed. (1992), lines 244–51, p. 98. By permission of Frank J. Frost.

won the affection of some of Miletus's leading citizens. It was probably while she was still in her early or mid-twenties that Aspasia
joined the growing flood of immigrants into imperial Athens, which
was prospering enormously amidst Pericles' great building program.
In Athens, she established an upper-class "house of assignation" and
staffed it with young women carefully chosen for their beauty, wit, and
charm. In time, the house of Aspasia became celebrated throughout
the Greek world, not only for the beauty of Aspasia and her girls but
also for the distinction of their clientele and the brilliance of the intellectual discourse between men and women. In classical Greek society,
such discourse could occur in no other context. The house of Aspasia
became a favorite meeting place of Athens's leading politicians, artists,
and playwrights. The philosopher Socrates became a close friend of
Aspasia's and dropped in often to converse with her.

Pericles himself fell deeply in love with Aspasia. He could not
legally marry her because the law provided that Athenian citizens
could marry only the daughters of citizens. But he divorced his wife
and took Aspasia as his constant companion, and by 441 B.C. she had
borne him a son and namesake. Her fame now reached new heights,
but her position at Pericles' side also drew much hostile comment from
citizens who suspected that the course of Athenian politics was being
influenced by a foreigner who was, worse yet, a woman. The comic
poet Cratinus, taking full advantage of Athens's freedom of speech,
attacked Aspasia viciously as "Pericles' Hera, the dog-eyed whore."
Rumors circulated that Aspasia was helping Pericles write his political
speeches or even, as Plato later alleged, ghostwriting some of them for
him. To the citizens of Periclean Athens, politics was a man's game, and
women had no business writing speeches or pulling strings behind the
scenes. Looking back on it today, it is quite impossible to sort fact from
rumor. We will never know to what degree Aspasia influenced politics,
diplomacy, and political oratory during the golden age of Athens.

Shortly after the onset of the Peloponnesian War in 431 B.C., a
plague carried off both of Pericles' sons by his ex-wife, leaving him
only his son by Aspasia, to whom Athenian law denied the right of citizenship. Pericles humbly pleaded with members of the Athenian Assembly to grant him a legal heir by extending citizenship to Aspasia's
son, and, pitying their bereaved leader, they did so. Pericles himself
died in 429 B.C., and in later years his son, the younger Pericles, became
a statesman and general.

Aspasia afterward became the companion of a wealthy wool
dealer named Lysicles, who, perhaps not coincidentally, was one of the
earliest non-noble merchants to strive for the political leadership of
Athens. Aspasia and Lysicles presented a standing target for the barbs

of comic poets, who could now give expression to their prejudices against both women and tradesmen in politics. How, they asked, could an unschooled merchant whose intellectual horizons had once been limited to sheep and wool suddenly become a great political orator? Aspasia, they said, was giving him a crash course in rhetoric. Lysicles became an Athenian general and died fighting in Anatolia. After his death in 428 B.C., Aspasia dropped from historical visibility, and we do not know how her life ended. Nevertheless, for a number of years, she was a unique figure in classical Athens—a woman who exercised political power and influence, and who did so not simply through her beauty and charm but by her skill and intelligence as well.

DRAMA

The civic culture of the golden age achieved its most remarkable triumphs in drama, architecture, and sculpture. All three illustrate the public orientation of Greek cultural life.

Greek tragedy probably arose out of the worship of Dionysus, as the songs (hymns called **dithyrambs**) and dance-dramas (called *saturikon*, which means a "satyrlike play," a play of mythological horselike creatures) of the worshipers gradually evolved into formalized drama with actors and a chorus. In the sixth century B.C., the Athenian tyrant Pisistratus gave vigorous support to the festival of Dionysus, and by the fifth century B.C. it had become a great civic institution. Wealthy citizens were expected to finance the productions, and each year a body of civic judges selected from the Athenian tribes awarded prizes to the three best tragedies. As in so many other areas of Greek life, competition was central to the development of this art form.

By modern standards, the performances were far from elaborate. The most important took place during the Athenian spring festival of Dionysos Eleuthereus in the outdoor Theater of Dionysus, which stands to this day on the southern slope of the Acropolis. The chorus sang and danced to simple musical accompaniment and commented at intervals on the action of the drama or engaged in alternating speech or song with the actors. In overall visual effect, an ancient tragedy was perhaps closer to modern opera than to an action movie, no doubt because tragedy originated in ritual.

The Acropolis
The Acropolis of the Athenians with the temple of Athena Parthenos (the Parthenon) at the summit. (© *Neil Beer/Getty Images/PhotoDisc*)

Behind the chorus were low broad steps on which the actors performed. There were never more than three actors on the stage at one time, and the sets behind them were simple in the extreme. The dramas were based on mythological or historical themes, often dealing with semilegendary royal families of early Greece, but the playwrights went beyond historical narrative to probe deeply into some of the fundamental problems of morality and religion.

The immense popularity of these stark, profound, uncompromising productions testifies to the remarkable cultural elevation of Athens in the fifth century B.C. The citizens who flocked to the Theater of Dionysus constituted a critical and sophisticated audience. Many had themselves participated in the numerous dramas that were constantly being performed both in the city and in the surrounding countryside of Attica. It has been estimated that each year some 3,000 citizens had the experience of performing in a dramatic chorus, and thousands more were trained, as a part of the normal Athenian curriculum, in singing, dancing, declamation, and acting. The drama was a central and meaningful element in the life of the polis and further illustrates the versatility of Athenian citizens during the fifth century B.C.

The three great tragedians of Athens during this period were **Aeschylus,** who wrote during the first half of the century; **Sophocles,** whose long productive period covered the middle and later decades of the century; and **Euripides,** a younger contemporary of Sophocles. All three exemplify the seriousness, order, and controlled tension that we identify as "classical," yet they also illustrate the changes the classical ideal of balance was undergoing.

Aeschylus, the first of the three, tended to emphasize traditional values and was deeply devoted to the polis and the Greek religious heritage. From his first to his last and most famous production in Athens, the *Oresteia* (in 458 B.C.), Aeschylus probed with majestic dignity the fundamental relationships of humanity and its gods, the problem of injustice in a righteous universe, and the terrible consequences of overweening pride. As pointed out earlier, on his epitaph no mention was made of the fact that Aeschylus had been Athens's greatest poet when the polis was at the height of its greatness; rather, his epitaph recorded that he had fought well at the battle of Marathon in 490 B.C. What mattered to Aeschylus was the contribution he had made as an Athenian citizen to keeping his beloved polis free.

Sophocles was less tradition bound than Aeschylus, but he was a supreme dramatic artist, with an unerring sense of plot structure and characterization, who made powerful use of props as well as entrances and exits. In most of his surviving plays, individual characters eventually must come to terms with the fact that what they believed to be true about reality has turned out not to be so—and that moment of recognition, when it is too late to undo what they have done based upon their faulty knowledge, is almost invariably connected to the individual's suffering or death. Nevertheless, Sophocles' plays, such as his immensely influential *Antigone,* treat the most violent and agonizing emotional situations with restraint and sobriety. In Sophocles, the classical equilibrium is fully achieved: intense passion under masterful control.

Sophocles' *Antigone,* which deals with (among other themes) the perennial conflict between individual conscience and public authority, exemplifies the depth and power of the century's dramatic tragedy. Antigone's brother has betrayed his country and has been killed. Her uncle, the king of Thebes, refuses to permit her brother's burial, even though burial was regarded as a sacred duty in the Greek religious tradition. Torn by the conflict between the royal decree and her sense of religious obligation, Antigone defies the king, buries her brother, and is condemned to death. She addresses the king in these words:

> I did not think that your decrees were of such force as to override the unwritten and unfailing laws of heaven. For their duration is not of today or yesterday, but from eternity, and no one knows when they were first put forth. And though men rage, I must obey these laws. Die I must, for death must come to all. But if I am to die before my time, I'll do it gladly; for when one lives as I do, surrounded by evils, death can only be a gain. So death for me is but a trifling grief, far better than to let my mother's son lie an unburied corpse.

The younger dramatist Euripides displayed (in his early plays at least) the logic, skepticism, and hard-headed rationalism of the Sophists, who were then the rage in Athens. One of his characters makes the audacious statement, "There are no gods in heaven; no, not one!" And Euripides, far more than his predecessors, demonstrated a deep, sympathetic understanding of human nature—its hopes and fears, its unpredictability and irrationality, and above all its individuality. Aeschylus's characters are chiefly types rather than individuals; he was far more interested in events or situations than in character development. In Sophocles, the individual emerges with much greater clarity, but Euripides portrayed his characters, especially women, with unparalleled realism and psychological insight. In one of his last and most disturbing plays, the *Bacchae* (performed after Euripides died in 407/406 B.C.), both men and women are destabilized and (in the case of at least one male character, Pentheus) literally torn to pieces as a result of their unhappy encounters with divinity.

The lighter side of drama is represented by the comic playwright **Aristophanes.** Taking advantage of the freedom of the Athenian theater, he subjected his fellow citizens great and small to merciless ridicule as he exposed the pretensions and follies of imperial Athens during and after the Peloponnesian War. A product of the age of Socrates and the Sophists, Aristophanes expressed his deep-rooted conservatism by lampooning them (although his satires of his fellow citizens are never made without qualification or complication). The character of Socrates appears in a comedy called *The Clouds* (from 423 B.C.), hanging from a basket suspended in the air so that he can contemplate the heavens at closer range, while below, his students study geology, their noses in the earth and their posteriors upraised toward the sky.

The plays of Aristophanes reflected and played to the political discontent of his audiences. He mocked Athens's leaders with a frankness that would seldom be tolerated by a modern democracy during wartime. The audacity of his criticism illustrates the degree of intellectual freedom that existed in Athens at that time. Yet his plays also betray a yearning for the dignity and traditionalism of former years and a disturbing conviction that all was not well.

ATHENIAN ARCHITECTURE AND SCULPTURE

Virtually every aspect of culture in the fifth century B.C. was influenced by the classical ideal of restrained excitement. We find it in Athenian drama, in which the most violent deeds and passions are

The Parthenon
The Parthenon was constructed in the Doric order of marble from nearby Mount Pentelicus, and the finished temple measured approximately 228 by 101 feet at its top step. There were eight columns at each of its ends and seventeen on the sides. Overall, the temple probably should be interpreted as a form of thanks offering to Athena for the victory over the Persians. (*Su Davies/Life File/Getty Images/PhotoDisc*)

presented in an ordered and unified framework. We find it in the history of Thucydides, who analyzes and presents the causes and events of the Peloponnesian War as objectively and dispassionately as possible. And we find it in the architecture and art of the Athens of this time: deeply moving, yet marvelously balanced and controlled.

When Xerxes burned the Acropolis of Athens, he left the next generation of Athenians with a challenge and an opportunity: to rebuild the temples in the new, classical style and crown the polis with structures of such perfection as the world had never known. Athenian imperialism provided at least some of the money with which to rebuild, and Pericles, against the opposition of a conservative minority, pursued a lavish policy of civic beautification as a part of his effort to make Athens the cultural center of Hellas. The age of Pericles was therefore a period of feverish public building, and its supreme architectural monument (designed by the architects **Ictinus** and

Head of Athena Lemnia (copy after Phidias)
Phidias was active from about 465 to 425 B.C. His statue of Athena Parthenos inside the Parthenon was almost forty feet high and was draped in more than a ton of gold. In antiquity, he was widely considered to be the greatest of Greek sculptors. (© *Alinari/Art Resource, NY*)

Hermes, by Praxiteles
Praxiteles is an Athenian sculptor who was active between about 375 and 330 B.C. His specialty was depictions of the younger gods, and he also was known for his nude sculpture of Aphrodite, the so-called Cnidia, supposedly modeled on his mistress Phryne. (© *Alinari/Art Resource, NY*)

Callicrates) was the central temple on the reconstructed Acropolis, the Parthenon. This structure, dedicated to the city's patron goddess Athena, is the ultimate expression of the classical ideal. It creates its effect not from a sense of fluidity and upward reaching, as in medieval Gothic cathedrals and twentieth-century skyscrapers, but from a superb harmony of proportions. Here, indeed, was "nothing in excess."

The genius of the architects was matched by that of the artists who decorated the temples and created the great statues that stood inside them. The most distinguished of these was **Phidias,** the master sculptor of the Parthenon, who was responsible, either directly or through his assistants, for its splendid reliefs. Among other statues, Phidias made a majestic statue of Athena in ivory and gold for the interior of the Parthenon (Athena Parthenos, The Virgin) and a still larger bronze statue of the same goddess (Athena Promachos), which was placed in the open and, like the Statue of Liberty, could be seen by ships several miles out at sea. The art of Phidias and his contemporaries comes at the great moment of classical balance. Their works portray human beings as types, without individual problems or cares, vigorous yet serene, ideally proportioned, and often in a state of controlled tension.

The architecture and sculpture of the Parthenon and its surrounding temples exemplify the synthesis of religious feeling, patriotic dedication, artistic genius, and intellectual freedom that characterized the age of Pericles. It would be pleasant to think of the Athenians of this period enjoying the beauty of these temples that so perfectly express the mood of the age. But such was not the case. The Parthenon, the first of the new Acropolis structures to be completed, was not finished until 432 B.C., a scant year before the outbreak of the Peloponnesian War that ultimately brought Athens to its knees. For centuries thereafter, Greek art would be a living, creative force; indeed, some of its most celebrated masterpieces were products of these later centuries. But the balanced, confident spirit of Periclean Athens—the spirit that shaped the works of Sophocles and Phidias and inspired the Parthenon—was never quite recovered.

CHAPTER 10

The Hellenistic Age

ALEXANDER THE GREAT

The political and military decline of the polis in the fourth century B.C. culminated, as we have seen, in the military triumphs of King Philip of Macedon and the submission of all Greece to his authority. After his climactic victory at Chaeronea in 338 B.C., Philip was murdered as a consequence of a palace intrigue. He was succeeded by his son Alexander, later to be called "the Great."

In his final months, Philip had been preparing a large-scale attack against the Persian Empire, hoping to transform the grudging obedience of the Greek city-states into enthusiastic support by leading a pan-Hellenic crusade against the traditional enemy of Hellas. His intention was to punish the Persians for alleged historical injustices committed against the Greeks. Alexander, during a dazzling reign of thirteen years, exceeded his father's most fantastic dreams. Leading his all-conquering armies from Greece through Persia to India, he changed the course of the ancient world—and the map of the Middle and Near East.

ALEXANDER'S CONQUEST OF GREECE

Although he was only twenty when he inherited the throne, Alexander possessed in the fullest measure the combination of physical attractiveness, athletic prowess, and intellectual distinction that had long been the Greek ideal. He had the face of a god. Although he was not big, he was an excellent athlete. Most important, he had a penetrating, imaginative mind. He was a magnetic leader who inspired intense loyalty and admiration among his followers, a brilliant general who adapted his tactics and strategy to the most varied circumstances, and at least initially, an ardent champion of Hellenic culture.

Alexander the Great
This marble portrait of Alexander the Great (late Hellenistic) is based upon
the model created by Alexander's favorite sculptor, Lysippus. Lysippus's
sculpture of Alexander portrayed the king with a slight leftward inclina-
tion of his neck and his hair thrown back from a part in the center. These
features were meant to suggest Alexander's divine associations and dynamism. *(The Louvre, Paris, France. © The Bridgeman Art Library, New York.)*

As a child and a young man, Alexander was deeply influenced by
three powerful figures: his mother, a princess from the nearby kingdom of Epirus, who instilled in him a sense of his special connection
to the gods; his father Philip, from whom he learned the skills to
become a great military leader; and the philosopher Aristotle, who
encouraged in him a love of Greek literature, especially Homer's
Iliad. Alexander's turn of mind is symbolized by the two objects he
kept beneath his pillow: the *Iliad* and a dagger.

At first, the Greek city-states were restive under Alexander's
rule. He quelled their revolts with merciless efficiency, destroying
rebellious Thebes and frightening the rest into submission. But there
was genuine support for his campaign against Persia. In the spring
of 334 B.C., he led a Graeco-Macedonian army of some 40,000 men
into Asia Minor and, during the next three and a half years, won a
series of stunning victories over the armies of the Persian Empire.

He freed the Ionian cities from Persian domination, bringing them under his own authority, and conquered the imperial provinces of Syria and Egypt. Then, striking deep into the heart of the empire, he won a decisive victory over the unwieldy Persian army at **Gaugamela,** near the Tigris, in 331 B.C. The triumph at Gaugamela enabled Alexander to seize the vast Persian imperial treasure, ascend the imperial throne, and bring an end to the Achaemenid dynasty of ancient Persia, which had ruled the Middle and Near East since the sixth century B.C.

ALEXANDER AND THE HELLENIZATION OF THE MIDDLE AND NEAR EAST

This was a glorious moment for the Macedonians and at least some of their Greek allies. The foe that had ruled so long over many Greeks was conquered. More than that, the ancient Near East was now under Macedonian control, open to Macedonian or Greek enterprise, culture, and exploitation. Alexander's conquest of the Persian Empire set the stage for a new epoch—a period known to modern historians as the Hellenistic Age. The Macedonians and the Greeks were now the military and political masters of the Middle East and a large part of the Near East, and under their sway a great cosmopolitan culture developed. It was distinctly Greek in tradition yet transmuted by the influence of the subject Near Eastern civilizations, by the huge new cities ruled by Macedonian or Greek kings, and by the spacious new environment in which Greeks now lived. The new culture has thus been termed "Hellenistic"—not purely Greek (Hellenic) but derived from Greece (as the culture of Macedon largely was).

The Hellenization of the Near East was facilitated by Alexander's policy of founding cities in the wake of his conquests and filling them with Macedonian or Greek settlers (although local peoples also were citizens of many of the cities). One historian has estimated that in the second half of the fourth century B.C., roughly 40 percent of all Greeks lived outside the Greek homeland in colonies, such as those founded by Alexander and his successors or in Hellenized communities. These communities, although intended chiefly as military and commercial bases, became islands of Greek culture that often exerted a powerful influence on the surrounding areas. Many of them were named, with charming, characteristic immodesty, after their founder.

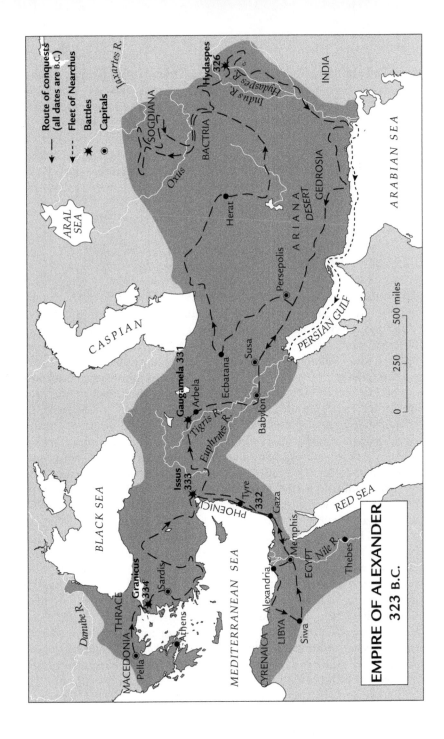

EMPIRE OF ALEXANDER 323 B.C.

Route of conquests (all dates are B.C.)
Fleet of Nearchus
Battles
Capitals

ARAL SEA

CASPIAN

BLACK SEA

MACEDONIA
Pella
THRACE
Danube R.
Athens
Granicus 334
Sardis

MEDITERRANEAN SEA

CYRENAICA
LIBYA
Siwa
Alexandria
EGYPT
Memphis
Nile R.
Thebes
RED SEA

Issus 333
Tyre 332
Gaza
PHOENICIA

Euphrates R.
Tigris R.
Babylon
Arbela
Gaugamela 331
Ecbatana
Susa

PERSIAN GULF

Persepolis

Herat
ARIANA

Oxus
SOGDIANA
BACTRIA
GEDROSIA
DESERT

Jaxartes R.

Hydaspes 326
Indus R.
Hydaspes R.
INDIA

ARABIAN SEA

0   250   500 miles

The greatest by far was Alexandria in Egypt, which Alexander established at the mouth of the Nile. Alexandria quickly outstripped the cities of Greece itself to become the commercial metropolis of the Hellenistic world. Before long, it had developed a cultural and intellectual life that put contemporary Athens to shame.

Once he ascended the throne of Persia, Alexander began preparations for further campaigns. The final seven years of his life were occupied in conquering the easternmost provinces of the Persian Empire and pushing on into India, impelled by a thirst for conquest and the lure of undiscovered lands. His spirit and ingenuity were taxed to the utmost by the variety of difficulties he encountered: the rugged mountains of Afghanistan, the hostile stretches of the Indus Valley, fierce armies equipped with hundreds of elephants. At length, his own army, its endurance exhausted, refused to go farther. It is the mark of a great leader, one of his officers told him, to know when to stop. Thus, Alexander returned in 323 B.C. to the city of Babylon (now in Iraq), where, in the midst of planning the conquest of the rest of the world, he fell ill and died, perhaps of malaria, at the age of thirty-two.

The empire of Alexander was the greatest that the world had yet seen, more extensive even than the Persian Empire. Wherever he went, Alexander adapted himself to the customs of the land. He ruled Egypt as a divine pharaoh and Persia as the Great King, demanding that subjects prostrate themselves in his presence. (Some of his Macedonian and Greek followers objected vigorously to this.) Although his great teacher Aristotle apparently had advised Alexander to treat the conquered peoples of his empire like plants or animals, Alexander married the daughters of the last two Persian kings and arranged for many of his officers to follow his example by taking wives from among the Persian aristocracy. He also incorporated Persians into the ranks of his incomparable Macedonian army. His goal was apparently nothing less than to create a homogeneous Macedonian-Persian aristocracy to rule over his world empire. To what extent this policy was the product of pragmatic calculation or his own genuine belief in the positive qualities of the once despised Persians is debated by scholars. But the project was scarcely under way when Alexander died, leaving behind a sense of loss and bewilderment and a vast empire that nobody but a second Alexander could have held together.

THE SUCCESSOR KINGDOMS

Alexander's greatest generals fought ferociously with one another for the rule of his empire. In the course of the bloodbath, his wife, son, and close kinfolk were all murdered. But after several decades, the struggle ended with some of Alexander's leading generals dividing the empire among themselves. The result was a series of Macedonian royal dynasties that ruled Greece and most of the ancient Near East until the Roman conquests of the second and first centuries B.C.

In broad outline, the succession went as follows: Ptolemy, one of Alexander's ablest generals (who also wrote an account of Alexander's campaigns), ruled Egypt, establishing the Ptolemaic dynasty that lasted until a Roman army deposed Cleopatra, the last of the Ptolemies, in 30 B.C. From their magnificent capital of Alexandria, the Ptolemies ruled with all the pomp and authority of the pharaohs, enriching themselves through the tight control the pharaohs traditionally had imposed on the Egyptian economy. Alexandria, with its imposing public buildings, its superb library and museum, its far-flung commerce, and its million inhabitants, was the wonder of the age.

Northern Syria and most of the remaining provinces of the old Persian Empire fell to another of Alexander's generals, Seleucus, who founded the Seleucid dynasty. The kingdom of the Seleucids was more loosely organized than that of the Ptolemies, and as time went on some of the Near Eastern peoples began to rebel against the Seleucid policy of Hellenization. This was particularly true of the Persians and Jews, who each had produced powerful transcendental religions and bitterly resented the influx of Greek religious thought. Farther to the east, the Parthians, originally a non-Persian nomadic people, had taken most of the Iranian plateau by the mid-third century B.C. The center of Seleucid power was the city of Antioch on the eastern Mediterranean, second only to Alexandria in population, wealth, and opulence.

The third important successor state, Macedon, passed in time to a dynasty known as the Antigonids, whose authority over the Greek poleis to the south was never very firm and whose power was usually inferior to that of the Ptolemies and Seleucids. A number of smaller states such as Pergamum, about fifteen miles inland from the western seacoast of Asia Minor, also developed out of the imperial wreckage, but the three dominant successor kingdoms—Ptolemaic

Egypt, Seleucid Asia, and Antigonid Greece—dominated the eastern Mediterranean world until the coming of the Romans.

POLITICAL AND SOCIAL CHANGE

These huge political units now overshadowed the old city-states as the characteristic sovereign units of the Greek world. The new political environment provided vast opportunities and encouraged a sense of cosmopolitanism that contrasted with the former particularism and civic cohesion of the polis. This was a prosperous age of vigorous and profitable business activity and successful careers in commerce and banking. It was an era in which women's ties to the home were loosened with the opening of new opportunities to hold and dispose of property and to engage in commercial enterprises. Shockingly, some Greeks even came to believe that husbands and wives should be equal partners in their marriages.

But as usual, the good life was reserved for the fortunate few. Slavery continued, even increased, and the peasants and urban commoners remained at an economic level of bare subsistence. The typical agrarian unit was no longer the small or mid-size farm but the large farm worked by gangs of slaves.

In Greece itself, the poleis retained throughout the new age a portion of their earlier autonomy. Old civic institutions continued to function, and citizens still had a voice in domestic politics. But the Greek peninsula was now something of an economic backwater, and cities such as Athens and Thebes were no match for the new super-states. Ambitious Greeks were lured by opportunity far from their homeland, as they had once been drawn to imperial Athens. No longer as involved in political affairs or in the intense life of a free community, overseas Greeks found themselves adrift in a wide and bewildering world over which they had little control.

The cosmopolitanism of the Hellenistic Age gave rise to a sense of estrangement and alienation, uncertainty and loneliness. The trend toward individualism, professionalism, and specialization accelerated. Writers and artists pushed the new impulse toward realism to its limits. Many Hellenistic artists turned to portraying the tragic and grotesque—ugliness, deformity, agony—often with powerfully effective results. The civic consciousness of the comic playwright Aristophanes in the fifth century B.C. gave way to the

Old Market Woman

In the Hellenistic era, artists moved away from depictions of the ideal toward explorations of emotion, age, and physical imperfections. This under-life-size Old Market Woman (second century B.C.) is not a portrait of a specific individual but a genre sculpture, of which many versions were made. (*The Metropolitan Museum of Art/Art Resource, NY*)

Laocoön
According to the Roman poet Virgil, Laocoön was a Trojan priest who had
protested against bringing the large wooden horse (inside which Greek
soldiers had hidden) into the city of Troy, and was punished, along with
his sons, by being slain by two serpents that came over the sea. The statue
group of Laocoön and his sons (late second century B.C.) was signed by
three Rhodian sculptors. (© *Timothy McCarthy/Art Resource, NY*)

highly individualized realism of the Hellenistic drawing-room comedy and bedroom farce. The Hellenistic sculptors, in contrast, produced superb works of art, lacking the serenity and balance of the
earlier period but surpassing it in psychological depth and emotional
impact.

RELIGION AND ETHICS

Hellenic religion, with its traditional civic orientation, was transformed in this new age. Ancient bonds and loyalties were broken, as many adventurous Greeks were uprooted from their poleis and had to fend for themselves. The result was a mood of individualism, which found expression in a variety of religious and ethical ideas stressing personal fulfillment or personal salvation. Individualism and cosmopolitanism went hand in hand, for, as some Greeks moved spiritually away from the polis and into themselves, they came to regard all humanity as a multitude of individuals. In an undifferentiated, universal community of this sort, intelligent Persians, Egyptians, and Jews were no worse than intelligent Greeks. For some Greeks, the traditional contrast between Greek and barbarian faded.

Yet the concept of *cosmopolis,* the idea of a common humanity, was too abstract to provide the sense of involvement and orientation formerly provided by the polis. For this reason, some Greeks turned away from the old Olympic gods and sought solace in more personal and potent religious concepts. Hellenistic religion is characterized by withdrawal from active social participation and the search for sanctuary in a restless, uncertain world. In that uncertain world, some Greeks also found religious fulfillment in the worship of their own rulers, paying them divine honors, as some of the contemporaries of Alexander the Great had done for him.

The Hellenistic Age saw a revival of mystery and salvation cults, such as Orphism and the worship of Dionysus and Demeter, which had always lurked behind the Olympic foreground. Many of these cults were centered on stories related to the death and resurrection of a god or goddess and the promise of safety or salvation of worshipers (but salvation during life, not as a guarantee against the unalterable fact of death). Although scholars have not been able to trace the rituals of these cults as practiced by the Greeks during the Hellenistic era to the Near East, it is clear that the Greeks themselves believed that many of the mystery cults originated there. Thus, from Egypt (they believed) came the cult of Osiris, who died, was reborn, and sat in judgment of the dead. From Asia Minor came a version of the ancient and widespread fertility cult of the Great Mother. From Persia, somewhat later, came the cult of **Mithras**, which, according to one interpretation, was a variation of Zoroastrianism that incorporated the traditional concept of a cosmic struggle between good and evil but added the idea of a savior-hero who redeemed humanity.

Alongside these and other Near Eastern cults came a revival of neo-Babylonian astrology, magic, witchcraft, and sorcery. Many ambitious Greeks of the upper class were devoted to the goddess of Fortune (Tyche), who rewarded talent and ambition and brought her worshipers material well-being. The Hellenistic world became a religious melting pot in which an individual might be a devotee of several cults. Many people adopted the idea of **syncretism**— the notion that the gods of different peoples are actually various manifestations of the same god and that Zeus, Osiris, and even Yahweh all symbolize a single divine spirit. (The more orthodox among the Jews found this doctrine abominable.)

SKEPTICS, CYNICS, STOICS, AND EPICUREANS

Many Greeks of the postclassical age turned neither to the old Orphic and Dionysian cults nor to the salvation cults but sought to adapt elements of Hellenic intellectual tradition to the new conditions. One group was the **Skeptics,** who originally were called Pyrrhonists after their founder, Pyrrhon of Elis (c. 365–275 B.C.). The Skeptics intensified the relativism of the Sophists by denying the possibility of any knowledge at all, whether of people, gods, or nature. The human mind, they maintained, is incapable of apprehending reality (if, indeed, there is any such thing as "reality"), and all beliefs and statements of fact are equally unverifiable. In doubting everything, they carried rationalism to its ultimate, self-destructive limit and reflected the profound uncertainty of the new age.

Another group, the **Cynics** ("doglike" in Greek), demonstrated through various forms of eccentric behavior their contempt for conventional piety and patriotism and their rebellion against the hypocrisy they detected in the lives and attitudes of their contemporaries. Thus Cynicism was not so much a philosophy as a way of life: specifically, a way of life based on the principle of living according to the Cynics' interpretation of nature rather than law or convention. Diogenes, the most famous of the Cynics, was a dropout who sought integrity amid a world of careerists and phonies (see accompanying biographical sketch).

Diogenes
Diogenes' minimum of possessions in this statue group (begging bowl, staff for support and protection, and girdle) is meant to suggest his rejection of material possessions and adoption of the natural life of primitive man, animals, and the gods. (© *Alinari/Art Resource, NY*)

The impulse toward withdrawal from society that characterized the Skeptics and Cynics was also evident in the two religio-ethical systems that emerged in the fourth century B.C. and influenced human thought and conduct for centuries thereafter: Stoicism and Epicureanism. Both were philosophies of resignation that taught believers to fortify their souls against the harshness of life.

Stoicism derives its name from an Athenian civic building, the Painted Stoa, in which Zeno, the founder of Stoic philosophy, taught his followers. (Its remains were excavated in the 1980s by a team of American archaeologists, including the author of this book.) Zeno came to Athens from his native Citium in 313 B.C. He developed

Stoicism as a related set of ideas separated into three parts: logic and the theory of knowledge, physics and metaphysics, and ethics. In his ethics, Zeno stressed, as the Cynics did, the worthlessness of worldly goods and the supreme importance of individual virtue. All people, whether rulers, nobles, artists, or peasants, should pursue their vocations honestly and seriously. The significant thing is not individual accomplishment but individual effort. Politics, art, and even farming are ultimately valueless, yet in working at them as best we can, we manifest our virtue. Since virtue is all-important, good Stoics are immune to the vicissitudes of life. They may lose their property, and may even be imprisoned and tortured, but except by their own will they cannot be deprived of their virtue—their one truly precious possession. By rejecting the world, Stoics created impenetrable fortresses within their own souls. Out of this doctrine there emerged a sense not only of individualism but of cosmopolitanism; the idea of the polis faded before the wider Stoic concept of an encompassing human community.

Ultimately, the Stoic emphasis on virtue (which alone was sufficient for happiness) was rooted in a cosmic vision based on the Greek conception of a rational, orderly, purposeful universe. Zeno taught that the harmonious movements of the stars and planets and the growth of complex plants from simple seeds all point to the existence of a Divine Plan that is both intelligent and good. We humans are incapable of perceiving the details of this plan as it works in our own lives, yet by living virtuously and doing our best, we are cooperating with it. The God of the universe, Zeno assured his followers, cares about humanity.

Epicurus (c. 341–270 B.C.), whose school, The Garden, was Stoicism's great rival, differed from Zeno both in his concept of human ethics and in his vision of the universe. He taught that people should seek happiness rather than virtue. Yet, happiness to the **Epicureans** was not the pursuit of thrills and euphoria but a quiet, balanced life (Greek, *ataraxia*), or freedom from disturbance. The life of the drunkard is saddened by countless hangovers, and the life of the libertine, by countless emotional complications. Happiness is best achieved not by chasing pleasures but by living simply and unobtrusively, being kind and affectionate to one's friends, learning to endure pain when it comes, and avoiding needless fears. In short, good Epicureans did not differ noticeably from good Stoics in actual behavior, for Stoic virtue was the pathway to Epicurean happiness.

The Epicureans, however, rejected the optimistic Stoic doctrine of divine purpose. Epicurus followed the teachings of the atomists, viewing the universe not as a great hierarchy of cosmic spheres centered on the earth but as a multiplicity of atoms, much the same in one place as in another. In the Epicurean belief, our world is not the handiwork of God but a chance configuration. The gods, if they exist, care nothing for us, and we ought to draw from this fact the comforting conclusion that we need not fear them or death, since what happens after death, as before birth, does not concern us.

Epicureanism, even more than Stoicism, was a philosophy of withdrawal. The members of Epicurus's school, which included women and slaves, were renowned for their devotion to privacy. Epicureanism was a wise, compassionate teaching that sought to banish fear, curb passions, and dispel illusions. Its doctrine of happiness was too bland to stir the millions and convert empires, but it gave solace and direction to an intellectual minority.

Diogenes

Accused along with his father, a moneyer, of defacing the currency of Sinope, Diogenes was exiled sometime after 362 B.C. and came to Athens. While in Athens, he became convinced that the times were out of joint. He asked to be buried face down when he died, "because before you know it, what's down will be up." He is said to have carried a lantern, by the light of which, he said, he was searching for an honest man but never did find one. He rejected all official and traditional religions and would not participate in civic life, marriage, the public games, or the theater. He ridiculed the prestige associated with wealth, power, and reputation and honored instead the simple life of courage, reason, honesty, and avoidance of all pretense. A life of virtue could best be attained by rejecting civilized life and returning to nature. The person of wisdom and integrity should live like a dog, without affectations or worldly possessions. The term "Cynic," associated with Diogenes' school of thought, originally meant "canine" or "doglike."

Thus, Diogenes wandered the streets begging for his food, homeless but free. His bedchamber was a large tub outside a temple of the Great Mother; his latrine was the public street. He used to eat and drink from a single crude wooden bowl until he saw a peasant boy drinking from the hollow of his hands, whereupon Diogenes promptly destroyed the bowl as an unnecessary social artifact.

Such stories about Diogenes, however, should not obscure the originality and appeal of his thought: he and his followers believed in the common humanity of all peoples and the unity of the universe (cosmopolitanism), including animals and the gods. There eventually were practicing Cynics in all the major Greek cities, and Cynicism remained influential into the Roman imperial era.

It is reported (probably apocryphally) that while on a voyage, Diogenes was captured by pirates and sold as a slave to a rich Corinthian named Xeniades. When Xeniades asked him what he did for a living, Diogenes answered waggishly that the only trade he knew was that of governing others and that he therefore wished to be sold to someone who needed a master. He spent his remaining years in Corinth, tutoring Xeniades' two sons and lecturing at public festivals on the subject of virtuous self-control.

Diogenes' growing fame brought him to the attention of the soon-to-be-greatest conqueror in Greek history, Alexander the Great. At their one recorded meeting, Alexander is said to have offered Diogenes any gift or favor he might choose. Diogenes replied that the single favor he wished was that Alexander would move over so as not to block the sunlight. Taking no offense, Alexander is said to have remarked, "If I were not Alexander, I would choose to be Diogenes." According to our most informative source, who might well be stretching matters, Diogenes died in Corinth in 323 B.C. on the very day that Alexander died in Babylon. Whether false or true, Diogenes had become, next to Alexander, the greatest celebrity of his generation.

We are not told whether Diogenes was in fact buried face down. We do know that his many admirers in Corinth erected a pillar in his memory, on top of which they set a marble dog.

HELLENISTIC SCIENCE

In the Hellenistic Age, Greek science reached maturity. The inspired guesswork of the earlier period gave way to a rigorous and highly creative professionalism. Hellenistic scientists followed and improved on Aristotle's example, collecting and sifting data with great thoroughness before framing their hypotheses.

Alexandria was the center of scientific thought in this age. Here, the Ptolemies built and subsidized a great research center, the **Museum** (literally, "a home of the Muses"), and established a library of unprecedented size and diversity containing some 500,000 papyrus rolls. At Alexandria and elsewhere, science and mathematics made rapid strides as Greek rationalism encountered the rich heritage of Near Eastern astrology, medical lore, and practical mathematics. The fruitful medical investigations of Hippocrates' school were carried on and expanded by Hellenistic physicians, particularly in Alexandria. Their pioneering work in the dissection of human bodies enabled them to discover the nervous system, to learn a great deal about the brain, heart, and arteries, and to perform a variety of new surgical operations. In mathematics, **Euclid** or his followers organized plane and solid geometry into a systematic, integrated body of knowledge. **Archimedes** of Syracuse did brilliant original work in both pure and applied mathematics, discovering specific gravity, experimenting successfully with levers and pulleys to lift tremendous weights, and coming very close to the invention of calculus.

The wide-ranging military campaigns of Alexander and the subsequent cultural interchange between large areas of the ancient world led to a vast increase in the Greeks' geographical knowledge. **Eratosthenes,** the head of the Alexandrian library in the late third century B.C., produced the most accurate and thorough world maps that had yet been made, complete with lines of longitude and latitude and climatic zones. He recognized that the earth was a sphere and was even able to determine its circumference with an error of less than 1 percent. He did so by measuring the altitude of the sun at different latitudes and calculating from this data the length of degrees of latitude on the earth's surface. Once that was known, Eratosthenes was able to determine the earth's 360-degree circumference by simple multiplication.

The same painstaking accuracy and dazzling ingenuity mark the work of the Hellenistic astronomers. **Aristarchus** of Samos suggested that the earth rotates daily on its axis and revolves yearly around the sun. This heliocentric hypothesis is a startling anticipation of modern astronomical conclusions, but Aristarchus's erroneous assumption that the earth's motion around the sun is uniform and circular rendered his system inaccurate. Aristarchus's theory was never widely accepted because it failed to explain the precise astronomical observations then being made at Alexandria and because it violated the hallowed doctrine of an earth-centered universe. Later, the great Hellenistic astronomer **Hipparchus,** who was heavily influenced by Babylonian astronomy, developed a complete system of circles and sub-circles, centered on the earth, that accounted exceedingly well for the observed motions of the sun and moon. Hipparchus's ingenious system, expanded and perfected by the Alexandrian astronomer **Ptolemy** in the second century A.D., represents antiquity's final word on the subject—a comprehensive geocentric model of the universe that, although it later proved incorrect, corresponded satisfactorily to the best observations of the day. And it should be remembered that a scientific hypothesis must be judged not by some absolute standard of correctness but by its success in accounting for and predicting observed phenomena. By this criterion, the Ptolemaic system stands as one of the impressive triumphs of Greek thought.

THE HELLENISTIC LEGACY

Greek culture exerted a fundamental influence on the Roman Empire, the Byzantine and Muslim civilizations, and the medieval West, and it did so largely in its Hellenistic form. The conclusions of the Hellenistic philosophers and scholars tended to be accepted by the best minds of later ages, but the Hellenistic spirit of free inquiry and intellectual daring was not. There is something remarkably modern about the Hellenistic world—with its confident scientists, its cosmopolitanism, its materialism, its religious diversity, its trend toward increasing specialization, its large-scale business activity, and its sense of drift and disorientation. But the Hellenistic economic organization, regardless of superficial similarities, was vastly different from ours. Ultimately based upon subsistence agriculture, often involving the labor of slaves or other dependent workers, rather than machines, it provided the benefits of its commercial prosperity to only a tiny fraction of the population. The great majority remained servile, illiterate, and impoverished.

Still, throughout the Mediterranean world and the Near East, the indigenous peoples were exposed to Greek culture and language. And the Greeks themselves were deeply influenced by the cultures of the Near East in particular. From Syria, Asia Minor, and the Nile Valley to Magna Graecia in the West, a common culture was developing with a common set of ideas and common gods. Although no one could have known it at the time, at least some of the conditions for the later political unification of the Mediterranean world under the authority of Rome and, much later still, for its spiritual unification under the authority of the Christian Church were being set. Alexander's dream of a world empire ruled by Macedonians and Persians would not come to pass. Instead, a small city on a river in Italy would eventually unify and rule the entire Mediterranean world.

SUGGESTED READINGS

General Works

For an immensely detailed and authoritative treatment of ancient Greek history, consult *Cambridge Ancient History* (1970–), 7 vols. A less detailed but similarly authoritative survey, emanating from the competition, is *The Oxford History of the Classical World* (1986), edited by J. Boardman, J. Griffin, and O. Murray, the Greek chapters of which have been published separately under the title *The Oxford History of Greece and the Hellenistic World* (1991).

Of the most recently published textbook histories, the best are C. Orrieux and P. Schmitt Pantel, *A History of Ancient Greece* (1999), a translation from an original French work; and S. Pomeroy, S. Burstein, W. Donlan, and J. Roberts, *Ancient Greece: A Political, Social, and Cultural History* (1999).

Over the last decade, dozens of Web sites focused upon ancient Greek history and culture have appeared. Not all of the sites provide accurate and reliable information. The most scholarly site can be found at www.perseus.tufts.edu. Another very rich site with links to all kinds of resources can be found at www.sas.upenn.edu/~ekondrat/greece.html.

Reference Works

S. Hornblower and A. Spawforth, eds., *The Oxford Classical Dictionary* (1996). An indispensable treasury of up-to-date information on all aspects of the classical world.

R. Talbert, ed., *Barrington Atlas of the Greek and Roman World* (2000). Far and away the best atlas of the classical world, with wonderfully detailed maps of every corner of the classical world.

Crete, Mycenae, and the Dark Age

M. Bernal, *Black Athena: The Afroasiatic Roots of Classical Civilization* (1987). Stimulating and learned but flawed by its overtly politicizing agenda.

T. Bryce, *The Trojans and Their Neighbors* (2006). Sets the Trojan War within its Near Eastern context. Fascinating and well written.

J. Chadwick, *The Decipherment of Linear B* (2nd ed., 1967). Discusses the achievement of Michael Ventris in cracking the code and the Bronze Age world that it disclosed.

J. Chadwick, *The Mycenaean World* (1976). A fine overview by a pioneering scholar, stressing social and economic history.

R. Drews, *The Coming of the Greeks: Indo-European Conquests in the Aegean and the Near East* (1988). Challenges traditional views on the date of the Indo-European entry into Greece and the location of the Indo-European homeland.

R. Drews, *The End of the Bronze Age: Changes in Warfare and the Catastrophe ca. 1200 B.C.* (1993). Argues that changes in chariot warfare helped to bring about the downfall of Bronze Age civilization.

M. I. Finley, *The World of Odysseus* (2nd ed., 1982). A penetrating work of synthesis, arguing that the material world of the Odyssey as presented in Homer's epic was not the world of the Bronze Age.

J. Graham, *The Palaces of Crete* (rev. ed., 1987). The fundamental work on Minoan buildings.

M. Lefkowitz and G. Rogers, eds., *Black Athena Revisited* (1996). Arguing, against the hypothesis of M. Bernal, for multicultural origins of Greek civilization.

W. McDonald, *Progress into the Past: The Rediscovery of Mycenaean Civilization* (2nd ed., 1990). A valuable treatment of Mycenaean scholarship and archaeology.

R. Osborne, *Greece in the Making 1200–479 B.C.* (1996). Far and away the best introduction available in English. For serious students of Greek history, the best book to purchase.

A. Samuel, *The Mycenaeans in History* (1966). A lively, concise, well-illustrated narrative of the Mycenaeans, from Neolithic times to the flowering of their culture in the late Bronze Age.

R. Simpson, *Mycenaean Greece* (1981). An excellent gazetteer keyed to a series of fourteen maps.

R. Willetts, *The Civilization of Ancient Crete* (2nd ed., 1991). The best comprehensive account, from the origins of Minoan civilization to the Roman conquest. Makes full use of archaeological evidence.

The Rise of Classical Greece

A. Andrewes, *The Greek Tyrants* (rev. ed., 1963). This relatively brief work is still the best account of its subject.

P. Cartledge, *Sparta and Lakonia: A Regional History, 1300–362 B.C.* (1979). A well-written regional history by an expert on Spartan history.

C. Fomara, ed. and trans., *Archaic Times to the End of the Peloponnesian War* (2nd ed., 1983). A volume in the series, *Translated Documents of Greece and Rome,* stresses lesser-known sources such as inscriptions and papyrus rolls over the often-translated works of the major literary figures (see below, under "Thought, Culture, Literature, Religion, and Art").

W. Forrest, *The Emergence of Greek Democracy, 800–400 B.C.* (1966). A short, lively, well-argued book.

A. Graham, *Colony and Mother City in Ancient Greece* (2nd ed., 1983). An expert treatment of the colonization movement.

M. Grant, *The Rise of the Greeks* (1987). An authoritative, stylishly written account of the history and archaeology of the early Greeks, 750–480 B.C.

M. Hansen, *Polis: An Introduction to the Ancient Greek City-State* (2006). Summarizes the results of a Danish center's research into the origins and spread of the polis. Provocative and the starting point for all future discussions.

G. Lloyd, *Early Greek Science: Thales to Aristotle* (1971). Brief but magisterial.

O. Murray, *Early Greece* (2nd ed., 1993). A social and economic history from the close of the Mycenaean era to the Persian Wars.

A. Snodgrass, *Archaic Greece: The Age of Experiment* (1980). A crucial period of Greek development, treated from an archaeological perspective.

The Zenith and Transformation of Classical Greece

J. Davies, *Democracy and Classical Greece* (2nd ed., 1993). A stimulating analysis and reinterpretation.

K. Dover, *Greek Homosexuality* (rev. ed., 1989). First published in 1978, this book stimulated most of the subsequent scholarship on the topic.

E. Fantham, H. Foley, N. Kampen, S. Pomeroy, and A. Shapiro, *Women in the Classical World* (1994). Especially good on visual representations of women in Greece.

Y. Garlan, *Slavery in Ancient Greece,* trans. J. Lloyd (1988). The best general account of the subject.

V. Hanson, *The Western Way of War: Infantry Battle in Classical Greece* (1989). A perceptive and engaged account with an introduction by John Keegan, perhaps the most prominent military historian of his generation.

S. Hornblower, *The Greek World, 479–323 B.C.* (rev. ed., 1991). The first volume in the series *Classical Civilizations,* this work makes full use of archaeological evidence and inscriptions as well as the more traditional literary evidence (all extensively quoted) in order to reexamine in broader perspective the civilization of classical Greece.

S. Hornblower, *Thucydides* (1987). The best short introduction to the greatest historian of antiquity.

D. Kagan, *The Peloponnesian War* (2003). A sensible one-volume account of the war made famous by Thucydides.

D. Kagan, *Pericles of Athens and the Birth of Democracy* (1990). The best biography of Pericles, this sympathetic account places him at the core of fifth-century-B.C. Athenian democracy.

M. Massey, *Women in Ancient Greece and Rome* (1988). An admirable work of scholarship, well written and absorbing.

R. Meiggs, *The Athenian Empire* (1972). Explores in technical detail the motives underlying Athenian imperialism in the fifth century B.C.

J. Ober, *Mass and Elite in Democratic Athens* (1989). A highly original sociological analysis of Athenian politics.

S. Pomeroy, *Goddesses, Whores, Wives, and Slaves: Women in Classical Antiquity* (1975). A skillful, illuminating account of women in contemporary literature and social reality.

P. Rhodes, *The Athenian Empire* (1985). Brief but valuable.

J. Roberts, *City of Socrates: An Introduction to Classical Athens* (1984). A meticulous study of the physical setting, society, constitutional arrangements, mentality, and culture of Athens in the fifth century B.C., the best such study in print.

Thought, Culture, Literature, Religion, and Art

The best approach to Greek literature is through the original writings themselves. Especially recommended is *The Norton Book of Classical Literature,* edited by B. Knox (1993), a comprehensive anthology covering both Greek and Roman literature. Similarly, *Archaic and Classical Greece: A Selection of Ancient Sources in Translation,* edited and translated by M. Crawford (1983), is a treasure trove of skillfully translated sources, as is C. Bowra's classic collection, *Landmarks in Greek Literature* (1966). For comprehensive introductory essays by noted modern scholars on individual classical authors see T. Luce, ed. *Ancient Writers: Greece and Rome* (1982).

A study of Greek literature must begin with Homer's *Iliad and Odyssey,* which have often been translated; I suggest the translations by R. Lattimore: *The Iliad and the Odyssey of Homer* (2nd ed., 1990). For the lyric poets see *Sappho's Lyre: Archaic Lyric and Women Poets of Ancient Greece,* translated by D. Rayor (1991); and the magisterial collection, *Lyra Graeca,* translated by J. Edmonds (rev. ed., 3 vols., 1979).

For the most recent translation of Herodotus's work, see R. Waterfield, trans., *The Histories* (1998), with a good introduction by C. Dewald. For Thucydides' *History of the Peloponnesian War,* see R. Crawley's translation, now revised with notes and maps under the title *The Landmark Thucydides: A Comprehensive Guide to the Peloponnesian War* (1996), edited by R. Strassler. Xenophon's *A History of My Times and The Persian Expedition* have been skillfully translated by R. Warner. Plutarch, a Greek-speaking Roman citizen of the early second century A.D., wrote a series of lives of famous Greeks and Romans, among whom were nine leading Greeks living around the time of the Peloponnesian War; their biographies have been well translated by I. Scott-Kilvert under the title *The Rise and Fall of Athens.* And M. Finley, in his *Greek Historians* (rev. ed., 1984), has edited and translated much of Herodotus, Thucydides, Xenophon, and Polybius with great skill.

For Greek philosophy, too, the original writings are recommended: H. Tredennick and H. Tarrant, ed. and trans., *The Last Days of Socrates* (rev. ed., 1993), presents four dialogues of Plato that cast particular light on the end of Socrates' career. *The Portable Plato* (1948), edited by S. Buchanan and translated by B. Jowett, provides well-chosen samples. For Aristotle, see B. Jowett and T. Twining, trans., *Aristotle's Politics and Poetics* (1972).

J. Boardman, *Greek Art* (3rd ed., 1985). A clearly presented survey by a distinguished scholar.

W. Burkert, *Greek Religion* (1983). The best introduction but very dense.

H. Kitto, *Greek Tragedy* (3rd ed., 1961). The fundamental work on tragic drama of the fifth century B.C.

A. Lawrence, *Greek Architecture* (4th ed., 1983). A valuable introduction to the subject.

R. Osborne, *Archaic and Classical Greek Art* (1998). Up-to-date and intelligently written. Perhaps the best short introduction.

J. Pollitt, *Art and Experience in Classical Greece* (1972). A sympathetic, thought-provoking interpretation.

L. Zaidman and P. Schmitt Pantel, *Religion in the Ancient Greek City* (1992). A thought-provoking account of the relationship between religion and the polis.

Alexander and the Hellenistic Age

Alexander the Great has attracted numerous modern biographers, most of them sympathetic, but not all. He emerges as a kind of religious visionary in W. Tarn, *Alexander the Great* (1948), but less so in A. Burn, *Alexander the Great and the Hellenistic World* (rev. ed., 1963), an early effort at demoting Alexander from a hero to a mere human. J. Hamilton, in his *Alexander the Great* (1973), sees Alexander as ruthlessly ambitious. For more balanced interpretations, see R. Lane-Fox, *Alexander the Great* (1973), and M. Renault, *The Nature of Alexander* (2nd ed., 1976), both stylishly written and intelligently argued. P. Green's *Alexander the Great* (1970) is a thoughtful and well-written work of biographical interpretation. A. Bosworth's more recent study of Alexander's career, *Conquest and Empire* (1988), is the best book available about the details of Alexander's campaigns but presents a somewhat distorted view of his character. G. Rogers, *Alexander: The Ambiguity of Greatness* (2004) argues for Alexander's moral ambiguity but maintains that Alexander was the greatest warrior the world has seen.

M. Austin, ed. and trans., *The Hellenistic World from Alexander to the Roman Conquest: A Selection of Ancient Sources in Translation* (1981). A comprehensive, broad-gauged collection of sources illuminating the politics, warfare, society, economy, and institutions of the Hellenistic Age.

M. Grant, *From Alexander to Cleopatra: The Hellenistic World* (1982). A masterful survey of the Hellenistic kingdoms and of Hellenistic culture and philosophy.

G. Lloyd, *Greek Science after Aristotle* (1973). A clearly written account by the reigning expert in the field of science in antiquity.

A. Long, *Hellenistic Philosophy: Stoics, Epicureans, Sceptics* (2nd ed., 1986). The best general account.

J. Pollitt, Art *in the Hellenistic Age* (1986). An excellent, well-illustrated survey.

A. Samuel, *The Shifting Sands of History: Interpretations of Ptolemaic Egypt* (1989). A valuable brief account of new interpretations, with a fine bibliography.

W. Tarn and G. Griffith, *Hellenistic Civilization* (3rd ed., 1966). A classic account of the postclassical age.

F. Walbank, *The Hellenistic World* (rev. ed., 1993). The greatest historian of Hellenistic history provides a short, skillful survey of Hellenistic politics and culture from the death of Alexander to the Roman conquest of Greece.

C. Bradford Welles, *Alexander and the Hellenistic World* (1970). An illuminating account that stresses social and economic history.

PART THREE

Ancient Rome

ANCIENT ROME: AN OVERVIEW

Rome's evolution from a set of small villages on the banks of the Tiber River in central Italy to the capital of a vast empire is the supreme political success story of the ancient world. The Romans had to struggle at first for mere survival and then for ascendancy over the neighboring villages of Latium, a countrified district on the Tyrrhenian coast of central Italy. Yet eventually, Rome ruled an empire that encompassed the entire Mediterranean basin and stretched northward across Gaul into remote Britain and southward down to the Persian Gulf. It was the greatest empire in the history of western Eurasia. The secret of the Romans' success was their extension of Roman citizenship to the conquered peoples of their empire.

But Rome's overall success was not achieved without setbacks and failures. The Roman Republic was almost annihilated by the armies and navy of its greatest rival, Carthage. After the Romans had conquered the Carthaginians, they turned against one another in savage political struggles. These internal conflicts abated for several generations with the emergence of powerful Roman emperors who took control of the republican military, political, and religious offices. Later, during the third century A.D., the empire was attacked by "barbarians" from outside the borders of the empire and also suffered from internal political instability. Civil order was finally restored by a series of authoritarian soldier-emperors of the late third and fourth centuries.

By then, Christianity, which had evolved out of Judaism during the first century A.D. as a small but determined cult, was a great force in the empire. After the emperor Constantine's "conversion" to Christianity during the early third century A.D. (and his powerful support of the Church) the cult spread swiftly, until by A.D. 400 it became the dominant religion of the Roman world. In the course of the fifth century, more Germanic barbarians flooded into Rome's western provinces and eventually overwhelmed them. Despite the political demise of the Western Empire, Christianity remained the religion of Western Europe. It was Rome's most enduring legacy to Western civilization. Meanwhile, the eastern part of the Roman empire survived the barbarian invasions of the fifth century fully intact as the Byzantine Empire, ruled by emperors from its capital city of New Rome, Constantinople. After the early seventh century A.D., the rulers of New Rome found themselves confronted by the adherents of Islam, another revealed monotheistic religion, born across the borders of the Roman Empire, in Arabia.

Significant Events of Early Roman History

All dates are B.C.

753	Traditional date for founding of Rome
753–509	Monarchic period
c. 450	Issuing of Twelve Tables, Rome's first law code
367	Plebeians eligible to be consuls
287	Plebiscites of the plebeians become legally binding upon all citizens
c. 265	Rome controls Italy south of the Po River
264–241	First Punic War
218–201	Second Punic War
149–146	Third Punic War
146	Corinth and Carthage destroyed
133	Tribunate and murder of Tiberius Gracchus
123–122	Tribunates of Gaius Gracchus
121	Murder of Gaius Gracchus
107	Consulate of Marius and enrollment of landless in Marius's volunteer army
82	Dictatorship of Sulla, followed by his legislation (81) reestablishing power in the hands of the Senate
49	Caesar crosses the Rubicon River into Italy and begins the Roman civil wars
44	Caesar assassinated on the Ides (15th) of March
43	Cicero murdered on 7 December
31	Octavian (later Augustus) defeats Mark Antony and Cleopatra at the battle of Actium

CHAPTER 11

The Rise of Rome

THE ROMAN REPUBLIC

Had Alexander lived to middle age instead of dying at thirty-two, he might well have led his conquering armies westward into Italy, Sicily, and North Africa. There, he would have encountered three vigorous cultures: Carthage, the city-states of Magna Graecia (Great Greece), and the rapidly expanding republic of Rome.

Carthage originally was a Phoenician commercial colony (founded c. 814 B.C.) strategically located on the North African coast (modern northeast Tunisia) just south of Sicily. It soon developed an extensive commercial empire that far outstripped Phoenicia in power and wealth. Carthage established a number of commercial bases in western Sicily, which brought it face-to-face with the Greek city-states that dominated the eastern sections of the island.

The Greek poleis of Sicily and southern Italy, known collectively as Magna Graecia, were products of the age of Greek colonization in the eighth and seventh centuries B.C. They evolved much like the city-states in Greece. And, as on the Greek mainland, Magna Graecia was disturbed by intercity warfare. By Alexander's time, the Sicilian polis of Syracuse had been the leading power of the area for many years, but the smaller poleis guarded their independence jealously. Real unification was delayed until the Roman conquests of the third century B.C. brought these Greek cities under the sway of a common political master.

EARLY ROME

The rise of Rome was relatively slow when compared with the dazzling imperialistic histories of Persia and Macedon, but it was far more lasting. There was nothing meteoric about the serious, level-headed early Romans—they built slowly and well. Their great military virtue was not tactical brilliance (although some later Roman military commanders were brilliant tacticians) but stubborn endurance; they lost many battles, but from their beginnings to the great days of their empire, they never lost a war. Since it was the Romans who ultimately provided the ancient world with its enduring, all-encompassing political framework, students of history always have been fascinated by the development of Roman political institutions. Rome's greatest contributions were in the realms of law, government, and imperial organization. At least part of the secret of Rome's success lay in the Romans' grasp of political realities.

The beginnings of Rome are obscure, and the surviving literary accounts about the early history of Rome all date to much later periods. Archaeological evidence, however, proves that settlers were living on the hills of Rome (including the Palatine) by about 1000 B.C. and that these hill villages of settlers had coalesced into a recognizable city-state by the end of the seventh century B.C. According to Roman sources, the population of this city-state included **Sabines** (a people who lived northeast of Rome along the western side of the Tiber River valley), Greeks, **Etruscans,** and **Latins.** From its very earliest days, Rome was an ethnically mixed community.

The strategic position of the cluster of hills where this mixed community lived, about fifteen miles inland on one of Italy's greatest rivers, was of enormous importance to Rome's future growth. Ancient seagoing ships could sail up the Tiber to Rome but no farther, while at the same time Rome was at the lowest point at which the river could be bridged easily. Hence, Rome was a key river crossing, road junction, and also, at least potentially, a seaport. It was at the northern limit of a fertile agricultural district known as **Latium,** whose inhabitants lived in about twenty city-states including Rome; these "Latins" eventually gave their name to the Latin language. North of Rome lay the district the Romans called **Etruria** (roughly modern Tuscany), a more urbanized region whose ruling class, the Etruscans, also helped to shape the religion and culture of early Rome.

Etruscan civilization flourished in central Italy between the eighth and fifth centuries B.C. in an assortment of independent hill-top towns and cities that shared a common culture. Scholars disagree about the question of whether the Etruscans arose in place or migrated into Etruria from elsewhere. (Asia Minor has been suggested.) Etruscan culture certainly shows Greek and Near Eastern influences, but it is highly distinctive at the same time. The Etruscans left no substantial literature, and their language, although employing a Greek alphabet in its written form, differs so sharply from other languages of the ancient world that scholars have had difficulty deciphering it.

The Etruscans were skilled engineers who equipped their cities with well-designed drainage systems. They grew wealthy from the abundance of metals within their hills—tin, copper, iron, gold—and wrought them into a marvelous variety of objects, from graceful bronze statues to dental braces. Their remarkable works of art, which include bronzes, frescoes, and decorated urns, disclose a vivacious, pleasure-loving civilization of great originality. Etruscan religion, which was revealed, unlike Greek and Roman religions, also made a lasting impression upon the Romans, who at least later considered the Etruscans to be "a nation more than any other devoted to religious rites, all the more as it excelled in the practice of them" (Livy, 5.1.6).

It was in Etruscan form that Greek civilization also made its first impact on Rome. The Romans adopted the Etruscan version of the Greek alphabet, and perhaps inspired by the Etruscan example, they organized themselves into a city-state, thereby gaining an inestimable advantage over the numerous half-civilized tribes in the region between Etruria and Magna Graecia. Although early Rome was never an Etruscan city, as some scholars previously have argued, Rome was ruled at times by kings with Etruscan names, which clearly indicates the influence that powerful Etruscan families and cities had upon early Roman history. The talented and aggressive leadership of Rome's Etruscan and Latin kings made the Romans an important power among the peoples of Latium by the end of the sixth century B.C. This ethnically mixed community of predominantly Latins, but also Sabines, Greeks, and Etruscans, grew in strength and wealth, and an impressive temple to the god Jupiter was built in Etruscan style atop one of the hills.

EMERGENCE OF THE ROMAN REPUBLIC

About 509 B.C., the last Etruscan king of Rome was overthrown as the result of an aristocratic coup d'état. That king, Tarquinius Superbus, was represented later in Roman sources as a kind of tyrannical populist. Most of the civil and military powers of the king subsequently were held by two magistrates known as **consuls,** who were elected annually for most of the history of the Republic in the so-called **Centuriate Assembly** (*comitia centuriata*). (For that assembly, see page 180.)

The annual and collegial character of Rome's most important political office reflected the Romans' distrust of concentrations of power: after the Romans had gotten rid of the kings, they were not inclined to let anyone have too much political authority for an extended period of time.

In practice, however, while the early consuls exercised their authority in the name of the Roman people, they usually did so in the interests of the upper classes from which they were almost invariably elected. The governing elite was composed of related wealthy landowners, known as **patricians,** who monopolized the most important religious offices of the state. They defended their prerogatives zealously against the encroachments of the poorer citizens, who comprised the **plebeians** or *plebs.* Marriage between plebeians and patricians was prohibited, and, for a time, the plebeians were almost entirely without access to the highest offices of the state. Moreover, many of Rome's poorer citizens lacked enough land to feed themselves and fell into debt to wealthier patricians.

But step-by-step the plebeians improved their condition and expanded their role in the government. They began by organizing themselves into an assembly known as the **Council of the Plebs** (*concilium plebis*). They elected their own representatives, called **tribunes** (*tribuni plebis*), who served as their spokesmen, defended their persons and property, and represented the interests of the plebs to the patrician-dominated government. The tribunes also eventually acquired the remarkable power of vetoing, in the name of the plebeians, any act performed by any Roman magistrate and elections as well as laws emanating from other organs of government. Moreover, anyone who violated the sanctity of the tribune's person was subject to execution. Under the leadership of the tribunes, the plebeians were able to act as a unit and to make their strength felt. Their most effective tactic in their struggle to gain rights and access to power within the state was secession: on at least three occasions during the early Republic, the plebs withdrew en masse to a hill outside the sacred boundary of the city and simply refused to work or perform military service. Since the plebs made up the vast majority of soldiers in the Roman army, plebeian secession left Rome essentially without any defense. In effect, plebeian secession was a devastatingly effective form of civil disobedience.

Under pressure from the plebeians, in about 451 B.C., the Romans committed their customary laws to a written record. The result was Rome's first law code—the **Twelve Tables**—although the code was yet far from comprehensive. By later standards, these laws were harsh (defaulting debtors, for example, could have strips cut from them or be enslaved or executed), but writing the customs down at least had the effect of protecting plebeians from the capricious authority of patrician consuls. The Twelve Tables are the first major landmark in the evolution of Roman law.

Having gained a measure of legal protection, the plebeians next sought additional farmlands. The Romans usually annexed a portion of the territory of conquered peoples, and with such military successes as the capture of the rich Etruscan city of Veii in 396 B.C., the Senate was persuaded to distribute land to the plebeians, both singly and in groups. By providing land to a growing Roman population, this policy removed some of the economic basis of plebeian discontent.

After centuries of struggle, in 287 B.C., resolutions passed by the Council of the Plebs (*plebiscita* or plebiscites) finally became legally binding on the entire Roman citizenry. Intermarriage also was eventually allowed between the two orders, the enslavement of Roman citizens for debt was abolished, and a law of 367 B.C. opened the consulship to plebeians. Later, in 342 B.C., it was stipulated that one of the consuls had to be a plebeian.

Nevertheless, the rise of the plebs by no means transformed Rome into an egalitarian democracy, even though plebiscites applied to plebeians and patricians alike. The most powerful Roman citizens exercised a disproportionately large influence over the politics of the state. Like the bosses in early-twentieth-century American cities, wealthy Roman landowners took large numbers of "clients" under their protection, seeing to their economic and legal needs and receiving political support in return. Through their clients, powerful patrons at times could exercise indirect control of Rome's assemblies and offices, including the Council of the Plebs itself. Historians have been engaged in a vigorous dispute as to how complete this control by wealthy Romans was. It used to be thought that the patron-client system rendered Roman democracy largely a sham. More recently, however, some scholars have argued that the politics of the Roman Republic were by no means a "frozen waste"; that the patron-client system was limited in its political effects; and that the political system had true democratic elements. Indeed, the Roman citizen body did possess the authority to vote for war or peace and passed all legislation in its assemblies. Some historians therefore have argued that Rome was in fact a direct democracy, at least in theory.

Whatever the case, the traditional domination by the patricians had by now given way to a more subtle influence exerted by a new nobility of wealthy, officeholding plebeian and patrician families. Although some plebeians did hold high political office during the early Republic, especially by the mid-fourth century B.C., a number of plebeians had accumulated extensive estates, and some of them began to rival patricians in wealth and political influence. Rich plebeians now became patrons themselves, with clients of their own. More and more, the plebeian tribunes tended to be drawn from noble and wealthy families. By 287 B.C., when plebiscites acquired the force of law, binding on the whole citizen population, the old division between patrician and plebeian was no longer as important. Although there was no official aristocracy, as defined by statute, a new patrician-plebeian nobility had been created, largely but not exclusively composed of men who either were holders of high political office or whose ancestors had held such positions. (Of course, because Roman officeholders were not paid during the republican period, they invariably came from wealthy families.)

Moreover, the machinery of Roman republican government was complex and changing. It included numerous civic officials with various titles and responsibilities and several different legislative assemblies, the most important of which were the Centuriate Assembly and the **Tribal Assembly** (*comitia tributa populi*)—the latter an official body patterned after the plebeians' Council of the Plebs. Both the Centuriate Assembly and the Tribal Assembly were made up of the entire Roman citizenry, but each had its own distinctive function and organization.

The Centuriate Assembly was divided into 193 groups known as "centuries," each with a single vote. These centuries were distributed according to socioeconomic class (five census classes in all), with the wealthiest citizens (whose wealth was measured in terms of agricultural produce) controlling a majority of the centuries. The number of centuries in any given class was not proportionate to the number of citizens who made up each century: thus, of the total of 193 centuries, 98 were allotted to the relatively small number of citizens with a considerable amount of property, whereas the mass of citizens who had little or no property (the *proletarii*) were lumped together into one century, with one vote. Since the centuries of the richer citizens voted first, and since balloting ceased as soon as a majority was reached, men who belonged to the poorer centuries often had no voice at all in the decisions of the Centuriate Assembly, which voted on issues such as war or peace and also enacted laws (*leges*). The unstated political theory behind the way that this assembly arrived at its decisions seems to have been that more weight should be given to the votes of citizens of the state who possessed more property.

The Tribal Assembly was likewise dominated, though less directly, by propertied families. Its members were organized by districts known as "tribes" (the Roman citizenry traditionally had been divided into tribal groups, originally three, then four, and so on up to thirty-five). During the republican period, tribal affiliation supposedly was based upon residence. Each tribe in the Tribal Assembly had one vote, and although the tribes consisted largely of the poorer citizens, the wealthier families were able to influence the Tribal Assembly through their clients. Of the republican tribes, four were urban and thirty-one rural, and the difficulty of coming in from the countryside resulted in the thirty-one rural votes being strongly influenced by the wealthy and the clients they brought with them (especially from Rome and its immediate environs).

The wealthier Roman citizens thus exercised political influence in both the Centuriate Assembly and the Tribal Assembly in ways that did not reflect the fact that the wealthy were a minority within the state. But the Roman Senate was really the instrument of power of the wealthy in republican Rome. Originally composed of selected patricians and plebeians who supposedly advised the kings and then the consuls after 509 B.C., the Senate by around 133 B.C. came to be made up of former holders of high political offices. The senators therefore constituted an impressive reservoir of political and military experience and talent (since consuls in particular served as the commanders of Roman legions). Constitutionally, the Senate was only an advisory body. It could not enact laws, although it did issue advisory opinions (*senatus consultum*) to magistrates, who traditionally submitted legislative proposals to it before the proposals came up for vote in the assemblies. But because of the prestige of its members, its influence was immense, exceeding that of any other organ of the state. Many wealthy plebeians entered the Senate after civic offices were opened up to their order, taking their place alongside the patricians. Thereafter, the Senate came to be dominated by an inner core of patrician-plebeian families.

This core of families in practice dominated Roman republican politics. Nevertheless, there was no shortage of disputes within the Senate and the assemblies, since Romans seldom voted on purely economic grounds. And the inclusion of the poorer citizens in the system of government, however limited by the organizational or procedural advantages given to the wealthy, was real and stands as a tribute to the pragmatic realism of the Romans. During the early Roman Republic, much Roman blood was spilled on the battlefields but relatively little on the streets of Rome itself. The willingness to settle internal conflicts by compromise—the ability of the patricians to bend before the strong winds of political change, which the poorer Roman citizens did much to encourage—preserved a sense of cohesiveness and a spirit of civic commitment without which Rome's political and military survival would have been impossible.

THE CAREER OF CONQUEST

Civic commitment was a hallmark of the early Romans. Devoted to the numerous gods of city, field, and hearth, the citizens of republican Rome tended to be hardworking, respectful of tradition, obedient to civil and military authority, and dedicated to the welfare of the state. According to the Romans' own understanding of their history, the backbone of Old Rome was the small, independent farmer who worked long and hard to raise crops and remained always vigilant against raids by tribes from the surrounding hills. Perhaps their stern resolution and rustic virtues were exaggerated by later Roman moralists looking back nostalgically from a later age, but there can be little doubt that the tenacious spirit and astonishing military success of early republican Rome owed much to the discipline and steadfastness of these citizen-farmers. As triumph followed triumph, as military booty and enslaved war captives flowed into Rome from far and wide, the character of its citizenry inevitably changed. One of the great tragic themes of Roman historiography is the gradual erosion of social morality by wealth and power—and the gradual expansion of huge slave-operated estates at the expense of the small farmer. But long before this process was complete, the empire had been won.

The expulsion of the last Etruscan king in about 509 B.C. was followed by a period of retrenchment and civil conflict (see pages 178–180 for the struggle between the patricians and the plebeians) during which the Romans fought for their lives against the attacks of neighboring tribes. After 400 B.C., the Etruscan cities, unwilling to unite for their mutual defense, fell one by one under Roman control. Veii, one of the most important Etruscan cities, was captured in 396 B.C. and eliminated as a rival. Battles were often lost—Rome itself was sacked in 386 B.C. by an army of Gauls from the north—but the Romans brushed off their defeats and pressed on. By 341 B.C., the Romans had come into conflict with their neighboring Latin cities; after Rome's victory in 338 B.C., some of the Latin cities were incorporated into the Roman state, and others were forced into bilateral alliances with Rome (but forbidden to have relations with each other).

The Romans were usually generous with the Italian peoples whom they conquered, allowing them a large measure of internal self-government, and were therefore generally successful in retaining their allegiance. Local aristocrats of conquered foes often were given Roman citizenship as a way of ensuring loyalty. At the same time, between 334 and 263 B.C., nineteen colonies were planted at strategic points throughout the Italian peninsula. In this fashion, Rome was able to construct an empire far more cohesive and durable than that of Periclean Athens. Gradually, the Roman conquests gained momentum. By about 265 B.C., all Italy south of the Po Valley was under Roman control. Even the Greek cities of Sicily acknowledged Roman supremacy. Thus, midway through the third century B.C., Rome took its place alongside Carthage and the three great Hellenistic successor states as one of the leading powers of the Mediterranean world.

Carthage and Rome now stood face-to-face. In 264 B.C., a dispute over a Sicilian city led to the first of three savage conflicts known as the Punic Wars (after *Poenus,* the Latin word for "Carthaginian"). To achieve success in the first war, Rome was forced to build a navy and take to the sea. At the conclusion of the first war in 241 B.C., Rome acquired its first overseas province, the fertile island of Sicily. (The English word "province" translates the Latin word *provincia,* which originally referred not to a physical area, but to a Roman magistrate's sphere of jurisdiction.)

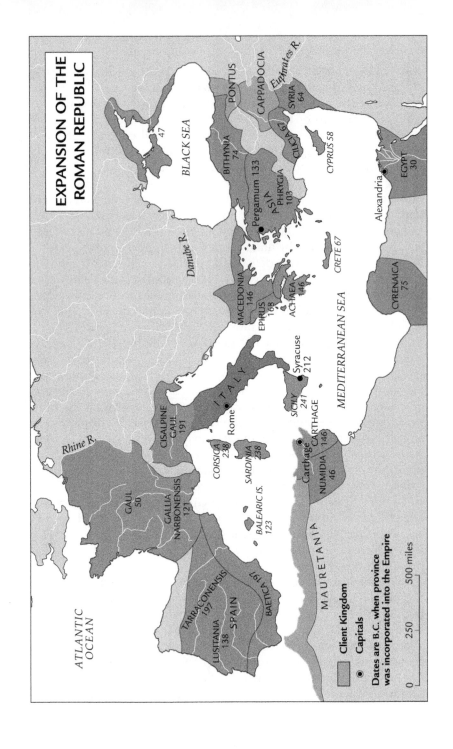

EXPANSION OF THE ROMAN REPUBLIC

ATLANTIC OCEAN

Rhine R.

Danube R.

BLACK SEA

47

PONTUS

BITHYNIA 74

CAPPADOCIA

Euphrates R.

CILICIA 67

SYRIA 64

Pergamum 133

ASIA

PHRYGIA 103

CYPRUS 58

Alexandria

EGYPT 30

GAUL 50

GALLIA NARBONENSIS 121

CISALPINE GAUL 191

CORSICA 238

SARDINIA 238

BALEARIC IS. 123

TARRACONENSIS 197

LUSITANIA 138

SPAIN

BAETICA 197

I T A L Y

Rome

MACEDONIA 146

EPIRUS 168

ACHAEA 146

CRETE 67

CYRENAICA 75

MEDITERRANEAN SEA

Syracuse 212

SICILY 241

Carthage

CARTHAGE

NUMIDIA 46

MAURETANIA

■ Client Kingdom
⦿ Capitals

Dates are B.C. when province was incorporated into the Empire

0 — 250 — 500 miles

The wars, especially the first two, were long and bitter. Rome lost numerous battles, scores of ships, and warriors and sailors by the hundreds of thousands. During the Second Punic War (218–201 B.C.), the armies of the masterly Carthaginian general Hannibal, having crossed the Alps, swept back and forth across Italy, winning victory after victory, and only the dogged determination of the Romans and the loyalty of their subject-allies saved the state from extinction. But the Romans hung on, always managing to win the last battle. At the conclusion of the Third Punic War in 146 B.C., Carthage lay in ruins—its population dispersed, its fields salted, and its far-flung territories in Africa, Sicily, and Spain in Roman hands.

In the meantime, Rome became involved in the rivalries among the Hellenistic kingdoms of the eastern Mediterranean. Ptolemaic Egypt, Seleucid Asia, Antigonid Macedon (Macedonia), and the several smaller Greek states had long been at one another's throats; Rome's victories over Carthage made it stronger than any one of them. Greek states frequently sought Roman aid against their enemies, and more often than not the Romans gave the requested support so as to maintain the balance of power in the East.

It has long been maintained that Rome entered the Greek world more as a pacifier and referee than as a conqueror. More recently, however, some historians have argued that not only were most Romans no more reluctant to engage in empire building than was Alexander the Great—or Napoleon—they were downright eager to acquire the riches of the eastern Mediterranean and the Near East. This fascinating debate will doubtless continue to generate scholarly sparks for some time.

Whatever the motives that underlay their conquests, the Romans gained control, directly or indirectly, of almost all the Hellenistic world during the course of the second century B.C. Rome won a decisive victory over the Seleucids in 189 B.C. and conquered Macedon in 168 B.C. In 146 B.C., it demolished the ancient city of Corinth and transformed Greece into a dependency under the authority of the Roman governor of Macedon. In 133 B.C. the Romans were bequeathed the kingdom of Attalus III of Pergamum, the most important kingdom in Asia Minor (roughly modern western Turkey). Acceptance of the bequest made the Romans a permanent presence in the eastern Mediterranean, with immense implications for world history. The remaining Hellenistic kingdoms were now overshadowed and had no choice but to bow to Rome's leadership. In time, they all became

Roman provinces. As the second century B.C. drew to a close, Rome was master of the Mediterranean world. There consequently arose the baffling problem of adapting a government designed to rule a city-state to the needs of an empire.

SOCIAL AND POLITICAL CHANGES: *264–146 B.C.*

Rome changed significantly during the Punic Wars, partly because the intoxicating effect of unimagined wealth and military success gradually undermined the old civic virtue and encouraged arrogance and materialism. More specifically, as Rome was conquering the Greek world, it was falling increasingly under the spell of Hellenistic culture. Roman writers of the time such as **Cato the Elder** lamented the corruption of Roman soldiers by the luxuries of eastern Mediterranean lands. Ultimately, Greece was perhaps the victor after all. The full tide of Hellenistic skepticism and individualism, which had earlier undermined allegiance to the Greek polis, began its transforming work on Roman conservatism and civic patriotism.

As in Greece, the effects of this process were both positive and negative. While the numbers of slaves were increasing, the status of women was improving. Whereas Roman women had previously been firmly under the control of their fathers, husbands, or guardians, they could now own property, attend public games, and move freely about the city. This development resulted not from changes in the laws but from less rigorous enforcement of them. And the growing popularity of a new, less binding form of marriage—marriage by *usus,* a kind of common-law marriage—gave wives much greater freedom from their husbands' authority than before. As a contemporary observer wrote: "Who among the Romans would be embarrassed to bring his wife to a dinner party? Or whose wife does not have first place at home or attend the public festivals?" *

What later republican Rome lost in old-fashioned Roman patriotism it gained in cultural and intellectual depth; for prior to its Hellenization, Rome certainly lagged behind the Greek city-states in the development of certain forms of literary culture. Moreover, the

---

*Cornelius Nepos, who wrote these words in the preface to his collection of biographies, is contrasting the freedom of Roman women with the circumscribed lives of Greek women.

Stoic notion of universal brotherhood was a singularly appropriate philosophy for a great empire, and it was a fortunate thing for the conquered peoples that in later years so many Roman statesmen became Stoics. But with Greek art, literature, and learning came the disquieting Hellenistic feeling of drift and alienation, aggravated by the shift from family farms to much larger plantations.

Both Carthage and the Hellenistic successor states had emphasized the large industrial farm over the small independent farm, and some Romans now began to do so as well. The conquests were bringing vast wealth and hordes of slaves into the hands of the Roman senatorial class, whose members regarded commerce and industry as sordid occupations and who were constrained by the strongest of social pressures to invest only in land. (A law passed in 218 B.C. forbade senators to engage in trade and moneylending.)

Accordingly, portions of central and southern Italy were now converted into extensive farms known as *latifundia*, worked by slaves and operated in accordance with the latest Carthaginian and Hellenistic techniques of large-scale farming. The latifundia existed in defiance of an old law that prohibited anyone from owning public tracts of land (Latin, *ager publicus*) in excess of about 300 acres. (These public tracts of land had come into the possession of the Romans as a result of military victories in Italy and were leased out by the state itself). Whereas the small farms had produced grain, the latifundia concentrated on the more lucrative production of wine and olive oil or the raising of sheep. The small farmers, whose energy and devotion had built the Roman Empire, were subjected to such heavy military demands that they found it increasingly difficult to maintain their farms. Their numbers were significantly reduced by continuous military conscription for overseas conquests. Many of those who were not conscripted sold out to latifundia owners and moved into the cities, especially Rome itself, where they joined multitudes of penniless immigrants and were transformed into a chronically unemployed mob. In later years, the riots of this underclass terrorized the government, and their hunger and boredom eventually gave rise to the custom of subsidized food and free entertainment of an increasingly sadistic sort—"bread and circuses" (*panem et circenses*).

During the Punic Wars, important changes were occurring in the social structure of the Roman elite. With the acceleration of commerce, a new, non-noble class of merchants, landowners, and public contractors emerged and eventually acquired such wealth as to rival the old nobility. This new class came to be known as the "equestrian order" because the wealth of its members enabled them to serve in the Roman army as cavalry rather than infantry. The equestrian order was effectively excluded from the Senate, but its members did not object. At first fundamentally apolitical except when their own interests were at stake, the equestrians were content to share with the nobility the rising living standards resulting from Roman military triumphs and increased contact with the Hellenistic world. As the equestrians and nobles came to live in increasing luxury, the gap between rich and poor steadily widened, and the pressures of social unrest began to threaten the traditional stability of the Roman state.

Meanwhile, the Roman government, which had earlier acted with restraint toward its subject-allies in Italy, was proving incapable of justly governing its newly acquired territories overseas. Most of Rome's non-Italian holdings were organized as provinces ruled by aristocratic Roman governors and exploited by Roman tax gatherers. Governor and tax gatherer often worked in partnership to bleed the provinces for personal advantage. The grossest kinds of official corruption were tolerated by the Roman courts of law, whose aristocratic judges hesitated to condemn dishonest officials of their own class for the sake of oppressed, but alien, provincials. After a time, some provincial governors began making it a practice to set aside a portion of their booty to bribe the courts.

VIOLENCE AND REVOLUTION: THE LAST CENTURY OF THE REPUBLIC

These deep-seated problems produced a century of violence and unrest (133–30 B.C.) that resulted ultimately in the downfall of the Republic and the advent of a new, imperial, government. The first steps toward revolution were taken by two reform-minded noblemen, the brothers **Tiberius** and **Gaius Gracchus,** who advocated a series of popular reform measures and thereby built up a powerful faction among the Roman commoners.

Tiberius Gracchus served as tribune in 133 B.C., and Gaius held the same office a decade later. Both recognized that the decline in citizen recruits for the Roman army and the deterioration of morale among the citizenry were caused by the virtual elimination of the small farm from central Italy (since there was a property qualification for recruits into the Roman legions). Their solution was to create a multitude of new farms for the dispossessed out of the vast public lands owned by the Roman state. This was a courageous and compassionate program, but the virtuous Roman farmer of yesteryear could not be conjured back into existence at this late moment. Most of the public lands had fallen under the de facto control of powerful noble families. Long accustomed to farming state lands for their own profit, the nobles reacted violently to the proposal that they should now surrender portions of these lands to create small farms for the impoverished, even though by law no one was supposed to hold more than about 300 acres of arable public land. In the political violence that followed, both Gracchi brothers were murdered—Tiberius in 133 B.C., Gaius in 121 B.C. The landed nobility demonstrated that, despite past concessions, it was still in control and willing to use mob violence to prevent change, even when that change was in the interests of the state. But it also betrayed its political and moral bankruptcy. The violence that was now unleashed would torment the Republic for a century and finally demolish it.

For a generation, the poorer citizens continued to press for the Gracchan reforms. The landed nobility found itself pitted not only against the masses but sometimes against the equestrian order as well. But the great political fact of the last republican century was the rise of individual adventurers who sought to use successful military careers as springboards to political power.

In 107 B.C., a skillful and ambitious military commander named **Marius** ignored the long-standing property qualification for military service and opened the army to volunteers from the poorest classes. The property qualification had been diminishing over the previous century in response to the decline in military manpower. Now the process was complete; Marius had the property qualification for service in the army abolished, and the jobless and homeless thronged into his volunteer army. Military service became, for many, the avenue to economic security, since the soldiers of a successful and politically influential general could often expect to receive a gift of land from the Senate upon retirement. The army began to acquire a more professional outlook than before, and soldiers came to identify themselves with their commanders rather than with the state. The opportunities for a ruthless general with a loyal army at his back were virtually limitless.

The subordination of the Roman Republic to the power of generals deepened during the decade of the eighties amid a struggle between the two foremost commanders of the age, Marius and **Sulla.** As the architect of open recruitment, Marius drew much of his support from the poorer classes, whereas Sulla tended to ally with the wealthier and more established. But both were strongly motivated by personal ambition.

In 88 B.C., Marius and Sulla were competing for the command of a major military campaign against King Mithradates Eupator of Pontos, one of Rome's most tenacious enemies. The Senate awarded the command to Sulla, but Marius, using terrorist tactics, forced a reversal of this decision and gained the command for himself. Sulla, part of his army already assembled, undertook to lead it in an unprecedented march on Rome. The Senate was outraged, but Sulla nevertheless compelled it to restore his command and then departed for four years' campaigning in the east. With Sulla busy elsewhere, Marius and his followers resumed control of Rome and slaughtered their political rivals with Assyrian thoroughness. In 83 B.C., Sulla returned from the east and wrested control of the city from Marius's faction, Marius himself having died in the meantime.

In 82 B.C., Sulla, in a spectacular break with tradition, got himself appointed *dictator* of the Roman Republic. In times of grave crisis, the Republic had traditionally concentrated all power in the hands of a dictator, permitting him to exercise virtually unlimited jurisdiction, but for six months only. Sulla compelled the Senate to vote him the dictatorship for an indefinite period, and he used his new power to settle old scores. He tortured and killed many of his enemies and dispossessed others, enriching himself from their confiscated fortunes. But Sulla had no intention of holding power indefinitely. A conservative at heart, he employed his dictatorial prerogatives to establish a series of laws that confirmed and strengthened the power of the Senate (such as giving senators control of the jury courts, which tried ex-governors accused of corruption). He retired in 79 B.C. to live in luxury on his country estate in Campania, leaving the Republic to stagger on.

In the decade of the sixties, the great senatorial orator **Cicero** strove desperately to unite senators and equestrians against the growing threat of adventurers, generals, and the riotous urban masses. Cicero's consummate mastery of Latin style, both in his orations and in his writings, earned him a lofty position in the field of Roman literature, but his political talents proved inadequate to the task of saving the Republic. In fact, in 63 B.C., when he was serving as consul, Cicero himself had to resort to extra-constitutional means (the execution of citizens without trial during the so-called conspiracy of **Catiline,** a corrupt aristocrat) to ensure the safety of the Republic.

Whatever the legality of his actions in 63 B.C., Cicero's dream of reconciling the interests of senators and equestrians was shattered by the selfishness of each. And his efforts to perpetuate the traditional supremacy of the Senate were doomed by the Senate's own incapacity, by the smoldering unrest of the city mobs, and by the hunger for power of the military commanders. It was Cicero's misfortune to be a conservative in an epoch of revolutionary turbulence—a statesman in an age of generals.

The Republic approached its final days in an atmosphere of chaos, naked force, and outright civil war. The dominant political figures of Cicero's generation were military commanders such as **Pompey** and **Julius Caesar,** who bid against one another for the backing of the poorer citizens, seeking to convert mob support into political supremacy. Characteristically, the three great political figures of their age—Pompey, Cicero, and Caesar—were all murdered. The failure of republican government was now manifest, and the entire imperial structure seemed on the verge of collapse. In the end, the institutions and leaders of what was originally a small city-state could not govern what had become a Mediterranean-wide empire.

But Rome emerged from this crisis transformed and strengthened, so much so that its empire endured for another 500 years in the west and 1,500 years in the east. The salvation of the Roman state out of the wreckage of the old order was one of antiquity's most stunning political achievements. To this transformation we now turn.

Spartacus

Spartacus, a slave and gladiator, escaped captivity in 73 B.C. and for the next two years led a large-scale insurrection against the Roman Republic. His rebellion illustrates not only the political insecurity of the Republic's last century but, more generally, the potential for local and regional violence that existed throughout the history of ancient Rome, owing to deep and widespread social discontent.

Only with difficulty can Spartacus's career be patched together from the accounts of several Roman writers, all of whom tended to be hostile toward him. A native of Thrace (see map on page 209), he became a Roman auxiliary soldier but then seems to have deserted. He was subsequently captured, enslaved, and assigned to a career of gladiatorial combat. While training for his new career at a gladiatorial school in Capua, he and a band of fellow gladiators made their escape. They took refuge near the top of the volcano Mount Vesuvius, where Spartacus became the commander of an army of brigands, including many runaway slaves. Responding swiftly, Rome sent an army of 3,000 legionaries to encircle the rebels and starve them out, but Spartacus and his men descended on the legionaries and routed them. As news of the successful insurrection spread, multitudes of paupers and runaway slaves swelled the ranks of Spartacus's band, enlarging it into an army that could hold its own against the Romans on the battlefield. Eventually, his army may have numbered between 70,000 and 120,000. A second, larger Roman army, led by the commander Varinius, found Spartacus's ex-slaves entrenched in regular formation on the open plain. Prudently declining battle, Spartacus led his army off secretly, and when the Romans advanced, they found his fortifications empty.

Varinius pursued the rebels across the length and breadth of the southern Italian countryside, but to no avail. Spartacus defeated Varinius in several pitched battles and just missed taking him prisoner. The rebels plundered a number of cities and, in time, extended their control over most of southern Italy.

The Roman Senate was by now deeply alarmed. It sent both consuls, each with his own army, against Spartacus, who routed each of the armies in turn. Spartacus then led his rebels northward toward the Alps in the hope of crossing into Gaul. Since Gaul had not yet been incorporated into the Roman Republic, it would have been a land of freedom for former Roman slaves.

But Spartacus's army of slaves refused to leave Italy and cross the Roman frontier. Spartacus had no choice but to turn back. His next move was to lead his men against the city of Rome itself, but his army's nerve seems to have failed again. The slaves drew back from attacking the city, and Spartacus led them south once more.

The Senate sent still another army against Spartacus, led by a magistrate named **Crassus,** whose far-flung commercial enterprises—including the buying and selling of slaves on a very large scale—had made him the richest man in Rome. More fortunate than his predecessors, Crassus defeated Spartacus in battle. Spartacus thereupon withdrew southward to the toe of the Italian boot with the idea of crossing the narrow Strait of Messina to the island of Sicily, where great numbers of restless slaves were eager to join his army. He made arrangements with pirates to ferry his men across the strait, but, as Crassus marched his army southward, the pirates betrayed and abandoned the rebels, leaving them trapped at the tip of the Italian toe.

Crassus tightened the trap by having a ditch and earthwork constructed all the way across the tip of the peninsula, but Spartacus and his army burst through and took to the hills of southern Italy once again. The morale of the rebels had been shaken by recent events, however, and dissension was increasing among them. One band seceded from the main army, only to be annihilated by the Romans. And the determined Crassus continued his pursuit. Spartacus crushed the vanguard of the advancing Roman army, but his troops disobeyed his command to retreat after inflicting the blow. As a result, the rebels were confronted with the full strength of Crassus's army, and in the course of a fiercely fought battle, Spartacus and most of his men were slain. Spartacus himself is reported to have died still gripping his sword.

Crassus's victory advanced his political career considerably, but even greater credit was given to another general, Pompey, called "the Great," who, curiously enough, had never really faced Spartacus in battle. Pompey and his army were returning from Spain when they encountered and destroyed a band of rebels fleeing from the battle that had claimed Spartacus's life. Yet, Pompey afterward boasted that he, and no other man, had ended the rebellion. As an example to other potential rebels, the slaves who survived the defeat of Spartacus's army were crucified by the Romans.

Catullus

Gaius Valerius **Catullus** (84–54 B.C.) is widely regarded as ancient Rome's foremost lyric poet. His life and poetry exhibit none of the somber old republican virtues, for Catullus was a young man of his times. He was sensitive to current styles and literary fashions that were just then flooding into Italy from the Greek world, from Hellenistic Alexandria in particular. His 114 surviving poems were influenced not only by the Hellenistic poets but also, going back much further, by the great lyric poets of archaic Greece, above all, by Sappho of Lesbos.

No contemporary biography of Catullus has survived; probably none was ever written. We must therefore piece together events in his life from passing references to him in the writings of others and from the evidence found in his own poems. A native of Verona in northern

Italy, Catullus moved with his family to Rome, which he much preferred to Verona. He remained in Rome for much of his life, living for at least a time in a modest villa. His father seems to have been relatively rich and politically well connected, indeed, a friend of Julius Caesar himself.

Although Catullus lived only thirty years, he lived them to the hilt. His brief lifetime was marked by the strongest of passions—intense loves and violent hatreds, directed in some cases toward the same person at different times. In his poetry, he mentions such contemporaries as Cicero, Pompey, and Julius Caesar, his father's friend. For reasons not altogether clear, Catullus absolutely despised Caesar and lampooned him scurrilously in his poetry, until Caesar, in an admirable display of diplomatic forbearance, invited the youth to dinner and managed to calm him down. Thereafter, Catullus and Caesar seem to have gotten along tolerably well.

Caesar's motive for undertaking to charm the young hothead was apparently an apprehension that Catullus, whose poetic gifts were winning him growing fame, could well damage Caesar's historical reputation. And although Catullus ceased his literary assaults against Caesar, he continued to heap scorn (and worse) on other, less celebrated contemporaries. His rapier wit and literary genius were beginning to strike fear in his enemies.

Catullus loved just as intensely as he hated. He wrote most affectingly of a dead brother, whose grave he visited while on a journey to Asia Minor (his one recorded trip abroad after settling in Rome). He wrote with flaming passion about his erotic loves—a homosexual love affair with a youth named Iuventius and, most notably, his adoration of a beautiful married woman whom he called "Lesbia" and who was evidently the great love of his life.

"Lesbia" has been identified, with a high degree of probability, as Clodia Pulchra, a beautiful patrician woman who was married to the prominent Roman politician Metellus Celer. He had earlier governed the district that included Catullus's native Verona, and it is likely that Catullus, while still a youth in the provinces, had fallen under Clodia Pulchra's spell. Whatever the case, Catullus wrote no fewer than twenty-five poems about her, which collectively exhibit, with the greatest passion and clarity, the pathology of a love affair—from extreme ardor to disenchantment and a potent brew of love and loathing. For Catullus, although clever in most respects, was evidently slow to realize what others well knew: that Clodia Pulchra, his beloved "Lesbia," was an unsavory character from an unsavory family. Her brother was a crooked politician, and she herself—according to the testimony of Cicero and Plutarch—was flamboyantly licentious.

Thus, Rome's greatest lyric poet, having soared to the heights, glided down into the depths. After pouring out his adoration, he ended the affair with a poetic dagger thrust:

> *My Lesbia, this fervent love I bear*
> *Exceeds all loves that other lovers knew.*
> *No love could persevere more faithfully*
> *Than this, the simple love I give to you.*
> *Your very faults, my Lesbia, bewitch*
> *My spirit and provide it blissful stress.*
> *So whether you be faithless or be true,*
> *I could not love you more, my love, or less.*
>
> *   *   *
>
> *I hate and love, nor can the reason tell;*
> *But that I love and hate I know full well.*
>
> *   *   *
>
> *Farewell, my love, Catullus now is done;*
> *Set fast in stone against this thankless one.*
> *But Lesbia, can you abide the slight—*
> *To have no lover come to spend the night?*

CHAPTER 12

The Principate

The new order saved Rome from the agonies of the civil wars of the late Republic and brought a long era of peace and stability to the Mediterranean world. It was chiefly the handiwork of two men: Julius Caesar and his grandnephew **Octavian Augustus.** For a time, Caesar ruled with two colleagues, and after his death a similar coalition guided Rome for a few years. A more centralized and lasting regime took shape under Octavian, who preferred the title *princeps* (first citizen) and whose new political system has thus been termed the Principate—even though it was clear to everyone that Octavian Augustus and his successors were in effect monarchs.

Significant Events of Roman Imperial History

Unless otherwise specified, all dates are A.D.

27 B.C.–A.D. 337   Principate

27 B.C.–A.D. 68	Iulio-Claudian dynasty
27 B.C.–A.D. 14	Augustus
14–37	Tiberius
37–41	Caligula
41–54	Claudius
54–68	Nero
68–69	Year of the Four Emperors
69–96	Flavian dynasty
69–79	Vespasian
79–81	Titus
81–96	Domitian
96–138	Nervo-Trajanic dynasty
96–98	Nerva
97–117	Trajan (97–98 with Nerva)

117–192	Antonine dynasty
117–138	Hadrian
138–161	Antoninus Pius
161–180	Marcus Aurelius (161–169 with Lucius Verus)
180–192	Commodus
193–235	Severan dynasty
193	Pertinax
193	Didius Julianus
193–211	Septimius Severus
211–217	Caracalla (211–212 with Geta)
217–218	Macrinus
218–222	Elagabalus
222–235	Alexander Severus
235–284	Crisis of the Third Century (eighteen "legitimate" emperors in the West and East)
284–305	Tetrarchic Period
293	Establishment of Tetrarchy of two Augusti and two Caesari
	West:
287–305	Maximian Augustus
305–306	Constantius Caesar
305–306	Constantius Augustus
305–306	Severus Caesar
307	Constantine Caesar
from 307	Constantine Augustus
	East:
284–305	Diocletian Augustus
293–305	Galerius Caesar
305–311	Galerius Augustus
305–309	Maximinus Caesar
308–324	Licinius Augustus
309–313	Maximinus Augustus
312–324	Constantine and Licinius joint rulers
324–337	Constantine sole ruler
330	Constantinople consecrated

337–1453   **Later Roman Empire(s)**

361–363	Julian
361–363	Failed revival of polytheism

379–395	Theodosius emperor of East
395	Pagan cults banned
410	Sack of Rome by Alaric and Visigoths
475–476	Romulus Augustulus, last western Roman emperor
1453	Sack of Constantinople by Ottoman Turks, end of Byzantine, or Eastern Roman, Empire

JULIUS CAESAR AND AUGUSTUS

Julius Caesar was a man of many talents—a superb general, an astute politician, and an author whose lucid and forthright *Commentaries on the Gallic Wars* was a significant contribution to the great literary surge of the late Republic. Above all, Caesar was a person of keen practical intelligence who could probe to the core of any problem, work out a logical solution, and then carry his plan to realization.

Caesar managed to ride the whirlwind of violence and ambition that was shattering Roman society during the mid-first century B.C. His political intuition and unswerving faith in himself and his destiny catapulted him to increasingly important political and military offices during the turbulent sixties. Opposed and distrusted by the conservative Senate, he allied himself with Pompey, a disgruntled general, and Crassus, an ambitious millionaire. These three formed an extralegal and unofficial coalition of political bosses, known to later historians as the **First Triumvirate,** which succeeded in dominating the Roman state.

Leaving Italy to his two colleagues, Caesar spent most of the following decade (58–50 B.C.) in Gaul, leading his army on a spectacular series of campaigns that resulted in the conquest of what is now France and Belgium and established his reputation as one of history's foremost military scientists. Caesar's conquest of Gaul pushed Roman civilization far northward from the Mediterranean basin into the heartland of western Europe. The long-range consequences of his conquest are immense, for in the centuries that followed, Gaul was thoroughly Romanized. The Roman influence survived the later barbarian invasions to give medieval and modern France a Romance tongue (i.e., a language that evolved from Latin) and to provide western Europe with an enduring Graeco-Roman cultural heritage.

While Caesar was winning Gaul, his interests in Italy were suffering. His advocacy of land redistribution and other policies dear to the hearts of the poorer classes earned him the hostility of the Senate. And his stunning military successes threatened to thwart Pompey's own ambitions. Out of common fear of Caesar, Pompey and the Senate joined forces, and in 49 B.C. they declared Caesar a public enemy. His career at stake, Caesar defied the Roman constitution by leading his own loyal army across the provincial boundary of the Rubicon River near modern Ravenna into Italy. In a series of dazzling campaigns (49–48 B.C.), he defeated Pompey and the hostile senators. Pompey fled to Egypt and was murdered there, leaving the Senate with no choice but to come to terms with the man who towered unchallenged over Rome.

Caesar was a magnanimous victor. He restored his senatorial opponents to their former positions and ordered the execution of Pompey's murderer. He could afford to be generous, for he was now the unquestioned master of the state. Caesar assumed the office of dictator and held it not for the traditional six months or, like Sulla, with the intention of early retirement, but year after year. Ultimately, he forced the Senate to grant him the dictatorship for life. He also assumed the key republican office of consul and retained the title *pontifex maximus* (supreme pontiff), or chief priest of the civic religion of Rome, which he had held for some years. In 44 B.C., he received the unprecedented honor of having a temple dedicated to his *genius* (family spirit), and the month of July was named in his honor. The political institutions of the Republic survived, but they were now under his thumb. The whole Roman electorate had become his clients.

Caesar used his power to reform the Republic along logical, practical lines. He introduced a radically new Julian calendar (based upon the solar year) that, with minor adjustments, is in almost universal use today. He organized numerous distant colonies that drained off a considerable number of Rome's unemployed and halved the bread dole. He did much to reform and rationalize Italian and provincial government and to purge the republican administration of its abuses. In short, his regime resembled that of a supremely talented and effective Greek tyrant.

Caesar's reforms were immensely beneficial, but he went too far, too fast—at least for the tastes of his conservative opponents. His disregard for republican institutions was too cavalier, and his assumption of the dictatorship for life alarmed powerful senators. On the Ides of March (15 March), 44 B.C., he was stabbed to death in the Senate by a group of senatorial conspirators led by **Brutus** and **Cassius.** As they rushed from the Senate, the assassins shouted,

"Tyranny is dead!" They were wrong: the Republic, which they claimed to be restoring, was dead, and Rome had only the choice between one-man rule and anarchy. By killing Caesar, they had given up the former for the latter.

Caesar's assassination resulted in fourteen more years of civil strife during which the traditionalist party of Brutus and Cassius struggled against would-be heirs to Caesar, while the heirs struggled among themselves. In the complex maneuvers of this civil war, some of the most famous figures in ancient history played out their roles. **Mark Antony,** Caesar's trusted lieutenant, defeated Brutus and Cassius in battle, and they both committed suicide. The golden-tongued Cicero, Rome's supreme literary craftsman, was murdered for his hostility to Mark Antony. And when the fortunes of war turned against Antony and his celebrated wife, Queen **Cleopatra** of Egypt, they took their own lives.

The ultimate victor in these struggles was a young man who had been virtually unknown at the time of Caesar's death. Octavian (later Augustus), Caesar's grandnephew and adopted son, was a young man of eighteen when Caesar died. Although inferior to Caesar in generalship and perhaps also in intellect, Octavian was Caesar's superior as a political realist—and a survivor. During his long, illustrious reign, Octavian completed the transformation of the Roman state from Republic to Empire, albeit an empire ruled by one man. But his reforms were more traditionalist in appearance than Caesar's, and he succeeded—where Caesar had failed—in soothing the Senate. He reformed the Romans and made them accept it.

THE AUGUSTAN AGE

In 31 B.C., Octavian's forces crushed those of Antony and Cleopatra at Actium. A year later, Octavian entered Alexandria as master of the Mediterranean world. He was then about the same age as Alexander at the time of his death, and it might be supposed that the two conquerors, both young, brilliant, and handsome, had much in common. But Octavian refused to visit Alexander's tomb in Alexandria, observing, so it was said, that true greatness lies not in conquest but in reconstruction—as well he might, given the fact that Alexander was an incomparably greater military leader and warrior. It is appropriate, therefore, that Octavian's historical reputation lies not in his military victories but in his accomplishment as architect of the Roman Empire's long peace.

The reformation of Rome, completed by Octavian, gave the Mediterranean world two centuries of almost uninterrupted peace during which classical culture developed and spread to the outermost reaches of the Empire. In the turbulent centuries that followed, people looked back longingly at the almost legendary epoch of the *Pax Romana* (Roman Peace). Octavian accomplished the seemingly impossible task of reconciling the need for one-man rule with at least some of the republican traditions of Old Rome (if not its republican form of government). He preserved the Senate; indeed, he increased its prestige. He retained the elected republican magistracies. He made no attempt to become dictator, for he preferred to manipulate the government in more subtle ways. He controlled the army, and like Caesar, he concentrated various key republican offices or the powers of those offices in his own person. Eventually he went beyond Caesar in being granted the power of a tribune (including the right to initiate legislation and the unlimited right of veto, which tribunes had originally exercised on behalf of the plebeian order). This power, with its great flexibility, was ideal for Octavian's needs and became a potent instrument of imperial control. Future emperors dated their reigns from their receipt of the tribunician power.

In 27 B.C., Octavian was given the novel name Augustus, a term that carried with it no specific power but had a connotation of reverence, almost sanctity. And like Caesar, he arranged to have a month (August) named in his honor. The necessity that his month should have as many days as Caesar's July resulted in a permanent asymmetry in our calendar, at the expense of luckless February.

Much as Augustus may have enjoyed these various distinctions, he took pains to maintain a relatively modest public image. He commonly used the simple title princeps, which, in its meaning of "first citizen," conveyed the suggestion that he was the leading Roman, nothing more. He lived fairly modestly, associated freely with his fellow citizens, revered the dignity of the Senate, and dressed and ate simply. It has been said that the government of the Principate was the opposite of the government of modern Britain: the former a monarchy masquerading as a republic, the latter a republic masquerading as a monarchy. But although the Principate was at heart a monarchy, it was by no means an arbitrary one. Augustus ruled with a keen sensitivity toward popular and senatorial opinion and a respect for

Augustus of Primaporta
This marble statue of Augustus (c. 20 B.C.) is a recognizable yet idealized
likeness of the first Roman emperor as military leader *(imperator)*. His
cuirass (breastplate) is decorated with figures of barbarians being defeated
by Romans. The cupid riding on the dolphin at his feet is a reference to
Augustus's descent from Venus through the Julian family line, which included his adoptive father Julius Caesar. *(© Erich Lessing/Art Resource, NY)*

tradition. Ancient Rome, like modern Britain, had no written constitution, but it had a venerable body of political customs—an unwritten constitution—that Augustus treated with cautious deference, lest he share the fate of his more brilliant but less politically sensitive adoptive father.

Still, Augustus was Rome's true master. Roman political liberty, defined as the freedom of action and speech of Roman citizens, especially those who belonged to the wealthy old senatorial class, was the single great casualty of the Principate, but its loss was rendered almost painless by the political deftness of the first princeps. (Of course, as noted by Tacitus, an astute historian of the late first century A.D., after all the bloodshed of the civil wars and the proscriptions, there was no one left alive who remembered what real freedom was.) In its place, Augustus provided peace, security, and justice. The administration of the provinces was more closely regulated, and corruption and exploitation reduced. In Rome itself, an efficient imperial bureaucracy gradually developed that was responsible to the princeps alone. Although class distinction remained strong, it was now possible for an able person from one of the lesser orders to rise in government service. And Augustus sought out and supported gifted writers and artists as a matter of policy.

The stable new regime, the promise of enduring peace, the policy of "careers open to talents," and the leadership of Augustus himself combined to evoke a surge of optimism, patriotism, and creative originality. In the field of arts and letters, the "Augustan Age" is the climax of Roman creative genius. Under Augustus, Roman artists and poets achieved a powerful synthesis of Greek and Roman elements. Roman architecture was obviously modeled on the Greek, yet it expressed a distinctively Roman spirit. Roman temples often rose higher than those of classical Greece and conveyed a feeling that was less serene and more imposing and dynamic. Augustan poetry—the urbane and faultless lyrics of **Horace,** the worldly, erotic verses of **Ovid,** the majestic cadences of **Virgil**—employed Greek models and ideas, but in original and characteristically Roman ways.

Rome's supreme poem, Virgil's *Aeneid,* is cast in the epic form of Homer and deals, as Homer's *Odyssey* does, with the voyage of an important figure in the Trojan War. But **Aeneas,** Virgil's hero, was also the legendary founder of the line that eventually would found Rome, and the poem is shot through with patriotic prophecies about the destiny of the state established by Aeneas's descendant, Romulus. Indeed, some readers have seen in Aeneas a symbol of Augustus himself. The *Aeneid* conveys the feeling of hope that the Roman people, descended from Aeneas and now led by the great peacemaker Augustus, had at last fulfilled their mission to bring enduring concord and justice to the tormented world:

> Let it be your charge, O Roman,
>> To rule the nations in your empire;
> This shall be your art:
>> To ordain the law of peace,
>> To be merciful to the conquered.
>> To beat the haughty down.*

IMPERIAL LEADERSHIP AFTER AUGUSTUS

Augustus died at the age of seventy-six in A.D. 14. During the decades following his death, the Principate grew steadily more centralized and more efficient. The imperial bureaucracy slowly expanded, but taxes remained relatively light and intelligently assessed, and the law became increasingly humane. The system that Augustus established proved sturdy enough to adapt and endure despite the relative incapacity of many of his imperial successors.

The abilities of the first-century emperors ranged from uninspired competence to (putting it mildly) mental illness. We encounter the childish cruelty of **Nero** and the bizarre antics of **Caligula,** who wallowed in the pleasure of watching his prisoners tortured to death. Caligula is reported to have allowed his favorite horse to dine at the imperial table during formal state dinners, consuming the finest food and wines from jeweled dishes and goblets. At the time of his assassination, Caligula was on the verge of raising the beast to the office of consul. Caligula and Nero were autocrats of the worst sort, and both were violently removed from power. On the whole, however, the emperors of the early Principate retained the traditional attitudes exemplified by Augustus himself, and the majority of them actually worked very hard to keep the Empire strong and safe. Given the size of the Empire itself, in practice the Roman emperors and the government as a whole were able only to react to events and requests from the inhabitants of the gigantic Empire. Although some Roman

---

Aeneid, book 6; adapted from *The Aeneid,* edited with introduction and commentary by J. W. Mackail (1930).

emperors did attempt to extend the borders of the Empire against Augustus's advice, the government of the Roman Empire, such as it existed, was fundamentally passive in character.

On a personal level, the second century A.D. witnessed a dramatic improvement in imperial leadership. Rome's rulers between A.D. 96 and A.D. 180—**Nerva, Trajan, Hadrian, Antoninus Pius,** and **Marcus Aurelius**—have been called the "five good emperors." At least part of their success can be attributed to the temporary solving of one of the knottiest dilemmas in the whole imperial system—the problem of succession. In theory, the Senate chose the princeps, but in fact the succession usually fell to a close relative of the previous emperor and was often arranged in advance by the emperor. Too often this led to a disputed succession that was settled by violence and even civil war. But none of the second-century emperors—Trajan, Hadrian, Antoninus Pius, or Marcus Aurelius—came to power by normal hereditary succession. In each case, the previous emperor adopted a younger man of outstanding ability as his son and successor.

This policy was both intelligent and necessary. Of the "five good emperors," only Marcus Aurelius, the last, had a son of his own.

Hadrian
Hadrian was a great lover of Greek culture and literature. As shown in this sculpture (c. A.D. 120), he was the first Roman emperor to be depicted consistently with a full beard, which was also characteristically worn by Greek philosophers. (© *Erich Lessing/Art Resource, NY*)

Yielding to a temptation that his four predecessors had not faced, Marcus chose his son, the incompetent **Commodus,** as his heir. With the disastrous reign of Commodus (A.D. 180–92), the age of enlightened imperial rule came to an end. It was followed by a century of invasion, civil strife, assassinations, economic and administrative breakdowns, and cultural and religious change, which certainly transformed, and nearly destroyed, the Roman state.

THE EMPIRE UNDER THE PRINCIPATE

Before plunging into the tumultuous third century, let us look briefly at the condition of the Roman Empire at its height. During the two centuries from the rise of Augustus (31 B.C.) to the death of Marcus Aurelius (A.D. 180), the Empire expanded gradually to include a vast area encircling the Mediterranean Sea and bulging northward across present-day France and England. It extended about 3,000 miles from east to west (a little less than the length of the United States)—from the Tigris-Euphrates Valley to the Atlantic. According to the best scholarly guesses, its inhabitants numbered some 50 million, heavily concentrated in the eastern provinces where commerce and civilization had flourished for thousands of years.

Augustus added a considerable amount of territory to the Empire, and several later emperors, most notably Trajan, made significant conquests. But most of the emperors were content to guard the frontiers and preserve what had already been won. To the east, Rome shared a boundary with the Parthian Empire, which gave way during the third century to a new and aggressive Persian dynasty. Elsewhere, however, Rome's expansion was halted only by deserts, mountains, wastelands, untamed forests, and the Atlantic. In short, the Empire encompassed virtually all the lands that could be reached by Roman armies and cultivated profitably by Roman landowners.

The burden of defending these frontiers rested on an imperial army of some 300,000 to 500,000 men, organized on principles laid down by Augustus. Infantry legions manned by Roman citizens serving long-term enlistments were supplemented by auxiliary forces, both infantry and light cavalry, made up of non-Roman citizens who were granted citizenship at the end of their extended terms of service. The army was concentrated along the frontiers except for the small, privileged praetorian guard that served the emperor in Rome itself.

The superb system of roads that linked the city of Rome with its most remote provinces ensured a high degree of military mobility. Paved with stones fitted closely together, and running in straight lines mile after mile, these roads were nearly as eternal as the city they served. They eased the flow of commerce as well as the movement of troops and remained in use many centuries after the Pax Romana was shattered.

The Empire's greatest commercial artery, however, was not built of stone; it was the Mediterranean itself, completely surrounded by imperial territory and referred to affectionately by the Romans as *mare nostrum* (our sea). Roman fleets patrolled the Mediterranean and cleared it of pirates for the first time in antiquity so that peaceful shipping could move safely among the Empire's many ports.

Roman institutions and classical culture spread far and wide across the Empire under the canopy of the Pax Romana. As distant provinces became increasingly Romanized, the meaning of the words "Rome" and "Roman" gradually changed. By the time of Augustus, these terms embraced the greater part of Italy. Later, as the decades of the Pax Romana followed one another, citizenship was extended to more and more provincials until finally, in A.D. 212, every free inhabitant of the Empire received citizenship, at least in principle. By then, the emperors themselves often came from the provinces; the second-century emperor Trajan, for example, was a native of Spain. In time, the terms "Rome" and "Roman" acquired a universal connotation: a Greek monarch in Constantinople, a Frankish monarch at Aachen, a Saxon monarch in Germany, a Habsburg in Vienna could, in later centuries, all refer to themselves as "Roman emperors." Thus, one of the most important themes in the history of the Roman Empire was the gradual extension of Roman culture to the provinces and the simultaneous adaptation of their inhabitants and their institutions to Rome, thereby changing what constituted "Rome".

ECONOMIC AND SOCIAL CONDITIONS

The most conspicuous effect of Romanization was the spread of cities. The city-state, the characteristic political unit of the Graeco-Roman world, now extended to the outermost provinces—to Gaul, Spain, the lands along the Rhine and Danube Rivers, even to remote

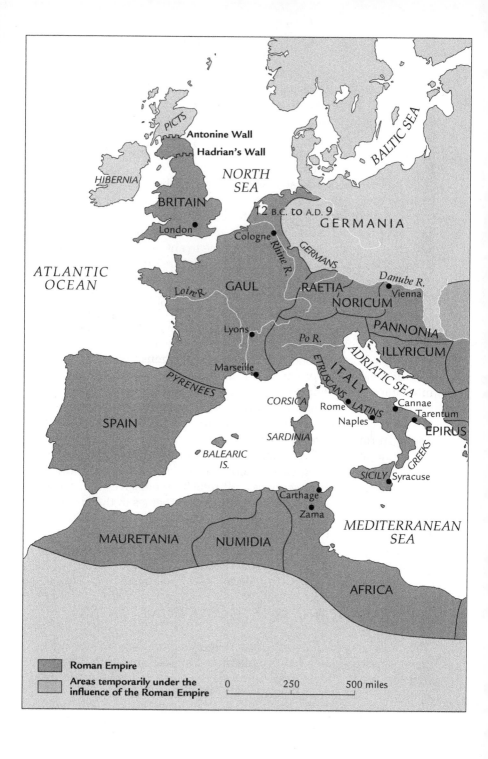

Antonine Wall
Hadrian's Wall
PICTS
HIBERNIA
NORTH SEA
BALTIC SEA
BRITAIN
12 B.C. to A.D. 9
London
GERMANIA
Cologne
ATLANTIC OCEAN
GERMANS
Rhine R.
Loire R.
GAUL
RAETIA
NORICUM
Danube R.
Vienna
PANNONIA
Lyons
Po R.
ILLYRICUM
ADRIATIC SEA
Marseille
ETRUSCANS
I T A L Y
PYRENEES
CORSICA
Rome
LATINS
Cannae
Tarentum
Naples
EPIRUS
SPAIN
SARDINIA
BALEARIC IS.
GREEKS
SICILY
Syracuse
Carthage
Zama
MEDITERRANEAN SEA
MAURETANIA
NUMIDIA
AFRICA

Roman Empire
Areas temporarily under the influence of the Roman Empire

0   250   500 miles

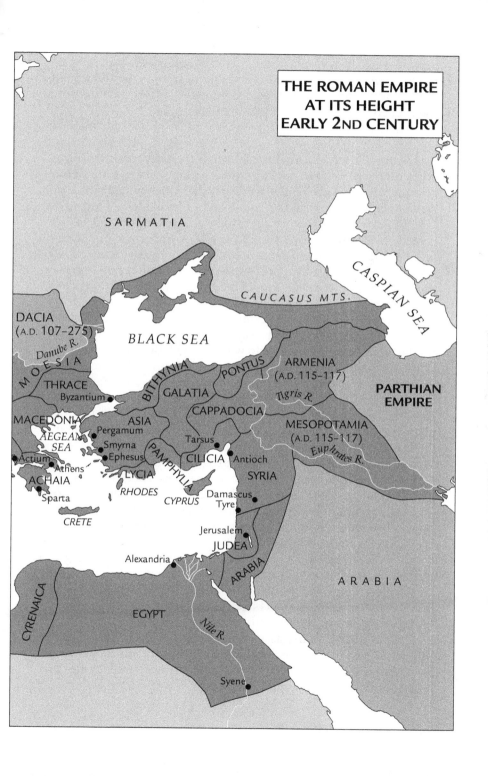

THE ROMAN EMPIRE
AT ITS HEIGHT
EARLY 2ND CENTURY

SARMATIA

CASPIAN SEA

CAUCASUS MTS.

DACIA
(A.D. 107–275)

BLACK SEA

Danube R.

MOESIA

THRACE
Byzantium

MACEDONIA

AEGEAN
SEA

Pergamum

ASIA

Smyrna
Ephesus

Actium

Athens

ACHAIA

Sparta

CRETE

BITHYNIA

GALATIA

PONTUS

ARMENIA
(A.D. 115–117)

Tigris R.

PARTHIAN
EMPIRE

CAPPADOCIA

MESOPOTAMIA
(A.D. 115–117)

Euphrates R.

Tarsus

PAMPHYLIA

CILICIA

Antioch

LYCIA

SYRIA

RHODES

CYPRUS

Damascus
Tyre

Jerusalem

JUDEA

ARABIA

Alexandria

ARABIA

CYRENAICA

EGYPT

Nile R.

Syene

Britain. The city still retained much local self-government and normally controlled the rural territories in its vicinity. In other words, the city was the key unit of local administration; the government of the Roman state remained fundamentally urban.

Paradoxically, the cities of the Empire, especially in the West, were of only modest importance as commercial and manufacturing centers. Although small-scale urban industry often flourished, particularly in the East, the Empire's economy remained fundamentally agrarian. Many of the western cities, including Rome itself, consumed far more than they produced—like modern Washington, D.C. Basically, these Roman cities were administrative and military centers whose mercantile significance was important but secondary. During the first two centuries of the Empire, the economy was prosperous enough to support them, but this would not always be the case. In time, the cities would decline, and with them the whole political structure of the Roman West.

By the first and second centuries A.D., the small family farms of the Roman past had given way across large areas of the Empire to the great latifundia, which were owned by the wealthy and tilled by slaves or half-free peasants. Although the products of Roman farming varied widely from region to region, the principal crops were grain, grapes, and olives—the old "Mediterranean triad" that had dominated agriculture in the Mediterranean basin for countless generations. Grain (chiefly wheat and barley) and grapes were cultivated throughout most of the Empire. From these, the Romans produced two of the basic staples of their diet: bread and wine. Olive trees were also grown in abundance, though their vulnerability to cold restricted their cultivation to the frost-free lowlands around the Mediterranean Sea. The people of the Mediterranean basin used olive oil in place of butter, which was favored by the Germanic tribes to the north and east but turned rancid in the southern heat. Throughout much of Italy, grain production had given way to the raising of grapes, olives, sheep, and cattle. The fertile wheat-growing provinces of Egypt and North Africa had by now become the primary suppliers of bread for the teeming populace (numbering perhaps half a million) of the city of Rome.

In the early Empire, as in the late Republic, slaves played an important role in the economy, especially in agriculture. But as the frontiers solidified and the flow of war captives dwindled, the chief source of slaves was cut off. Landowners now began to lease major portions of their estates to sharecroppers called *coloni,* who tended to fall more and more under the control of their landlords and sank into a semi-servile status akin to that of medieval serfs. Agricultural slavery persisted in western Europe, however, far into the Middle Ages, dying out only in the years around A.D. 1000.

The condition of the slaves, coloni, and urban poor should warn us against viewing the Roman Principate through the rose-tinted microscopes of nineteenth-century historians, who considered it humanity's happiest age. Roman classical literary culture was impressive, but it was also narrowly limited, shared largely by the Empire's upper crust. And although everybody benefited from the Pax Romana, the great majority were impoverished and undernourished and lived only one failed harvest away from starvation.

Such conditions persisted throughout the Principate and beyond, not as economic misfortunes that might be remedied by economic stimulus programs but as the means necessary for the functioning of great estates, mines, and wealthy households. The leisured lives of the Empire's elite, and the very survival of the imperial economy, depended on the muscles of slaves and poor laborers, who constituted 80 to 90 percent of the total population.

Even the Pax Romana, so widely and properly admired, was not as complete as one might suppose. Germanic tribes hammered repeatedly at Rome's frontiers and sometimes pierced them, while deep within the Empire, towns and countryside suffered a degree of local violence and mayhem exceeding that of European societies today. By modern standards, the provinces of the Roman Principate were drastically underpoliced and undergoverned.

Roman women, even the wealthiest, were barred from political office, although some women did hold important political and religious offices in cities and towns outside of Rome itself. By longstanding tradition, they were expected to stay home and obey their husbands, but during the imperial era, as in the late Republic, many Roman wives owned property, and most of them traveled freely within their cities. Indeed, in the Empire's later centuries, women acquired considerable independence with respect to marriage, divorce, and property ownership, and many upper-class women were well educated. The Roman father, however, was the master of his family in legal theory and exercised the power of life or death over his newborn children. If he liked their looks, he let them remain in the family; if they were scrawny or handicapped, or if the family already had enough children—particularly female children—they were taken from the home and abandoned. Some had the good fortune to be rescued by adults in need of children, but others simply died of exposure. Infanticide was yet another brutal consequence of Rome's marginal economy: the Empire could not afford excess mouths.

But all ancient civilizations were afflicted by slavery, poverty, malnutrition, internal violence, the suppression of women, and the killing of unwanted infants (although the religion of the Hebrews prohibited infanticide). In these respects, Roman imperial civilization was no worse than others, and in the larger cities, where public baths and free bread were available, it was significantly better.

Under the emperors of the second-century A.D., imperial policy was humane and, to a degree, compassionate. It was influenced by the Stoic emphasis on human brotherhood and social and political responsibility. Unlike Caligula and Nero, who used their power to indulge their sadistic whims, emperors such as Hadrian, Antoninus Pius, and Marcus Aurelius viewed their authority as a trust—a commission to govern in the interests of their people, whether rich or poor. They funded charities, provided food to orphans and paupers, launched building programs, and assisted cities in financial distress. Hadrian won wide popularity by canceling all private debts to the imperial government. But given the nature of the Roman economy, such policies could effect no fundamental, structural improvement. Roman life under the "five good emperors" could be pleasant enough if one were male, adult, rich, and naturally immune to various epidemic diseases.

THE SILVER AGE

The cultural epoch from approximately the death of Augustus (A.D. 14) to the death of Marcus Aurelius (A.D. 180) is known as the silver age. Less celebrated than the golden Augustan Age, it nevertheless produced literary, intellectual, and artistic works of the first order. Some critics have seen in silver-age writers such as the Stoic **Seneca** and the essayist **Pliny the Younger** a decline in creative genius from predecessors such as Cicero, Catullus, Virgil, Ovid, and Horace. These critics have stressed the pretentious, ornate style of second-century literature and the sometimes stale conformity of second-century art. And they have attributed these supposed shortcomings to the "homogenization" of imperial society and the dullness engendered by peace and security. Such judgments are necessarily relative, and many sensitive people across the centuries have viewed writers of the silver age with enormous admiration.

However one may judge the originality of silver-age literature, there can be no question that it produced major works of synthesis. **Plutarch** (c. A.D. 46–120), in his *Parallel Lives,* provided biographies of famous Romans along with notable figures from his native Greece. One of the most widely read works in antiquity, Plutarch's *Lives* undertook to educate youth in the nature of virtue as exemplified by models from both the Greek and the Roman past.

Less edifying is *Lives of the Caesars,* by **Suetonius.** A treasure chest of court scandal, it educates its reader as much in the nature of vice as in the nature of virtue. More significant is the work of **Tacitus** (c. A.D. 56–118), whose histories carefully and vividly trace the course of the early Empire—though with an old-fashioned republican bias. Tacitus also wrote an important ethnographic study of the early Germanic peoples, titled *Germania,* and a biography of a Roman governor of Britain named Agricola, who was Tacitus's father-in-law. This last work is a source of fundamental importance for the history of Roman Britain.

During the silver age, classical culture spread outward and downward. Remote provincial cities built temples and baths, theaters, and triumphal arches in the Roman style. Libraries and schools were scattered abundantly across the Empire, and the extent of urban literacy is demonstrated by the many irreverent and obscene scribblings and campaign slogans discovered by modern excavators on the buildings of Pompeii, buried and preserved by the eruption of Mount Vesuvius in A.D. 79.

Alexandria, the Hellenistic metropolis, retained its commercial and intellectual importance throughout the age of the Principate, producing brilliant early Christian and Jewish theologians as well as several distinguished scientists who developed and synthesized the achievements of their Hellenistic predecessors. Ptolemy of Alexandria, who died about A.D. 180, developed Greek and Hellenistic astronomical thought into a sophisticated and comprehensive geocentric model of the universe. He also wrote the most complete geography of antiquity. **Galen** (A.D. 131–201), a medical scientist from Hellenistic Pergamum, produced a series of works on biology and medicine that dominated these fields for more than a thousand years. The

Meditations of Marcus Aurelius, the last of the "five good emperors," is a moving expression of the Stoic philosophy that deepened and humanized much of the era's best thought. In literature and art, science and philosophy, the silver age produced an effortless blend of Greek and Roman traditions. Its cosmopolitanism is echoed in the varied languages, religions, and homelands of its writers. Alongside Latin-speaking Romans such as Tacitus, Suetonius, and Seneca stand the Epicurean satirist **Lucian** from Syria, the Greek-speaking biographer Plutarch, and the Jewish historian **Josephus,** a Roman citizen who wrote in Greek and whose monograph *The Jewish War* (which describes the great Jewish Revolt against Roman rule of around A.D. 66 to 73, including the destruction of the Jewish Temple in Jerusalem by the Romans) is a classic of historiography. In the works of these and other silver-age writers, the rich, complex, and occasionally tragic interactions and legacies of Greece, Rome, and the ancient Near East are summarized and fused.

ROMAN LAW

Of all the achievements of this epoch, perhaps the most far reaching—certainly the most distinctively Roman—was the development of imperial law. The rigid code of the Twelve Tables was gradually broadened and humanized by the magistrates of the later Republic and early Empire, by the great Roman lawyers of the second and third centuries A.D., and through the enlightened intervention of the emperors themselves. As the Romans became acquainted with more and more peoples, each with its unique set of laws and customs, they gradually emancipated themselves from the peculiarities of their own law and strove to replace it with a body of fundamental principles drawn from the laws of all people. The *ius gentium,* or "law of nations," slowly transformed the Roman code into a legal system suitable to a vast, heterogeneous empire.

The evolution of Roman law into a universal system of jurisprudence owed something also to the Greek concept of the *ius naturale* (law of nature), which has played a prominent role in the history of Western thought. More abstract than the ius gentium, the law of nature, or natural law, is based on the belief that, in a divinely ordered world, there are certain universal norms of human behavior that all people tend to follow, regardless of their own customs and traditions. Most human societies, for example, have laws or taboos against such acts as murder, theft, and rape. Such ethical norms, based on general principles of political and social justice, served to rationalize and humanize the law of the Empire and to provide it with a sturdy philosophical foundation.

Roman law, a product of Latin practical political genius influenced by Greek speculative thought, gave substance to the Augustan ideal of justice. Codified at enormous effort by the sixth-century emperor **Justinian,** it has become a crucial part of the Western heritage—the basis of many legal systems to this day in Europe and its former colonies.

CHAPTER 13

The Spiritual Metamorphosis

The second and third centuries A.D. witnessed a shift in religious attitudes. While many traditional Graeco-Roman cults remained popular, so-called mystery cults, many of which dated from the sixth century B.C., clearly gained momentum. The ultimate beneficiary of this ferment was the Christian faith.

GODS, MYSTERY CULTS, AND NEOPLATONISM

The Romans honored many gods. Like the Greek city-states, Rome had its official civic deities—**Jupiter** and **Juno, Minerva** and **Mars,** and many others—who by the later Republic had become identified with parallel gods of the Greek Olympic religion. The Roman Jupiter was thought of as equivalent to the Greek Zeus, the Roman Minerva was the Greek Athena, the Roman **Venus** was the Greek Aphrodite, and so on. Besides these state deities, there were innumerable local gods and cults that enjoyed official toleration. None of them claimed a monopoly on truth, and a single individual might without compromise participate in the cults of several of them. The Principate added an important new element to the state religion: the cult of the emperor. Even before his death, Augustus had cults devoted to him in Pergamum and Nicomedia, and Augustus and his successors (with a few notorious exceptions) were deified by the Senate after their deaths. It became customary for Romans and provincials alike to participate in formal religious observances to the deified emperors as well as to the major deities of the city of Rome. These observances encouraged the allegiance of diverse peoples, and few objected to the addition of a handful of new deities to the divine multitude that they worshiped already.

But to the Jews, and later the Christians, these religio-patriotic observances were intolerable, for the God of the Jews permitted the worship of no other. Rome had long legally recognized the Jews as a people apart and had excused them from participation in the official cults. The Christians, in contrast, suffered greatly from their refusal to worship the emperors and gods of Rome. To the Romans, such intransigence smacked of both atheism and treason. It is no accident that Christianity, alone of the religions of the Empire, was the object of serious persecution.

But the imperial centuries witnessed something of a shift in Roman religious attitudes. While veneration of the traditional gods of household, clan, and city continued, the worship of deities imported from the eastern Mediterranean gained momentum. The gods of Old Rome, like those of Greek Olympus, had safeguarded the welfare of social and political groups; the gods of the eastern cults, who were worshiped in the context of mystery cults, appealed more to individuals. As the Roman imperial age progressed, religious allegiances drifted from the gods of the Graeco-Roman Olympic cult—Jupiter, Juno, Venus, Apollo, Minerva, and the rest—to the Egyptian Isis, the Persian Mithras, the Phrygian Great Mother, the Syrian sun god, and other deities who usually offered initiates some kind of personal experience of the divine, which might give them better hope for the future, at least during this life. The majority of these cults, however, did not make any promises to initiates about avoiding death or any sort of redemptive afterlife. The salvation they promised related to the here and now. Such immediate salvation was important in the fragile and uncertain Mediterranean world.

This surge in the popularity of mystery cults was a continuation and expansion of a trend we have already observed among the Hellenistic Greeks. The same forces that had encouraged rootlessness and disorientation in the Hellenistic world were now at work throughout the Roman Empire: cosmopolitanism, gradually increasing autocracy, and, among the underprivileged majority, grinding poverty and loss of hope. The shift from civic god to savior god gained additional momentum as the peace of the second century gave way to the anarchy of the third, making the high hopes of classical humanism—the dream of a rational universe, an ideal republic, a good life—seem like cruel illusions.

The older Graeco-Roman cults were by no means dead, but they were altered by the growth of otherworldliness. The trend is especially conspicuous in the leading philosophical movement of the third century, **Neoplatonism.** The Egyptian philosopher **Plotinus**

(A.D. 205–270), one of the most influential minds of the Roman imperial era, popularized the doctrine of a single "One," or the "Good"—infinite, unknowable, and unapproachable except through a mystical experience. This One was the ultimate source of everything, spiritual and physical. All existence was conceived of as a series of circles radiating outward from the One, like concentric ripples in a pond, diminishing in excellence and significance as they grew more distant from their divine source. Human reason, which the Greeks had earlier exalted, lost its fascination, for at the core of reality was a god that lay beyond reason's scope. Plotinus and his followers regarded the gods of Olympus as crude but useful symbols of the true Platonic god.

Though poorly suited to the deepening mood of otherworldliness, the Graeco-Roman cults were given new life by the overarching structure of Neoplatonic philosophy. They were themselves brought into line with the trend toward mysticism and monotheism. The distinction between Jupiter and the new eastern deities was steadily blurring. By the fourth century A.D., Greek rationalism and humanism had been superseded by a spirit of otherworldliness and a yearning for eternal life. Neoplatonic philosophy and Near Eastern religion were accompanied by astrology, magic, and similar arcane practices, which had never been absent from Graeco-Roman society but which now dominated popular thinking as never before.

CHRISTIANITY

It was in this atmosphere of heightened religious sensibility that the Christians eventually found many converts within the Roman Empire. Some of their beliefs and practices resembled those of older and competing religions. Eternal salvation, the death and resurrection of a savior god, baptism, the sacramental meal, human brotherhood under a divine father—none was completely new. Yet, Christianity differed from the majority of mystery cults in two fundamental ways. First, its founder and savior was an actual historical personage who had lived and died during the Roman Empire. Second, its god was not merely the best of many gods but the One God, the God of the Hebrews, unique in all antiquity in his claims to exclusiveness and omnipotence, and now detached by Christianity from his association with a chosen people to become the God of all peoples.

Jesus had lived and died a Jew, and almost all of his early followers were Jews as well. He announced that he had come not to abolish Judaism but to fulfill it. In his earliest quasi-biographies, the four Gospels, he is pictured as a warm, magnetic leader who miraculously healed the sick, raised the dead, and stilled the winds. His ministry was chiefly to the poor and outcast, and in Christianity's early decades it was they who accepted the new faith most readily. He preached a doctrine of love, compassion, and humanity; like the Hebrew prophets, he favored a simple life, generosity toward both friend and enemy, and devotion to God. He did not object to ritual as such but only to ritual infected with pride and divorced from love of God and neighbor. He angered some leaders of the Jewish priesthood by criticizing their complacency and by claiming to speak with divine authority. In the end, he was arrested by soldiers under the command of the Roman government and was accused before the Roman governor, **Pontius Pilate,** of claiming to be king of the Jews, which could be seen as an act of treason against the emperor. Pilate had Jesus lashed and condemned him to crucifixion, a common means of executing non-Romans who were nevertheless under the jurisdiction of the Roman prefect (Pilate).

According to the Gospels, Jesus' greatest miracle was his resurrection—his return to life on the third day after his death on the cross. He is said to have remained on Earth for a short period thereafter, giving solace and instruction to his disciples, and then to have ascended into heaven with the promise that he would return in glory to judge all souls and bring the world to an end. The first generation of Christians expected this second coming to occur quickly, which may be one of the reasons that formal organization was not stressed in the early Church.

From the beginning, Christians not only accepted the ethical teachings of Jesus but also worshiped him as the Christ, the "anointed" one. In the Gospels, Jesus repeatedly distinguishes between himself ("the Son of Man") and God ("the Father"), but he also makes the statement "I and the Father are one." And in one account, he instructs his followers to baptize all persons "in the name of the Father and the Son and the Holy Spirit." Hence, Christianity became committed to the difficult and sophisticated notion of a single divinity with three aspects. Christ was the "Son" or "Second Person" in a **Holy Trinity** that was nevertheless one God. The doctrine of the Trinity produced a great deal of heated theological controversy over the centuries. But it also gave Christians the unique advantage of a single, infinite, philosophically respectable God who could be worshiped and adored in the person of the charismatic, lovable, tragic Jesus.

THE EARLY CHURCH

The first generation of Christians witnessed the beginning of a deeply significant process whereby the Judeo-Christian heritage was modified and enriched through contact with Graeco-Roman culture. Jesus' own apostles were little influenced by Greek thought, and some of them sought to keep Christianity strictly within the ritualistic framework of Judaism. But **Saint Paul,** an early convert who was both a Jew and a Roman citizen, succeeded in steering the Church toward a more encompassing goal. Christians were not to be bound by the strict Jewish dietary laws or the requirement of circumcision (which would have severely diminished Christianity's attraction to adult, non-Jewish males). The new faith would be open to all people everywhere who were willing to accept Jesus as God and Savior— and open also to the bracing winds of Graeco-Roman thought.

Saint Paul traveled far and wide across the Roman Empire, winning converts and establishing Christian communities in many towns and cities of the Mediterranean basin. Other Christian missionaries, among them Saint Peter and Jesus' other apostles, also devoted their lives to traveling, preaching, and organizing, often at the cost of ridicule and martyrdom. Their work was tremendously effective, for by the end of the apostolic generation, Christianity had become a force to be reckoned with among the impoverished towns-people of Italy and the east. Within another century, it had spread through most of the Roman Empire. The urban poor found it easy to accept a savior who had worked as a carpenter, had surrounded himself with fishermen and ex-prostitutes, had been crucified by the imperial authorities, and had promised salvation to all who followed him—free or slave, man or woman.

From the first, Christians engaged regularly in a sacramental meal of bread and wine that came to be called the Eucharist (the Greek word for "thanksgiving"), or Holy Communion. It was viewed as an indispensable channel of divine grace through which the Christian was infused with the spirit of Christ. By means of another sacrament, baptism, one was initiated into the fellowship of the Church, had all sins forgiven, and received the grace (moral strength) of the Holy Spirit. A person could be baptized only once, and baptized people alone could consider themselves members of the Christian community. In the early Church, baptism was often delayed until adulthood, and many unbaptized persons were therefore associated with Christian communities without being Christians in the full sense. Because baptism erased all sins, some put it off until they were nearing death.

As Christian historical documents become more common, in the second and third centuries A.D., the organization of the Church begins to emerge more sharply. These documents disclose an important distinction between the clergy, who governed the Church and administered the sacraments, and the laity whom they served. The clergy, initiated into the Christian priesthood through the ceremony of ordination, were divided into several ranks. The most important were the **bishops,** who served as spiritual leaders of Christian urban communities, and the ordinary priests, who conducted religious services and administered the Eucharist under a bishop's jurisdiction.* The most powerful of the bishops were the "metropolitans," or archbishops, of the more important cities, who supervised the bishops in their districts. Atop the hierarchy were the bishops of the three or four greatest cities of the Empire: Rome, Alexandria, Antioch, and later Constantinople. These leaders, known as "patriarchs," exercised spiritual authority (often more theoretical than real) across vast areas of the Mediterranean world.

In time, the bishop of Rome came to be regarded more and more as the highest of the patriarchs. His preeminence was based on the tradition that Saint Peter, foremost among Jesus' twelve apostles, had spent his last years in Rome and suffered martyrdom there. Saint Peter was held to have been the first bishop of Rome—the first pope—and later popes regarded themselves as his direct successors. Nevertheless, the establishment of effective papal authority over even the Western part of the Church was to require the efforts of many centuries.

---

*The Latin word for bishop is *episcopus,* from which are derived such English words as "episcopal" (having to do with a bishop or bishops) and "Episcopalian" (a member of the Anglican communion in America or associated with church government by bishops).

CHRISTIANITY AND CLASSICAL CULTURE

Medieval and modern Christian theologies are products of both Jewish and Greek traditions. The synthesis began not among Christians but among Jews, especially those who had migrated in large numbers to the Graeco-Egyptian metropolis of Alexandria. Here, Jewish scholars—in particular a religious philosopher of the early first century A.D. named **Philo Judaeus**—worked toward the reconciliation of Jewish biblical revelation and Greek philosophy. Drawing from Aristotle, the Stoics, and particularly Plato, they developed a symbolic interpretation of the Old Testament that was to influence both Jewish and Christian thought across the centuries.

Following the lead of Philo Judaeus, Christian theologians strove to demonstrate that their religion was more than merely an appealing myth. Plato and the Bible agreed, so they argued, on the existence of a single God and the importance of living an ethical life. As the expectation of an immediate second coming faded, Christians started to explore their faith more analytically and began to differ among themselves on such difficult issues as the nature of Christ (How could he be both God and man?) and the Trinity (How can three be one?). Some opinions were so inconsistent with the views of most Christian leaders that they were condemned as "heresies." As questions were raised and orthodox solutions agreed on, Christian doctrine became increasingly specific and elaborate.

The early heresies sought to simplify the nature of Christ and the Trinity. A group known as Gnostics, claiming apostolic origins and echoing Persian dualism, insisted that Christ was not truly human but only a divine phantom: because the material world was evil, God could not have degraded himself by assuming a flesh-and-blood body. Others maintained that Christ was not fully divine, not an equal member of the Trinity. This last position was taken up in the fourth century by a group of Christians known as Arians (after their leader, Arius), who spread their view throughout the Roman Empire and beyond.

The position that came to be defined as orthodox lay midway between **Gnosticism** and **Arianism:** Christ was fully human and fully divine. He was a coequal member of the Holy Trinity who had always existed and always would, but who had assumed human form and flesh at a particular moment in time and had walked the earth, taught, suffered, and died as the man Jesus. In this way, the characteristic Christian synthesis of matter and spirit was strictly preserved, and Christ remained the bridge between the two worlds.

The intellectual defenders of early Christianity are known as "apologists." In upholding Christian orthodoxy against polytheist attacks from without and heterodox attacks from within, they played a crucial role in formulating and elaborating Christian doctrine, coping with problems that had not occurred to the apostolic generation. It is of the highest significance that many early Christian writers worked within the framework of the Greek philosophical tradition. The greatest of them, the Alexandrian theologian **Origen** (d. A.D. 254), constructed a coherent, all-inclusive Christian philosophical system on Platonic foundations. Origen's religious system did not win over the pagan intellectual world with one blow. Indeed, several of his conclusions were rejected by later Christian orthodoxy, but he and other Christian theologians succeeded in making their faith meaningful and intellectually attractive to those whose thinking was cast in the Graeco-Roman philosophical mold. The greatest of the Greek philosophers, so these Christian writers said, had, without realizing it, been led toward truth by the inspiration of the Christian God.

CHRISTIANITY AND THE EMPIRE

At the very time that Christian theology was being Hellenized, the thoughts of some polytheists were shifting increasingly toward otherworldliness. Origen's greatest polytheist contemporary was the Neoplatonist Plotinus. With the growth of a transcendental outlook throughout the ancient world, Christianity increasingly appealed to an age hungry for a consoling doctrine of personal redemption. Yet, its triumph was by no means assured, for it faced competing promises of salvation (at least during this life), such as those offered by Mithraism, the Isis cult, and traditional Graeco-Roman polytheism in its new, Neoplatonic armor.

Against these rivals, Christianity could offer the immense appeal of the historic Jesus, the growing profundity of its theology, the infinite majesty of its God, and the compassion and universalism of its message, which was preserved and dramatized in its canonical books, the Hebrew Bible and the so-called New Testament. Few social groups were immune to its attraction. The poor, humble, and underprivileged probably made up the bulk of its early converts, and it was to them that Jesus had directed much of his message. Intellectuals were drawn by its Hellenized theology, townspeople by its mysticism, and bureaucrats by the ever-increasing effectiveness of its administrative hierarchy. For in administration no less than in theology, the Church was learning from the Graeco-Roman world.

Before the collapse of the Roman Empire in the West, Christianity had absorbed and turned to its own purposes much of Rome's heritage in political organization and law, carrying on the Roman administrative and legal tradition into the medieval and the modern world. The Church modeled its canon law on Roman civil law. The polytheist leadership of the Roman Empire gave way to the spiritual leadership of the Roman Church. The pope assumed the old republican and imperial title *pontifex maximus* (supreme pontiff) and preserved much of the imperial ritual of the later Empire. In this organizational sense, the medieval Church has been described as a ghost of the Roman Empire. Yet it was far more than that, for the Church reached its people as Rome never had, giving the poor majority a sense of participation and involvement that the Empire had failed to provide.

From the beginning, the Christians of the Empire had been a people apart—convinced that they alone possessed the truth and that the truth would one day triumph. Eager to win new converts, they were uncompromising in their rejection of all other religious theologies and practices. They were willing to learn from the pagan world but unwilling ever to submit to it. They angered their polytheist contemporaries by their sense of destiny and by their cohesiveness (which doubtless appeared to outsiders as clannishness). Their refusal to offer sacrifices to the state gods resulted in imperial persecution, but only intermittently. Horrifyingly violent purges such as those under Nero and Marcus Aurelius were very limited in scope and alternated with long periods of official inaction. The persecutions could be cruel and terrifying, but they were neither sufficiently ruthless nor sufficiently sustained to exterminate the whole Christian community, and the martyrdoms only strengthened the resolve of those who survived.

Most emperors, if they persecuted Christians at all, did so reluctantly. The "good emperor" Trajan instructed a provincial governor, the administrator and letter writer Pliny the Younger, neither to hunt Christians down nor to heed anonymous accusations. Such a procedure, Trajan observed, is inconsistent with "the spirit of the age."

Christians were to be punished only if they were formally accused, tried, and convicted and then persisted in their refusal to venerate the imperial gods. One can admire the Christian who would rather face death than worship false gods, but one can also sympathize with emperors who hesitated to apply their traditional policy of religious toleration to these obstinate, exasperating people who seemed bent on subverting the Empire.

The persecutions of the first and second centuries A.D., although occasionally severe, tended to be limited to specific local areas. The Empire-wide persecutions of the third and early fourth centuries were products of a crisis in Roman civilization. The greatest imperial persecution, and the last, occurred at the opening of the fourth century under Emperor **Diocletian.** By then, Christianity was too deeply entrenched to be destroyed, and the failure of Diocletian's persecution made it evident that the Empire had little choice but to accommodate the Church.

A decade after the outbreak of this last persecution, **Constantine,** the first Christian emperor, dramatically reversed imperial religious policy. He legalized and favored the Church while continuing to tolerate the traditional Graeco-Roman cults. His successors, with one exception, supported Christianity more and more vigorously until, toward the end of the fourth century A.D., Christianity became the official religion of the Empire, most of whose inhabitants had by then been brought into the Christian fold. Rome and Jerusalem had come to terms at last.

CHAPTER 14

The Dominate

THE THIRD CENTURY A.D.

The turbulent third century A.D.—the era of Origen and Plotinus—brought major changes to the Roman Empire. The age of the "five good emperors" (A.D. 96–180) was followed by a hundred troubled years during which civil anarchy alternated with military despotism. Under increased pressures from external peoples, imperial survival came to depend more than ever on military defense. And the Roman legions, well aware of that fact, made and unmade emperors. Roman armies battled one another repeatedly for control of the imperial office until (to exaggerate only slightly) a man might be a general one day, emperor the next, and dead the third. There were no fewer than eighteen emperors during the calamitous half-century between A.D. 235 and 284, not to mention innumerable usurpers and pretenders whose plots contributed to the general chaos. In this fifty-year period, every emperor save one died violently—by assassination or in battle. The silver age had given way to what one contemporary historian described as an age of "iron and rust."

CAUSES OF THE THIRD-CENTURY ANARCHY

Imperial succession was a crucial problem, and all too often it was solved by force alone. As the power of the army increased and military rebellions became commonplace, the succession depended more and more on the whim of the troops. Perhaps the most successful emperor of the period, **Septimius Severus** (A.D. 193–211), maintained his power by expanding and pampering the army, opening its highest offices to every class, and broadening its recruitment. A military career was now the logical springboard to high civil office, and the bureaucracy began to display an increasingly military cast of mind. The old ideals of Republic and Principate were less and less meaningful to those now in power, many of whom had risen from the dregs of society through successful army careers to positions of high political responsibility. These new administrators were often strong and able, but they were not the sort who could be expected to be sensitive to old Roman political traditions. As emperors such as Septimius Severus increased taxes to fatten their treasuries and appease their troops, the civilian population was becoming powerless and impoverished. Septimius's deathbed advice to his sons "not to disagree, give money to the soldiers, and ignore the rest" is characteristic of his reign and his times.

But Rome's troubles in the third century cannot be ascribed entirely to the problem of imperial succession. As early as the reign of Marcus Aurelius (A.D. 161–180), the empire had been struck by a devastating plague that lingered on for a generation and by Germanic tribes that spilled across the Rhine-Danube frontier as far as Italy itself. Marcus Aurelius, the philosopher-emperor, was obliged to spend the greater part of his reign campaigning against the invaders, and it was only by enormous effort that he was able to drive them out of the Empire. During the third century, the Germans attacked repeatedly, penetrating the frontiers time and again, forcing the cities to erect protective walls, and threatening for a time to destroy the Empire altogether. And the Germanic onslaught was accompanied by attacks from the east by the recently reconstituted Persian-Iranian Empire, led by the able kings of its new **Sassanid** dynasty (A.D. 224–651).

But Rome's crucial problems were internal. During the third century, political disintegration was accompanied by social and economic breakdown. The ever-rising fiscal demands of the mushrooming bureaucracy and insatiable army placed a crushing burden on the inhabitants of town and countryside alike. Peasants fled their fields to escape the hated tax collector, and the urban middle classes became shrunken and demoralized. The self-governing city, the bedrock of imperial administration and, indeed, of Graeco-Roman civilization itself, was beginning to experience grave financial difficulties, and as one city after another turned to the emperor for financial aid, civic autonomy diminished. These problems arose partly from the parasitical nature of many of the Roman cities, partly from rising imperial taxes, and partly from the economic stagnation that was slowly gripping the Empire. Long before the death of Marcus

Aurelius, Rome had largely abandoned its career of conquest in favor of a defensive policy of consolidation. As the flow of booty ceased, the Empire was thrown back on its own resources and forced to become economically self-sufficient. For a while, all seemed well, but as administrative and military expenses mounted without corresponding growth in commerce and industry, the imperial economy began to suffer. The army, once a source of riches from conquered lands, was becoming an economic deadweight.

By the third century, if not before, the Roman economy was shrinking. Plagues, hunger, and a sense of hopelessness resulted in a gradual decline in population. At the very time when imperial expenses and taxes were rising, the tax base was contracting. Prosperity gave way to depression and desperation, and the flight of peasants from their farms was accompanied by the flight of the savagely taxed middle classes from their cities. The Empire was now clogged with beggars and bandits, and those who remained at their jobs were taxed all the more heavily.

It was the western half of the Empire that suffered most. What industry there was had always been centered in the East, and money was gradually flowing eastward to productive centers in Syria, Asia Minor, and beyond to pay for luxury goods, some of which came from outside the Empire altogether—from Persia, India, and China. In short, the Empire as a whole, and its western part especially, suffered from an unfavorable balance of trade that resulted in a steady reduction in Rome's supply of precious metals.

The increasingly desperate financial circumstances of the third-century Empire forced the emperors to reduce the value of the coinage, blending the precious metals in their coins with baser metals. This policy provided only temporary relief. In the long run, it resulted in runaway inflation that further undermined the economy and hastened the decline of the commercial class. Between A.D. 256 and 280, the cost of living rose 1,000 percent.

The third-century anarchy reached its climax during the 260s A.D. By then, the Roman economy was virtually in ruins. Germanic armies had burst through the frontiers. Gaul and Britain in the West and a large district in the East had broken loose from imperial control and were pursuing independent courses. The population was shrinking, and cities were decaying. Pirates once again roved the Mediterranean, and robbers waylaid travelers on the Roman roads. Total political collapse seemed imminent.

The Empire survived this crisis, but only through the tremendous efforts of a series of determined leaders who rose to power in the later third century A.D. The Roman state survived in the West for another two centuries and in the East for more than a thousand years. But the agonies of the third century left an indelible mark on the reformed Empire. The new imperial structure that brought order out of chaos was vastly different from the government of the Principate: it was an autocracy undisguised by republican trappings.

THE REFORMS OF DIOCLETIAN

Even at the height of the anarchy, there were emperors who strove desperately to defend the Roman state. After A.D. 268, a series of able, rough-hewn emperor-generals from the Danubian provinces managed to turn the tide. They restored the frontiers, smashing the invading armies of Germans and Persians and recovering lost provinces in Gaul and the East. At the same time, the emperors took measures to stem social and economic decay. These policies were expanded and brought to fruition by Diocletian (A.D. 284–305) and Constantine (A.D. 306–337), to whom belong the credit—and responsibility—for reconstituting the Empire along authoritarian lines. No longer merely a *princeps* (in theory, a first among equals), the emperor was now *dominus et deus* (lord and god), and it is appropriate that the new despotic regime that replaced the Principate should be called the Dominate.

In the days of Augustus, it had been necessary to disguise the power of the emperor so as not to offend republican sensibilities. In Diocletian's day, the imperial title had for so long been abused that it was necessary to exalt it. Borrowing from Hellenistic and Persian court ceremonial, Diocletian and his successors employed all the known techniques of costume, makeup, and drama to make themselves appear majestic. Everyone had to fall prostrate in the emperor's presence, and Constantine added the touch of wearing a diadem on his head.

Diocletian's most immediate task was to bring to a close the turbulent era of short-lived "barracks emperors" and military usurpers. In order to stabilize the succession and share the ever-growing burden of governing the Empire, he decreed in A.D. 293 that there would thenceforth be two emperors—one in the East, the other in the West—who were to work together harmoniously for the welfare and defense of the state. Each would be known by the title Augustus, and each would adopt a younger colleague, with the title Caesar, to share his rule and ultimately succeed him. Diocletian reorganized the Empire into four administrative districts, each supervised by an Augustus or a Caesar.* At the same time, the Old Roman provinces (about forty-four of them) were divided into about 100 smaller units to ensure closer control.

Well aware of the increasing importance of the eastern over the western half of the Empire, Diocletian made his capital in the East and did not set foot in Rome until the close of his reign. A usurper would now, presumably, be faced with the daunting task of overcoming four widely scattered personages instead of one. The chances of military usurpation were further reduced by Diocletian's rigorous separation of civil and military authority. He enlarged the army, chiefly by incorporating Germanic forces, which now assumed much of the burden of guarding the frontiers. But by restricting the jurisdiction of generals over civilian districts, he reduced their power and increased his own.

Imperial control was the keynote of the new regime. Diocletian based his power not only on the authority of the army but also on that of the gods, closely associating himself with Jupiter (as seen on his coins). The Senate was now largely ornamental, and the emperor ruled through his obedient and continuously expanding bureaucracy, issuing edict after edict to regulate and regiment the state. He circumvented the shortage of money by imposing a new land tax to be collected in kind every year after an assessment, and he reduced the widespread flight from productive labor by issuing new laws freezing peasants, artisans, and merchants in their jobs. A system of hereditary social orders quickly developed, a virtual caste system in which sons were required by law to take up the careers and tax burdens of their fathers. Peasants were bound to the land and city dwellers to their urban professions. Workers in the mines and quarries were literally branded.

The quasi-caste system, however, was more theoretical than real, for these measures were difficult to enforce, and a degree of social mobility remained. Nevertheless, the Dominate was a relatively regi-

---

*Scholars sometimes refer to the resulting system of government as the **Tetrarchy**, literally, "fourth part of an *arche* (rule)."

mented society. Economic collapse was temporarily averted, but at the cost of social petrification and loss of hope. The once autonomous cities lay in the grip of the imperial government. Commitment to the Empire was rapidly waning among the tax-ridden urban middle class, which had formerly been among its most enthusiastic supporters but was now (as one historian has put it) condemned for life.

But it was Diocletian's mission to save the Empire whatever the cost, and it may well be that authoritarian measures were necessary. For every problem, Diocletian offered a solution—often heavy-handed, but a solution nevertheless. A thoroughgoing currency reform had retarded inflation but had not stopped it altogether, so Diocletian issued an edict in late A.D. 301 fixing the prices of most commodities by law. To the growing challenge of Christianity, Diocletian responded in A.D. 303 with a persecution of unprecedented severity, which eventually included the burning of Scriptures and the destruction of churches, the banning of meetings of worshipers, the imprisonment of clergy, and an order for universal sacrifice. As it turned out, neither the imperial price controls nor the imperial persecution achieved their ends. But the very fact that they were attempted illustrates the lengths to which the emperor would go in his effort to hold together the Roman state.

The four-part division of the Empire among the two Augusti and the two adopted Caesari was an imaginative attempt at political reform, but it worked effectively only as long as Diocletian himself was in command. Once his hand was removed (after he abdicated voluntarily in A.D. 305), a struggle for power brought renewed civil strife. The principle of adoption, which the sonless Diocletian had revived without serious difficulty, was challenged by the sons of his successors. The era of chaos ran from the end of Diocletian's reign in A.D. 305 to the victory of Constantine over the last of his rivals in A.D. 312 at the battle of the Milvian Bridge.

THE REIGN OF CONSTANTINE (A.D. 306–337)

Constantine's triumph at the Milvian Bridge near Rome marked the return of political stability and the consummation of Diocletian's economic and political reforms. In an edict of A.D. 332, Constantine tightened Diocletian's policy of freezing occupations and making them hereditary. He increased imperial authority and embellished imperial ceremony. But in certain respects, Constantine moved in radical new directions. In place of the abortive principle of adoption, Constantine founded an imperial dynasty of his own.

For a time, Constantine shared his authority with an imperial colleague (his brother-in-law), but in A.D. 324 he conquered him and thereafter ruled alone. Nevertheless, the joint rule of an eastern and a western emperor became common in the years after Constantine's death, and he himself contributed to the division of the Empire by building a magnificent eastern capital, Constantinople (Constantine's City), on the site of the ancient Greek colony of Byzantium (now modern Istanbul).

Constantinople was a second Rome. It had its own Senate, its own imposing palaces and public buildings, and its own hungry proletariat fed by the bread dole and diverted by chariot races in its enormous Hippodrome. A few decades after its foundation, it even acquired its own Christian patriarch. Constantine plundered the Graeco-Roman world of artistic treasures to adorn his new city, and he lavished his vast resources on its construction. Consecrated in A.D. 330, Constantinople was to remain the capital of the Eastern Empire for well over a thousand years, impregnable behind its great landward and seaward walls and perpetually renewing itself through its control of the rich commerce flowing between the Black Sea and the Mediterranean. The age-old survival of the Eastern Empire owes much to the superb strategic location that Constantine chose for its capital. The lands that its emperors ruled are known to historians as the Byzantine Empire, after old Byzantium, although the proud inhabitants of the Eastern Empire simply called themselves "Romans."

Even more momentous than the building of Constantinople was Constantine's controversial conversion to Christianity and his (much better documented) reversal of imperial policy toward the Church. Constantine's conversion has been dated by historians to a religious vision he claimed to have had before the battle of the Milvian Bridge in A.D. 312: a vision of a single cross (presumably a symbol of the crucifixion) above the sun, with the words "Be victorious in this." Careful analysis of the sources for this Christian vision has shown, however, that Constantine made this claim only many years after the battle. Moreover, it is also evident that he continued to permit polytheistic practices well after A.D. 312, the date of his supposed conversion to Christianity. Constantine's dedication of his great new city of Constantinople in A.D. 330, for instance, included both polytheistic rites and Christian ceremonies. In Italy itself, Constantine also allowed the continuation of the Old Roman cult of the emperors.

There can be no doubt, however, that after A.D. 312 Constantine issued a series of pro-Christian edicts ensuring full toleration, legalizing bequests to the Church (which accumulated prodigiously over the subsequent centuries), and granting a variety of other privileges. He also built many churches, granted compensation to Christians who had suffered persecution, and involved himself in church organization and theological disputes. Although he put off baptism until his dying moments (as many Christians did), there is no reason to doubt his clear commitment to the Christian God after A.D. 312, at any rate. Like Diocletian, he based his authority on divine sanction, substituting Christ for Jupiter. The Church, he hoped, would serve as a source of unity—a cement to bind together a fragmented empire. Christianity was now an officially recognized, legal religion. It was not yet the official religion of the state, but it would become so before the end of the fourth century A.D.

THE CHRISTIAN EMPIRE

The respite gained by Diocletian's reforms and Constantine's promotion of the Church made it possible for the Church to develop rapidly under the benevolent protection of the Empire. In the generations following Constantine's reign, Christianity enjoyed the active support of a line of Christian emperors. Several of the great aisled churches that remain standing in Rome today—Santa Maria Maggiore, Santa Sabina, Saint John Lateran, Saint Paul Outside the Walls—were built at imperial expense. The fights to the death by gladiators, which had traditionally provided savage amusement for the urban masses, gave way (in popularity) under Christian influence to the less bloodthirsty sport of chariot racing. The practice of crucifixion ceased. Finally, infanticide was prohibited by imperial law. It was repugnant to Christians, as it had always been to Jews, and it was losing much of its social utility in an era of declining population. Slavery continued, for the imperial economy could not survive without it. The Church urged its members to free their slaves, but few, including churchmen themselves, were willing to comply and suffer the resulting economic ruin.

Interior of Santa Sabina, Rome
Like the original Saint Peter's in Rome, Santa Sabina (A.D. 422–432) follows
the traditional basilica form, which was developed by the Romans for public judicial and commercial use: rectangular, with a wide main aisle, narrow side aisles separated by arched colonnades, and an apse at the end of
one long side. (© *Archivo Iconografico, S.A./Corbis*)

Rich and poor alike now flocked to the Christian faith. Although
polytheism continued to survive, particularly in the countryside,
Christianity had grown by the end of the fourth century to become
the dominant religion of the Mediterranean world. In A.D. 312, perhaps less than 10 percent of the inhabitants of the Western Empire
were Christians (in the Eastern Empire, the figure might have been
higher), whereas by the century's end the Christians were in the majority. No longer persecuted and disreputable, Christianity was now
official, conventional, and respectable. But it lost some of its former
spiritual intensity in the process. Bishops and patriarchs now tended
to come from wealthy aristocratic families. And as so often happens
in human institutions, victory was accompanied by an intensifica-

tion of internal disputes and increasingly aggressive intolerance of different views, in this case, polytheism.

Fourth-century Christianity was wracked by doctrinal struggles to such a degree that a contemporary Latin historian, Ammianus Marcellinus, could remark, "No wild beasts are such enemies to mankind as are most Christians to each other." In theological controversies, as in so many other matters affecting the fourth-century Church, the Christian emperors played a determining role. It was only with imperial support that Arianism, the most powerful of the fourth-century heresies, was at length suppressed within the Empire.

To their opponents, the Arian belief in Christ's subordination to God the Father was a perversion of the true doctrine of the Trinity—the equality and co-divinity of Father, Son, and Holy Spirit. Constantine sought to heal the Arian-Trinitarian dispute by summoning an ecumenical (universal) council of Christian bishops at **Nicaea** in A.D. 325. He had no strong convictions himself, but the advocates of the Trinitarian position managed to win his support. With imperial backing, a strongly anti-Arian creed was adopted almost unanimously. The three divine Persons of the Trinity were declared equal: Jesus Christ was "of one substance with the Father."

But Constantine was no theologian. In later years, he waffled— sometimes favoring Arians, sometimes condemning them—and imperial policy remained ambiguous throughout most of the fourth century. Indeed, one of Constantine's fourth-century successors, **Julian the Apostate,** reversed Constantine's policy of favoring the Christian Church and attempted to revive the old polytheistic cults. Julian was unsuccessful, however, largely because his reign lasted for only a few years, from A.D. 361 to A.D. 363. (Julian was wounded and subsequently died during some kind of melée while campaigning against the Persians.)

Eventually, however, the sternly orthodox **Theodosius** I (A.D. 379–395) banned the teachings of the Arians and broke their power, making orthodox Christianity the one legal religion of the Empire. Theodosius outlawed polytheism as well, and the old gods of Rome, deprived of imperial sanction, gradually shuffled offstage (although there is abundant evidence that polytheists continued to make their traditional sacrifices to the ancient gods and goddesses into the sixth century A.D.).

Christianity now dominated the Empire, but its triumph, won with the aid of political force, was far from complete. For one thing, the mass conversions of the fourth century tended to be superficial. Conversion to Christianity was the path of least resistance, and the new converts were on the whole a far cry from the earlier society of saints and martyrs. It was at this time that many ardent Christians, discontented with mere membership in a respectable, workaday church, began taking to the desert as hermits or flocking into monastic communities. Religious communities for women grew and flourished, offering a new kind of freedom from male authority previously unknown to women of the ancient world.

Despite the policies of Emperor Theodosius, the imperial program of enforced orthodoxy proved difficult to carry out. Old heresies lingered and vigorous new ones arose. Even Arianism survived—not widely among the citizens of the Empire but among the Germanic peoples. For, during the mid-fourth century, at a time when Arianism was still strong in the Empire, several Germanic tribes had been converted to Christianity by Arian missionaries, and the Trinitarian policies of Theodosius I had no effect on them. Consequently, when these tribes poured into the Western Empire and established successor states on its ruins, they found themselves divided from their Roman subjects not only by language and custom but by religion as well.

By accepting imperial support against polytheism and heresy, the Church sacrificed much of its earlier independence. Many Christians of Constantine's day were so awestruck by the emperor's favoritism toward Christianity that they tended to exalt him. As a Christian, although of somewhat uncertain orthodoxy, Constantine could no longer claim divinity, but Christian writers such as the historian Eusebius allowed him a status that was almost godly. To Eusebius and some of his contemporaries, Constantine was the thirteenth apostle, the master of all churches, the divinely chosen ruler of the Roman people. His commanding position in ecclesiastical affairs is illustrated by his domination of the Council of Nicaea, and the ups and downs of Arianism in the following decades depended largely on the whims of his successors.

In the Eastern Empire, this glorification of the imperial office ripened into the notion that the emperor was God's agent on earth. Church and state tended to merge under the sacred authority of the emperors at Constantinople. Indeed, the Christianization and sanctification of the imperial office were potent forces in winning for the eastern emperors the allegiance and commitment of the masses of their Christian subjects. Religious loyalty to the Christian emperor provided indispensable nourishment to the eastern Roman state over the ensuing centuries. Conversely, widespread hostility toward imperial orthodoxy in those districts of the Near East that were dominated by heretical groups resulted in the alienation and eventual loss by the Byzantine Empire of several of its wealthiest provinces.

The veneration of Christian emperors was less marked in the West, for as the fifth century dawned the Western Empire was visibly failing. Western churchmen were beginning to realize that Christian civilization was not irrevocably bound to the fortunes of Rome. Gradually, the western Church began to assert its independence of state control—with the result that church and state in medieval western Europe were never fused but remained in a state of tension.

In the era of the Christian Empire, the culture of Graeco-Roman antiquity was all but transformed. The sense of otherworldliness, which had long been gaining momentum, produced profound changes in literature and art. Rome drifted far from the classical Greek culture that it had inherited—the straightforward, superbly proportioned architecture, the deeply human drama, the bold flights into uncharted regions of rational thought, and the tensely controlled, naturalistic sculpture. Greek classicism had undergone important modifications in the Hellenistic Age and again during the Principate. Now, in the late Empire, the otherworldly mood brought a virtual transmutation of the classical aesthetic.

There had always been a spiritual-mystical element in Graeco-Roman culture, which coexisted with the earthly and concrete. Now the mystical element grew far stronger. More and more of the better minds turned to religious thought, spiritual fulfillment, and the quest for individual salvation. Artists were less interested in portraying physical perfection than in portraying the inner person. The new Christian art depicted slender, heavily robed figures with solemn faces and deep eyes that were thought of as windows into the soul. Techniques of perspective, which the artists of classical antiquity had developed to a fine degree, mattered less to the artists of the late Empire (as they have mattered less to artists of the twentieth century) De-emphasizing physical realism, they embelli[...] rich, dazzling colors that stimulated in the beh[...] enly radiance and religious grandeur. Church[...] glistening mosaics portraying saints and rulers[...] his virgin Mother on luminous backgrounds c[...]

Mosaics, San Apollinare Nuovo
Mosaics on the nave wall of San Apollinare Nuovo, Ravenna (sixth century A.D.), show a procession of Christian virgins holding crowns of martyrdom (below), Old Testament prophets (window level), and scenes from the New Testament (top). The mosaics of this church are characteristic of the anti-classicism of early Christian art: the figures are flat, rigid, presented without background, staring straight at the viewer. They are depicted in glittering, brilliantly colored stones and are meant to evoke awe and reverence rather than to convey a sense of naturalism. (© *Archivo Iconografico, S.A./Corbis*)

was an art vastly different from that of Greek classical antiquity, with different techniques and different goals, yet just as successful as the art of the Athenian golden age and more fundamentally original than anything the Roman Empire had produced before.

DOCTORS OF THE LATIN CHURCH

Constantine's intervention into questions of Church theology has-
ned the process of fusion between Christianity and Graeco-Roman
re. During the generations following his death, the process was

brought to completion by three celebrated scholar-saints—**Ambrose, Jerome,** and **Augustine**—honored in later generations as "Doctors of the Latin Church." Working at a time when the Christianization of the Roman state was far advanced but before the intellectual vigor of the Western Empire had diminished, they used their mastery of Graeco-Roman thought to interpret the Christian faith. Nearly seven centuries were to pass before Western Europe regained the intellectual level of late antiquity, and the writings of these three Latin Doctors therefore exerted a commanding influence on succeeding generations.

Although Ambrose, Jerome, and Augustine made their chief impact in the world of thought, all three were immersed in the political and ecclesiastical affairs of their day. Saint Ambrose (c. A.D. 340–397) was bishop of Milan, which by the later fourth century had replaced Rome as the western imperial capital. He was famed for his eloquence and administrative skill, for his vigor in defending Trinitarian orthodoxy against Arianism, and for the ease and mastery with which he adopted the literary traditions of Cicero and Virgil and the philosophy of Plato to his own Christian purposes. Significantly, he was the first major churchman to assert that in the realm of morality the emperor himself is accountable to the Christian priesthood. After the massacre of thousands in the circus of Thessalonica at Theodosius's order (which had followed the death of the general Butheric in a riot), Ambrose excommunicated the emperor, barring him from the church in the imperial capital of Milan until he had formally and publicly repented. Ambrose's bold stand and Theodosius's submission set a long-remembered precedent for the principle of ecclesiastical superiority in matters of faith and morals.

Saint Jerome (c. A.D. 347–420) was the most celebrated biblical scholar of his time. He was a restless, troubled man with a touch of acid in his tongue. He once remarked to an opponent, "You have the will to lie, good sir, but not the skill to lie." Wandering far and wide throughout the Empire, Jerome studied in Rome for a time but then fled the worldly city eastward to the desert of Chalcis, where he began to learn Hebrew. Later, he returned to Rome, where his association with a widow named Paula helped to make him unpopular with Christians in the city. Hounded from Rome, Jerome made his way to Bethlehem (followed by Paula), where he founded a monastery and a convent. Jerome's monks devoted themselves to the copying of Latin manuscripts, a task that was to be carried on by countless monks in centuries to come and which, in the long run, resulted in the preservation of important works of Graeco-Roman antiquity that otherwise would have perished. The modern world owes a large debt to Jerome and his successors for preserving and transmitting the tradition of Latin letters.

Jerome feared that his love of pagan literary figures such as Homer, Virgil, Horace, and Cicero might dilute his Christian fervor. He told of a dream in which Jesus banished him from heaven with the words, "You are a Ciceronian, not a Christian!" For a time, Jerome renounced all classical writings, but he was much too devoted to the charms of classical literature to persevere. In the end, he concluded that Graeco-Roman letters might properly be used in the service of the Christian faith.

Jerome's supreme achievement lay in the field of scriptural commentary and translation. It was he who produced the definitive translation of the Hebrew Bible and revision of the Gospels from their original Hebrew and Greek into Latin, the language of the Western Roman Empire and subsequently of medieval Western Europe. Despite Jerome's deeply rooted knowledge of classical Greek and Roman authors, his translation of the Bible was executed in simple, accessible Latin. The ultimate result of Jerome's efforts (and his decision to translate the Bible into ordinary, vernacular Latin) was the Latin Vulgate Bible, which Roman Catholics continued to use well into the twentieth century and which has served as the basis of innumerable translations into modern languages. It was an achievement of incalculable significance to Western civilization.

Saint Augustine of Hippo (A.D. 354–430), whose conversion and career are sketched in the accompanying biographical sketch, was the foremost Christian philosopher of Roman antiquity. As bishop of Hippo, he was deeply involved in the political and religious problems of his age. Like Jerome, he worried about the dangerous attractions of classical culture, finally concluding, much as Jerome did, that Graeco-Roman learning, although not to be enjoyed for its own sake, might properly be used to elucidate the faith.

Augustine was the chief architect of medieval theology. Even more than his contemporaries, he succeeded in fusing Christian doctrine with Greek thought, especially the philosophy of Plato and the Neoplatonists (since Augustine never mastered Greek). It has been said that Augustine "baptized" Plato. As Saint Thomas Aquinas later observed, looking back from the thirteenth century, "Whenever Augustine, who was expert in the Platonists, found in their teaching anything consistent with faith, he adopted it; those things which he found contrary to faith, he amended."

Plato had taught that abstract ideas were more important than tangible things (see pages 126–129). As a Platonist, Augustine therefore stressed the importance of ideas, or archetypes, over material objects, but instead of locating his archetypes in the abstract Platonic "heaven," he placed them in the mind of God. The human mind had access to the archetypes through an act of God that Augustine called "divine illumination."

Against the several heretical doctrines that threatened Christian orthodoxy in his day, Augustine wrote clearly and persuasively on the nature of the Trinity, the problem of evil in a world created by God, the special character of the Christian priesthood, and the nature of free will and predestination. His most influential work, *City of God,* was prompted by a barbarian sack of Rome in A.D. 410, which the polytheists ascribed to Rome's desertion of its old gods. Augustine responded by developing a Christian theory of history that interpreted human development not in political or economic but in moral terms. As the first rigorous Christian philosopher of history, Augustine drew heavily on the historical insights of the ancient Hebrews. Like the Hebrew prophets, he asserted that kingdoms and empires rose and fell according to a divine plan, but he insisted that this plan lay forever beyond human comprehension. Augustine rejected the theory, common in antiquity, that history was an endless series of cycles, arguing instead that history was moving toward a divinely appointed goal. This linear view of history set something of a precedent for the modern secular concept of historical progress. As did other Christians, Augustine rejected the Hebrew notion of tribal salvation, emphasizing instead the Christian notion of individual salvation. The ultimate units of history were individual mortal souls, not tribes and empires.

The salvation of souls, Augustine stated, depends not on the fortunes of Rome but on the grace of God. Christ is not dependent on Caesar. And if we look at history from the moral standpoint—from the standpoint of souls—we see not the clash of armies or the rivalry of states, but a far more fundamental struggle between good and evil, which has raged through history and rages even now within each soul. Humanity is divided into two classes: those who live in God's grace and those who do not. The former belong to what Augustine called the City of God, the latter to the Earthly City. The members of the two cities are hopelessly intermixed in this world, but they will be separated at death by eternal salvation or damnation. It is from this transcendental standpoint, Augustine believed, that the Christian must view history. Only God could know what effect Rome's decline would have on the City of God. Perhaps the effect would be beneficial, or perhaps even irrelevant.

Augustine is one of the seminal minds in Christian history. His Christian Platonism governed medieval theology until well into the twelfth century and remains influential in Christian thought today. His emphasis on the special sacramental power inherent in the priestly office remains a keystone of Catholic theology. His emphasis on divine grace and predestination, although softened considerably by the medieval Church, reemerged in the sixteenth century to dominate early Protestant doctrine. And his theory of the two cities, although often in simplified form, had an enormous influence on Western historical and political thought over the next millennium.

Ambrose, Jerome, and Augustine were at once synthesizers and innovators. The last great minds of the Western Empire, they operated at a level of intellectual sophistication that the Christian West would not reach again for 700 years. The strength of the classical tradition that underlies medieval Christianity and Western civilization owes much to the fact that these men, and others like them, struggled with the issue of how to be both Christians and Ciceronians.

Saint Augustine of Hippo

In his *Confessions*—the first major autobiography ever written—Augustine (A.D. 354–430) described his long intellectual and moral journey along a twisting path from youthful hedonism to Christian piety. He did so in the form of a long prayer, a confession to God, written in the hope that others, lost as he once was, might enter the spiritual haven of the Church.

Augustine told of his dissolute boyhood and early manhood in the North African portion of the Roman Empire. Despite the prayers and admonitions of his Christian mother, Monica (later known as Saint Monica or Santa Monica), he rejected her faith. He took a mistress, who bore him a son. He studied Greek philosophy and rhetoric as translated into Latin. And he drifted from one philosophy or popular creed to another: from Ciceronian philosophy to Manicheism, from Gnostic wisdom to Christianized Neoplatonism, and finally, from Neoplatonism to Catholicism. It was not until the age of thirty-two that he was fully converted to the "Divine Philosophy" of Christianity.

Indeed, Augustine's conversion occurred in stages while he was teaching rhetoric in Milan. Out of curiosity, he went to hear the preaching of Milan's eloquent and renowned Christian bishop, Ambrose, and he was profoundly moved. "I came to damn," Augustine said, "and stayed to praise."

Nevertheless, Augustine was not yet prepared to abandon his life of wine and women. While in Milan, he became betrothed to a wealthy heiress not yet of marriageable age, and out of respect for his betrothal he parted from the mistress who had borne his son. But as one of Augustine's mid-Victorian biographers disapprovingly and discreetly remarks, "Neither the pain of this parting nor consideration for his not yet marriageable bride prevented him from forming a fresh connection of the same kind." Augustine prayed to God to deliver him from his slavery to the pleasures of the flesh but then added, "Let me wait a little longer."

But Ambrose's sermons and Augustine's own intellectual quest were drawing him more and more deeply into the Christian religion, and the tension between his growing faith and the worldliness of his life was becoming all but unbearable. The great emotional crisis of his life occurred late in the summer of A.D. 386, when a friend told him about the development and spread of Christian monasticism and about how two young imperial officials, betrothed as Augustine was, had abandoned the world and the prospect of marriage to become monks. Profoundly moved, Augustine said to his friend, "What's the matter with us? What does this story mean? These two men have none of our education, yet they rise up and storm the gates of heaven while we, for all our learning, lie here wallowing in this world of flesh and blood."

Overcome by his emotions, Augustine rushed from the house: "I now found myself driven by the torment in my breast to take refuge in the garden, where nobody could interrupt that fierce struggle, in which I was my own opponent, until it reached its conclusion." Augustine tore at his hair and beat his forehead. His past sins seemed to speak to him in tempting whispers: Did he really intend to renounce them forever? His conscience countered: "Close your ears to the unclean whispers of your body." Then, as Augustine reports, "A great storm broke within me, bringing with it a deluge of tears." He flung himself beneath a fig tree, continuing to weep, when he heard a child's voice repeating a phrase over and over again: "Take it and read, take it and read."

In the belief that those words were a divine command, Augustine sought out his copy of Saint Paul's Epistles, opened it at random, and read a passage from the Epistle to the Romans: "No drunken orgies, no promiscuity or licentiousness, and no strife or jealousy. Let your armor be the Lord Jesus Christ, and forget about satisfying your bodies with all their lusts." Augustine wrote: "I had neither the desire nor the need to read further. As I finished the sentence, as though the light of peace had been poured into my heart, all the shadows of doubt dispersed."

Augustine gave up his wealthy bride-to-be, his licentiousness, and his teaching career. Saint Ambrose baptized him in Milan the following Easter, A.D. 387, to the overwhelming joy of his mother Monica, who was at his side.

Augustine subsequently returned to his native North Africa, where he formed a small religious community and headed it for a time. His writings were by now winning him fame throughout the Western Empire. In the 390s, he was dragged unwillingly into Church administration and was appointed bishop of the important North African port city of Hippo in A.D. 395. There, he produced a great quantity of literary and philosophical works of immeasurable importance, including *Confessions* (A.D. 397–400) and *City of God* (A.D. 413–426).

As he wrote, Augustine was also occupied with the day-to-day cares of his diocese and his flock. His contribution to religious thought arises not from the dispassionate working-out of an abstract system of theology but rather from his responses to the urgent issues of the moment. One such issue was the survival of the Roman Empire itself. And by strange, and perhaps revealing, coincidence, in A.D. 430, within months of the death of the man who wrote *City of God*, the Vandals seized his episcopal city of Hippo.

CHAPTER 15

The Waning
of the Western Empire

THE SPLITTING OF EAST AND WEST

Ever since Diocletian's time, the Roman imperial office had been split from time to time between a western and an eastern emperor, and by the close of the fourth century, the split had become permanent. From then on, although the Empire continued to be regarded as a single unit, one emperor ruled the eastern half from Constantinople while another ruled the western half—no longer from Rome but from some more strategically situated capital, first Milan, then Ravenna.

The political split reflected a cultural and linguistic division of long standing. The Latin tongue of the early Romans had spread across the western provinces, but Greek had remained the major language of the East. (The educated elite throughout the Empire tended to be bilingual.) The eastern half of the Empire—Greece, Egypt, and the eastern Mediterranean provinces—had its cultural roots in civilizations that dated back to the fourth millennium B.C. The Eastern Empire contained the bulk of the population; its agriculture was dominated less by owners of vast plantations who, in the West, resisted imperial taxation and, to a degree, imperial authority. The eastern cities were larger, more numerous, and more commercially active than the newer cities of the West, which necessarily suffered from an unfavorable balance of trade.

During the fourth and fifth centuries, the Western Empire's balance of trade with the East grew worse than ever. In exchange for eastern silks, spices, jewels, and grain, it had little to offer except slaves and hunting dogs—and a diminishing supply of gold coins. Thus, with the coming of large-scale Germanic invasions in the fifth century, the Eastern Empire managed to survive, while the political superstructure of the western provinces disintegrated.

"DECLINE AND FALL"

The catastrophe of the "decline and fall of the Roman Empire" has fascinated historians across the centuries, for it involves not only the collapse of one of humanity's most impressive and enduring universal states but also the demise of Graeco-Roman civilization itself. Many reasons have been proposed—no fewer than 210 different causes, according to one survey. They include such factors as climatic changes, diseases, bad ecological habits, sexual orgies, slavery, Christianity, and even lead poisoning. None of them alone is completely persuasive. Classical civilization began and ended with slavery, although it was rather less common in the late Empire than in the Principate. Christianity had deeper roots in the Eastern Empire than in the Western, yet the Eastern Empire carried on for another thousand years. As for orgies, the more spectacular of them occurred during the Principate; Christian conversion made them unstylish, and the fifth-century invasions came long after the age of orgies had passed. One historian proposed the bizarre idea that the fall of Rome was a result of homosexuality—a practice that is much more easily documented in the fifth century B.C. than the fifth century A.D.

More likely causes were the failure of the Roman economy to change or expand and the parasitical character of the western cities. Then, too, the fifth-century western emperors tended to be less competent than their eastern colleagues and more open to the hazardous policy of filling their armies with Germanic troops under Germanic generals. The first-century Empire was sufficiently powerful to endure the rule of Nero and Caligula; the far weaker Western Empire of the fifth century was hard put to survive the rule of such imperial incompetents as **Honorius, Valentinian III,** and **Romulus Augustulus.**

The riddle of Rome's decline and fall will probably never be completely solved, and even the question itself is misleading. For Rome did not literally fall. Instead, it underwent an immense strategic withdrawal from the less productive West to the wealthier, long-civilized provinces of the eastern Mediterranean. Some historians have found it puzzling that the Western Empire endured as long as it did.

The political collapse culminated in the deposition of the last western emperor in A.D. 476, but the true period of crisis was the chaotic third century, when the Empire nearly disintegrated. Viewed against the background of the third-century anarchy, the work of reconstruction under Diocletian and Constantine seems a remarkable achievement. The strong imperial government that emerged at that time became the basis of Byzantine political organization for centuries thereafter. But in the West, the reforms succeeded only temporarily. The death of the body politic was delayed, but the disease remained uncured.

During the generations after Constantine, the economic problems that had plagued the Western Empire in the third century grew more intense. Industrial production continued to lag. Instead of importing manufactured goods from major urban centers, the various regions of the Empire tended more and more to produce them locally, and therefore somewhat less efficiently. The Roman aristocracy generally held aloof from trade and manufacturing; its members preferred to draw their wealth from their great plantations, their status from high public office, and their pleasure from the good company of fellow aristocrats.

The Roman economy remained agrarian to the end, and basic farming techniques advanced very little during the imperial centuries. The Roman plow was adequate but rudimentary, and windmills were unknown. There were some water mills, but nowhere near as many as in, say, eleventh-century England; Roman landowners, continuing to rely on their slaves and coloni, seemed uninterested in labor-saving devices. The horse could not be used as a draft animal on Roman plantations because the Roman harness crossed the horse's windpipe and could strangle the beast under a heavy load. Consequently, Roman agriculture was powered by oxen, slaves, and peasants.

The economic exhaustion of the Western Empire was accompanied by population decline, runaway inflation, and deepening poverty. The army and bureaucracy grew ever larger. The urban middle classes continued to suffer the burden of higher and higher taxes on fewer and fewer taxpayers until, by the fifth century, the western cities were declining sharply in wealth and population. Only the senatorial aristocracy, the small, exclusive class of great landowners, managed to prosper. As early as the third century, they were withdrawing from civic affairs, abandoning their town houses, and retiring to their estates in the country. They warded off marauders and imperial tax collectors alike by assembling armies of their own and fortifying their villas. Having deserted the cities, the aristocracy would remain an agrarian class for the next thousand years.

The decline of the city was damaging to the urbanized administrative structure of the Western Empire. More than that, it crippled the civic culture of Graeco-Roman antiquity. The civilizations of Athens, Alexandria, and Rome could not survive in the fields. It is in the decay of urban society that we find the crucial connecting link between political collapse and cultural transformation. In a very real sense, Graeco-Roman culture was dying long before the demise of the Western Empire; the deposition of the last western emperor in 476 was merely a delayed entombment. By then, the cities were shrinking. The rational outlook of Graeco-Roman classicism had been transformed. The army and even the civil government had become Germanized as the desperate emperors, faced with a growing shortage of people and resources, turned more and more to non-Romans to defend their frontiers and keep order in their state. In the end, Germans abounded in the army, entire tribes were hired to defend the frontiers, and Germanic military leaders came to hold positions of high authority in the Western Empire. Survival had come to depend on the success of Germanic defenders against Germanic invaders.

THE GERMANIC MIGRATIONS

Germanic peoples from central and southeastern Europe had long been pressing against the Empire. They had defeated a Roman army in the first century; they had probed deeply into the Empire in the second century and again in the mid-third. But until the late fourth century, the Romans had always managed eventually to drive the invaders out or absorb them into the Roman political structure. Beginning in the 370s, however, an overtaxed Empire was confronted by renewed Germanic pressures of great magnitude. Lured by the relative wealth, the productive agriculture, and the sunny climate of the Mediterranean world, the Germanic tribes tended to regard the Empire as something to enjoy, not destroy. Their age-long yearning for the fair lands across the Roman frontier was suddenly made urgent by the westward thrust of a tribe of Asiatic nomads known as the **Huns.** These mounted warriors conquered one Germanic tribe after another and turned them into satellites. They subdued the **Ostrogoths** and made them a subject people. Another Gothic group, known subsequently as the **Visigoths,** sought to preserve their independence by appealing for sanctuary behind the Empire's

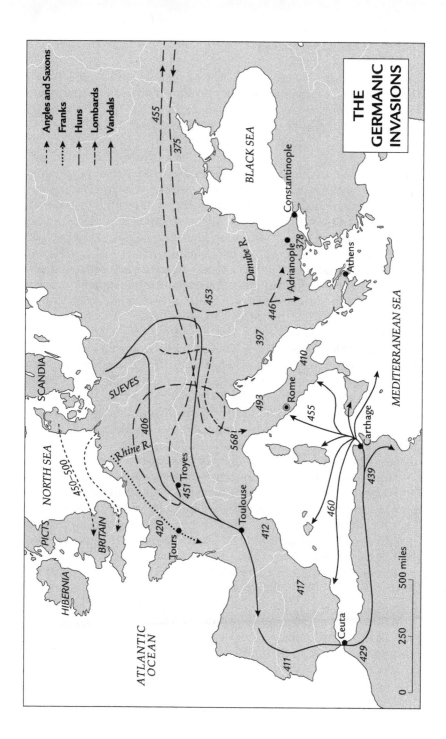

THE GERMANIC INVASIONS

- - - - Angles and Saxons
··········· Franks
⟶ Huns
─ ─ ─ Lombards
⟶ Vandals

NORTH SEA

ATLANTIC OCEAN

HIBERNIA

PICTS

BRITAIN

450–500

Tours
420

Troyes
451

Toulouse

412

417

411

Ceuta
429

SCANDIA

SUEVES

Rhine R.
406

493

568!

397

453

455
375

Danube R.

Adrianople
378

446

Athens

Constantinople

BLACK SEA

Rome
410

455

Carthage

439

460

MEDITERRANEAN SEA

0   250   500 miles

Danube frontier. The eastern emperor **Valens** (c. A.D. 364–378), a devout Arian, sympathized with the Visigoths because they were themselves converts to Arian Christianity. In A.D. 376, he took the unprecedented step of permitting a multitude of Visigoths and associated peoples to cross peacefully into the Empire.

There was trouble almost immediately. Corrupt imperial officials cheated and abused the Visigoths, who retaliated by going on a rampage. At length, Emperor Valens himself took the field against them, but his military incapacity cost him his army and his life at the battle of **Adrianople** in A.D. 378. Adrianople was a military debacle of the first order. Valens's successor, Theodosius I, managed to pacify the Visigoths, but he could not expel them.

When Theodosius died in A.D. 395, imperial authority was split between his two youthful sons. **Arcadius,** barely eighteen, became emperor in the East; Honorius, a child of eleven, assumed authority in the West. As it happened, the two halves were never again rejoined under a single ruler. Not long after Theodosius's death, a new Visigothic leader named **Alaric** led his people on a second pillaging campaign that threatened Italy itself. In A.D. 406, the desperate Western Empire recalled most of its troops from the Rhine frontier to block Alaric's advance, with the disastrous result that in the dead of winter, the Vandals and a number of other Germanic tribes crossed the frozen, ill-guarded Rhine into Gaul. Shortly thereafter, the Roman legions abandoned distant Britain, and the island was gradually overrun by Angles, Saxons, and other Germanic war bands.

In A.D. 408, Emperor Honorius engineered the murder of his ablest general, a man of Vandal ancestry named **Stilicho.** Honorius was by now an adult in his mid-twenties, but the evidence suggests that he was mentally deficient.* He apparently suspected, perhaps with reason, that Stilicho's devotion to the imperial cause was less than fervent. But without Stilicho, Italy was virtually defenseless. Honorius and his court barricaded themselves behind the impregnable marshes of Ravenna, leaving Rome to the mercies of Alaric. On 24 August 410, the Visigoths entered the city unopposed, and Alaric permitted them to plunder it for three days.

The sack of Rome had a devastating impact on imperial morale. "My tongue sticks to the roof of my mouth," wrote Saint Jerome on

---

*For a most ingenious (if not altogether convincing) rehabilitation of Honorius as an astute strategist, see Roger Collins, *Early Medieval Europe, 300–1000* (1991), pp. 51–57.

hearing of the catastrophe, "and sobs choke my speech." But in historical perspective, the event was merely a single milestone in the disintegration of the Western Empire. Leaving Rome to its witless emperor, the Visigoths turned northward into southern Gaul and Spain. There, they established a Visigothic kingdom that endured until the Muslim conquests of the eighth century.

Meanwhile, other Germanic peoples were carving out kingdoms of their own. The Vandals swept through Gaul and Spain and across the Strait of Gibraltar into Africa. In A.D. 430, the year of Saint Augustine's death, they captured his episcopal city of Hippo. They established a North African kingdom centering on ancient Carthage and took to the sea as buccaneers, devastating Mediterranean shipping and sacking coastal cities, including Rome itself in A.D. 455. The Vandal conquest of North Africa cost Rome much of its grain supply, while Vandal piracy shattered the peace of the Mediterranean and dealt a crippling blow to the waning commerce of the Western Empire.

Midway through the fifth century A.D., the Huns moved against the Western Empire, led by **Attila,** the "Scourge of God" (see accompanying biographical sketch). Defeated by a Roman-Visigothic army in Gaul in A.D. 451, the Huns returned the following year, hurling themselves toward Rome and leaving a path of devastation behind them. The western emperor left Rome undefended, but the Roman bishop, Pope **Leo I** (c. A.D. 400–461), somehow persuaded Attila to withdraw from Italy, and Attila died shortly afterward. His empire collapsed, and the Huns vanished from history. They were not mourned.

In its final years, the Western Empire, whose jurisdiction now extended scarcely beyond Italy, fell under the control of hardbitten military adventurers of Germanic birth. Emperors continued to reign for a time, but their Germanic generals were the power behind the throne. In A.D. 476, the general **Odovacar,** who saw no point in perpetuating the farce, deposed the last emperor, a boy named Romulus Augustulus (little Augustus). Odovacar sent the emperor's crown and related paraphernalia to Constantinople and asserted his sovereignty over Italy by diverting a third of the agrarian tax revenues to his Germanic troops. Odovacar claimed to rule as an agent of the Eastern Empire, but in fact he was on his own. A few years later, the Ostrogoths, now free of Hunnish control and led by an astute king named **Theodoric,** advanced into Italy. Theodoric invited

Odovacar to a peace conference, murdered him, and established his own rule over Italy.

THEODORIC AND CLOVIS

Theodoric (c. A.D. 454–526) was king of Italy from A.D. 493 to 526. Although apparently illiterate, he respected Roman culture: Arian Ostrogoths and orthodox Romans worked together harmoniously under his governance, repairing aqueducts, creating new buildings, and bringing a degree of prosperity to the long-troubled peninsula. The improving political and economic climate gave rise to a modest intellectual revival that contributed to the transmission of Graeco-Roman culture into the Middle Ages. At a time when knowledge of Greek was dying out in the West, the philosopher **Boethius** (c. A.D. 480–524), a high official in Theodoric's regime, produced a series of Latin translations of Greek philosophical works that served as fundamental texts in Western schools for the next 500 years. Boethius wrote his masterpiece, *The Consolation of Philosophy,* at the end of his life, when he had fallen from official favor and was in prison awaiting execution. The book's central theme is that earthly misfortunes cannot affect the inner life of a virtuous individual. Although such a notion is consistent with Christianity, Boethius drew his ideas primarily from the thought of Plato and the Stoics. Boethius was himself a Christian, yet he never mentioned Christianity explicitly in his *Consolation of Philosophy.* Nevertheless, this work remained immensely popular throughout the Middle Ages.

Theodoric's secretary, **Cassiodorus,** was another scholar of considerable distinction (though incorrigibly long-winded). A wealthy Roman aristocrat, Cassiodorus spent his later years as abbot of a monastery that he had erected on his own lands in southern Italy. Like Jerome, he set his monks to the task of copying and preserving the literary works of antiquity, both Christian and pagan.

During the years of Theodoric's rule in Ostrogothic Italy, another Germanic king, **Clovis** (A.D. 481–511), was carving out a Frankish kingdom in the former Roman province of Gaul. Although far less Romanized than Theodoric, Clovis possessed a keen instinct for political survival. Going well beyond Theodoric, he adopted the straightforward policy of murdering *all* possible rivals. **Gregory of Tours,** a sixth-century bishop and historian, quotes him as saying, "Oh woe, for I travel among strangers and have none of my kinfolk to help me!" But Gregory adds, "He did not refer to their deaths out of grief, but craftily, to see if he could bring to light some new relative to kill."

It will perhaps seem odd that Bishop Gregory approved wholeheartedly of Clovis's rule. That savage monarch—who lacked even the family loyalty of a mobster—is pictured in Gregory's *History of the Franks* as one who "walked before God with an upright heart and did what was pleasing in His sight." The explanation is that Clovis, untouched by Arianism, was converted directly from Germanic polytheism to orthodox Christianity. He respected and favored the churches, whereas other Germanic rulers were handing them over to the Arians. Clovis himself regarded Christianity as a kind of magic that would help him to win battles (much as the emperor Constantine had done), but the Church supported him as a hero of Christian orthodoxy.

Another reason for Clovis's good press was the relatively warm relations he maintained with the old landholding aristocracy (to which Bishop Gregory of Tours belonged). Because of the depopulated condition of the countryside, there were adequate lands for all, Frank and Gallo-Roman alike. The great landowning families of Roman times were for the most part left in place—to enjoy their fields and their bishoprics and to serve as high officials in the Frankish regime. From their point of view, Clovis's victory was not so much a conquest as a coup d'etat.

In succeeding generations, Frankish and Gallo-Roman landowners, sharing a common religion, fused through intermarriage into a single aristocratic order. As centuries passed, the royal name "Clovis" was softened to "Louis" and the "Franks" became the "French." And the friendship between the Frankish monarchy and the Church developed into one of the determining elements in European politics.

EUROPE IN A.D. 500

As the sixth century dawned, the Western Empire was only a memory. In its place was a group of Germanic successor states that vaguely prefigured the nations of modern Western Europe. Theodoric headed an Ostrogothic-Arian regime in Italy. The orthodox Clovis, still murdering his kinsmen, was completing the Frankish conquest of Gaul. The Arian Vandals lorded it over a restive orthodox Christian population in North Africa, seizing the wheat plantations

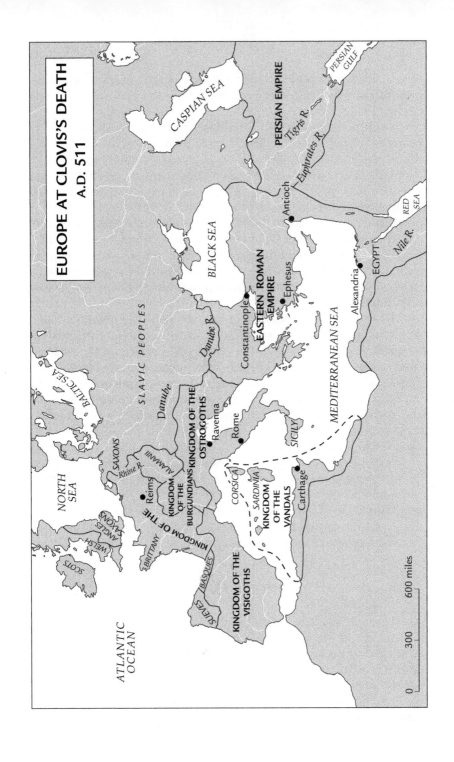

EUROPE AT CLOVIS'S DEATH
A.D. 511

and introducing former aristocratic landholders to the joys of field work. The Arian Visigoths were being driven out of southern Gaul by the Franks, but their regime continued to dominate Spain for the next two centuries. And the Angles and Saxons were in the process of establishing a group of small, non-Christian kingdoms in Britain that would one day coalesce into "Angle-Land," or England.

While Germanic kingdoms were establishing themselves in the West, the Roman papacy was beginning to play an important independent role in European society. We have seen how Leo I, who was pope from A.D. 440 to 461, assumed the task of protecting the city of Rome from the Huns, thereby winning for himself the moral leadership of Italy. Leo and his successors declared that the bishops of Rome—the popes—constituted the highest authority in the Church, and, following the example of Saint Ambrose, they insisted on the supremacy of Church over state in spiritual matters. In proclaiming its doctrines of papal supremacy and ecclesiastical independence, the papacy was wisely disengaging itself from the faltering western emperors. The mighty papacy of the twelfth and thirteenth centuries was yet far off, but it was already foreshadowed in the boldly independent stance of Leo I. The Western Empire was crumbling, but eternal Rome still claimed the allegiance of the Christian world.

THE GRAECO-ROMAN LEGACY

Notwithstanding the collapse of imperial government, the decline of cities, and the victory of a great Near Eastern religion, Graeco-Roman culture never really died in the West. It exerted a profound influence on the fourth-century Doctors of the Latin Church and, through them, on the thought of medieval and early modern Europe. Even the Roman administration survived, through the Middle Ages and beyond, in the organizational structure of the Church. Just as papal Rome echoed imperial Rome, so, too, did the ecclesiastical dioceses and provinces, headed by bishops and archbishops, reflect imperial administrative units that had borne identical names. The bishops of the late Empire had become increasingly involved in imperial governance, participating in numerous civic functions and checking on the activities of Roman officials. When the imperial government perished, bishops filled the vacuum by assuming political control of their dioceses, seeing to the maintenance of the food supply and supervising the repair of walls and fortifications. Since most bishops were by then drawn from officeholding families of the old senatorial aristocracy, such duties came easily to them.

The classical past was the source of repeated cultural revivals great and small down through the centuries: in the era of Charlemagne, in the High Middle Ages, in the Italian Renaissance, in the northern humanist movement of the sixteenth century, and in the neoclassical movements of more recent times. Roman law endured to shape Western jurisprudence. The examples of democratic Athens and republican Rome inspired the framers of modern constitutions, including our own. (Not by accident was the upper house of the American legislature named the "Senate.") The Latin tongue remained the language of educated Europeans for well over a thousand years as it evolved into the Romance languages: Italian, French, Spanish, Portuguese, and Romanian. And the dream of imperial Rome obsessed empire builders from Charlemagne to Napoleon.

In these ways, and countless more, the legacy of classical antiquity has molded our civilization. Across the centuries, the West has been nourished by Graeco-Roman culture and haunted by the memory of Rome.

Attila the Hun, the "Scourge of God"

Attila, leader of the Huns during their invasions of the Roman Empire, is well known but not well loved. His atrocities, although reported in hair-raising detail by contemporary Roman observers, were probably no worse than those of the Roman armies. To the Romans, one of the most terrifying things about the Huns was that, being Asiatic nomads from Mongolia, they did not resemble Romans or Germans in appearance. They were therefore regarded by people of the West as foul and hideously ugly—short and skinny, with low foreheads, high cheekbones, and ritually scarred faces. As one contemporary put it, "Their swarthy aspect was fearful and they had a kind of shapeless lump for a head, with pinholes rather than eyes."

Less biased contemporaries described Attila as brown skinned and broad chested, with deep eyes, an upturned nose, and prematurely gray hair. He ruled the Huns from A.D. 435–453, at first jointly with his brother (who vanished under mysterious circumstances). By about A.D. 440, he and his horsemen had made themselves virtually supreme over the Germanic tribes of central Europe and had frightened the Eastern Roman Empire into paying an annual tribute. Attila established his capital in Pannonia, present-day Hungary, not far from modern Budapest. A report by an ambassadorial mission from Constantinople in A.D. 448 provides a vivid description of Attila and his court. He walked around the wooden buildings of his headquarters with a "dignified strut" and entertained the envoys from Constantinople in his large wooden banquet hall, where attendants served food on silver plates and drink in silver cups. Attila himself drank from a wooden cup typical of older, less elegant, days. At nightfall, "torches were lit and two barbarians approached Attila and sang songs they had composed celebrating his victories and brave deeds in war." Afterward, Attila retired to his bed, on a raised platform in the same hall, to sleep under "linen sheets and jewelled coverlets." The ambassador's sense of cultural superiority over the newly rich Hun is dimmed by the fact that the mission from Constantinople had hired an assassin to murder Attila. Discovering the plot, he contemptuously sent the envoys home.

In A.D. 450, the Eastern Empire discontinued its tribute payments to the Huns, and rather than seeking revenge on Constantinople, with its formidable walls, Attila turned to the vulnerable Western Empire. Accompanied by his Huns and tributary Germans, he crossed the Rhine in A.D. 451. He claimed that he was coming as a kind of Prince Charming to rescue the Roman princess Honoria, who had been put under house arrest for having an affair with a palace chamberlain. In a fit of anger, Honoria had sent her ring to Attila with the plea that he marry her and carry her off to freedom. Although Honoria is said to have been beautiful, Attila's chief motive for coming west was doubtless plunder rather than marriage. His army was met by an allied Roman-Visigothic force near Troyes in central Gaul, where, after a day of mutual carnage, Attila withdrew his warriors from the battlefield and led them back home to Pannonia.

In the following year, Attila descended on Italy, sacking and pillaging cities as he moved toward Rome. It was at this point that he was confronted by Pope Leo I at the head of a delegation of Roman senators. According to the best account, Pope Leo, "an old man of harmless simplicity, venerable in his gray hair and majestic clothing," was suddenly and miraculously joined by Saints Peter and Paul, swords in their hands and clad in bishops' robes. Whether because of this marvel or because his army was dying from heat and plague, Attila withdrew once again from the Western Empire. He died in A.D. 453 during the night following a great banquet celebrating his marriage to a young Germanic woman named Ildico. Perhaps he had too much to drink at the banquet; perhaps Ildico was more than the middle-aged Hun could cope with. There were rumors of violence, but more probably his death was natural and (as one Victorian writer put it) "due to his own intemperate habits."

SUGGESTED READINGS

General Histories

A fundamental resource is the *Oxford Classical Dictionary* (1996), edited by S. Hornblower and A. Spawforth. Roman civilization is also well served by learned and well-illustrated essays in *The Oxford History of the Classical World* (1986), of which the separate Roman volume, also produced by J. Boardman, J. Griffin, and O. Murray, is titled *The Roman World* (1988). Of the older general histories of Rome, H. H. Scullard, *A History of the Roman World from 753 to 146 B.C.* (1980 ed.) remains useful, especially when read in tandem with Scullard's *From the Gracchi to Nero: A History of Rome from 133 B.C. to A.D. 68* (1982 ed.). M. Grant's *History of Rome* (1978) is a lively and clearly written general account. Of the more recent works, M. Le Glay, J. L. Voison, and Y. Le Bohec, *A History of Rome* (2000 ed., updated by D. Cherry), is perhaps the best student textbook. G. Alföldy, *The Social History of Rome* (1988), provides an adept blend of social history and politics. J. Matthews's and T. Cornell's *Atlas of the Roman World* (1982) is a useful, carefully executed reference tool. Thus far, for reasons that are not entirely clear, Roman history has not been as effectively represented on the internet as has Greek history. One good site can be found at www.bbc.co.uk/history/ancient/romans. The BBC site has articles written by top-notch scholars and is very reliable. Another site with lots of useful links and resources can be found at www.fordham.edu/halsall/ancient/asbook09.html.

The Roman Republic and Early Empire: Histories and Themes

E. Badian, *Publicans and Sinners* (1983) and *Roman Imperialism in the Late Republic* (2nd ed., 1968). Rigorous studies of the acquisition and financial management of the Empire.

M. Beard and M. Crawford, *Rome in the Late Republic* (1985). New perspectives on a much-discussed topic.

K. Bradley, *Slaves and Masters in the Roman Empire: A Study in Social Control* (1984) and *Slavery and Society at Rome* (1994). Authoritative accounts.

J. Campbell, *The Empire and the Roman Army* (1984). A study of the army's role in both foreign conquests and domestic politics.

T. Cornell, *The Beginnings of Rome: Italy and Rome from the Bronze Age to the Punic Wars (c. 1000–264 B.C.)* (1995). Far and away the best book in English on the early Roman Republic.

R. Duncan-Jones, *The Economy of the Roman Empire* (1984). A highly sophisticated economic analysis.

S. Dyson, *The Creation of the Roman Frontier* (1985). This major study, covering the late Republic and early Empire, makes expert use of both documentary and archaeological evidence.

W. Eck, *The Age of Augustus* (2002). A concise synthesis by a major scholar.

E. Gabba, *Republican Rome: The Army and the Allies,* trans. P. J. Cuff (1976). A collection of studies by a distinguished scholar of late-republican Rome that, among other things, represents the army of the late Republic as an avenue of advancement for the Italian peasantry.

J. Gardner, *Family and Familia in Roman Law and Life* (1998). An important study of the Roman family, especially in its relation to law.

P. Garnsey and R. Saller, *The Roman Empire: Economy, Society, and Culture* (1987). A skillful, multifaceted account that paints a relatively dark picture of the effect of the economy on the lower levels of society.

K. Greene, *The Archaeology of the Roman Economy* (1986). An astute multidisciplinary study.

E. Gruen, *The Hellenistic World and the Coming of Rome* (1984). A synthesis in which Rome's eastward expansion is seen in its Hellenistic context.

W. Harris, *War and Imperialism in Republican Rome, 327–70 B.C.* (1970). An important and original work of scholarly analysis.

L. Keppie, *The Making of the Roman Army: From Republic to Empire* (1984). Intended for the general reader, this is a well-written, thoroughly researched account of the Roman army from the time of its emergence as a town militia to the mid-first century A.D.

D. Kleiner, *Roman Sculpture* (1992). A comprehensive overview of Roman sculpture from the Republic through the Empire.

E. Luttwak, *The Grand Strategy of the Roman Empire from the First Century A.D. to the Third* (1976). An expert on modern strategic defense presents a fresh, comprehensive analysis of Roman imperial military policy, showing similarities and contrasts to the role of the United States as a world power.

R. MacMullen, *Roman Social Relations, 50 B.C. to A.D. 294* (1974). A more somber picture than the traditional one.

F. Millar, *The Crowd in Rome in the Late Republic* (1998). Challenges the dominant scholarly interpretation that Roman republican politics were dominated by the senatorial elite.

F. Millar, *The Emperor in the Roman World, 31 B.C.–476 A.D.* (1977). The fundamental work on the Roman emperor and how the Roman Empire worked in practice.

F. Millar, *The Roman Near East, 31 B.C.–A.D. 337* (1993). A masterpiece of scholarship.

C. Nicolet, *The World of the Citizen in Republican Rome,* trans. P. Falla (1980). A masterful portrayal of the civic life of ordinary Romans and their political institutions.

R. Ogilvie, *Early Rome and the Etruscans* (1976). A deft summary of historical and archaeological findings.

M. Pallottino, *The Etruscans,* trans. J. Cremona (1975). The basic work on the subject, translated from the 6th Italian edition of 1973.

E. Rawson, *Intellectual Life in the Late Roman Republic* (1985). In this landmark study of intellectual life in Rome during the 50s and 40s B.C., the author explores with impressive erudition the interaction of Greek and Italian intellectual elites and stresses the eagerness of Romans to assimilate Hellenistic culture.

A. Rousselle, *Pornea: On Desire and the Body in Antiquity,* trans. F. Pheasant (1993). A social history of sexuality during the Roman imperial era.

C. Starr, *The Beginnings of Imperial Rome in the Mid-Republic* (1980). A very short, challenging work of reinterpretation which argues that Rome between 338 and 264 B.C. was larger and more active commercially than was previously thought.

R. Syme, *The Roman Revolution* (1960 ed.). A great pioneering work that downplays constitutional factors and stresses the political significance of families and factions in the late Republic. The most important twentieth-century work of scholarship about the Roman Republic.

R. Talbert, *The Senate of Imperial Rome* (1984). Detailed and comprehensive, the definitive account.

M. Todd, *Roman Britain, 55 B.C.–A.D. 400* (1981). A learned and readable study that makes full use of both textual and archaeological evidence to show the creative fusion of British and Roman cultures across the centuries of Roman rule.

C. Wells, *The Roman Empire* (1984). A brief, up-to-date survey emphasizing the era of the Principate and showing the burdens it imposed on those outside the ruling elite.

Polytheism, the Mystery Cults, Christianity, and the Conversion of the Empire

T. Barnes, *Constantine and Eusebius* (1981). By far the most important critical study.

M. Beard, J. North, and S. Price, *Religions of Rome* (1998), 2 vols. Provides narrative and sources; fundamental to understanding polytheism in the Roman world.

P. Brown, *Augustine of Hippo: A Biography* (2000 ed., with new epilogue). A wise and learned study, extraordinarily sensitive to Augustine and his world.

W. Burkert, *Ancient Mystery Cults* (1987). The best general synthesis on the subject.

H. Chadwick, *Early Christian Thought and the Classical Tradition: Studies in Justin, Clement, and Origen* (1966, paperback 1984); *The Early Church* (1967); *Augustine: A Very Short Introduction* (2001 ed.). Fundamental works by the greatest historian of the early Christian church.

R. Lane Fox, *Pagans and Christians* (1987). Stimulating and highly original.

W. Frend, *The Rise of Christianity* (1984). Perhaps the best current account for the material remains. See also his *The Archaeology of Early Christianity: A History* (1996).

J. Liebeschuetz, *Continuity and Change in Roman Religion* (1979). Shifts in religious sentiment from the late Republic to Saint Augustine.

R. MacMullen, *Christianizing the Roman Empire,* A.D. *100–400* (1984). A succinct survey, engagingly written. See also his more recent *Christianity and Paganism in the Fourth to Eighth Centuries* (1997).

R. Markus, *Christianity in the Roman World* (1974). A clear, brief, learned overview of the era from the origins of Christianity to the end of the Western Empire.

J. McManners, ed. *The Oxford History of Christianity* (1993). Early chapters by Chadwick and Markus on the Church from A.D. 330 to 1050 are authoritative.

W. Meeks, *The First Urban Christians: The Social World of the Apostle Paul* (1983). A fascinating, groundbreaking study.

G. Vermes, *Jesus the Jew: A Historian's Reading of the Gospels* (1981). Rightly making the case that Jesus and his mission must be understood within the world of first-century Judaism(s).

The Later Empire and the Germanic Invasions

T. Barnes, *The New Empire of Diocletian and Constantine* (1982). The best treatment of the period.

P. Brown, *The World of Late Antiquity:* A.D. *150–750* (1971). A classic, sympathetic study of social and cultural change in eastern and western Europe and the Near East; this pioneering work argues persuasively against the traditional notion of a fifth-century break separating the ancient from the medieval world. See also, by the same author, *The Rise of Western Christendom: Triumph and Diversity,* A.D. *200–1000* (1996).

A. Cameron, *The Later Roman Empire,* A.D. *284–430* (1993) and *The Mediterranean World in Late-Antiquity,* A.D. *395–600* (1993). Two superb works of original scholarly synthesis, cast in the mold of Peter Brown's concept of "Late Antiquity."

A. Ferrill, *The Fall of the Roman Empire: The Military Explanation* (1986). A persuasive reexamination.

E. Gibbon, *The History of the Decline and Fall of the Roman Empire* (ed. J. B. Bury, 1896–1900; reprinted 1974), 7 vols. A shortened version of Gibbon's eighteenth-century masterpiece is the one-volume edition edited by D. M. Low (1960).

W. Goffart, *Barbarians and Romans, A.D. 418–584: The Techniques of Accommodation* (1980). A provocative work that argues strongly against the idea of the Western Empire sinking under a barbarian deluge and stresses the separateness of individual Germanic groups.

M. Grant, *The Fall of the Roman Empire* (1990 ed.). An important work that provides revealing insights into Roman social development and change.

P. Heather, *Goths and Romans, A.D. 332–489* (1991). Revises older views on the Ostrogoths and Visigoths as distinct, coherent tribes long before their entry into the Empire and shows that the reality was far more complex. See also, by the same author, *The Fall of the Roman Empire* (2005), which focuses on the period from c. A.D. 376 to the deposition of Romulus Augustulus.

A. Jones, *The Later Roman Empire, 284–602: A Social, Economic, and Administrative Survey* (1986). A major classic, building on a great body of this scholar's earlier work on the subject of society.

D. Kagan, ed., *The End of the Roman Empire: Decline or Transformation?* (3rd ed., 1992). A short anthology of modern scholarly views, showing that historians remain at odds.

R. Krautheimer, *Three Christian Capitals: Topography and Politics* (1983). A penetrating and highly original study of architecture, society, and culture in late-antique Rome, Constantinople, and Milan.

F. Lot, *The End of the Ancient World and the Beginnings of the Middle Ages* (1961). Reprint and translation of a seminal study of 1927 stressing the economic factors in Rome's decline.

M. Todd, *The Early Germans* (1992). A readable, sophisticated archaeological and historical study of the Germanic peoples in their "preinvasion" setting, their movements into the Empire, and the resulting cultural synthesis.

R. Van Dam, *Leadership and Community in Late Antique Gaul* (1985). An original, persuasive interpretation of the receding imperial administration, the regional and local aristocracy, the evolution of Christian communities and heresies, and the growing social importance of the cult of saints and relics—Saint Martin of Tours in particular—in late Roman and early medieval Gaul.

B. Ward Perkins, *The Fall Of Rome* (2005). Makes use of the archaeological data to argue that Rome's fall led to a real break in the standard of living for most of the inhabitants of the Roman Empire in the West.

S. Williams, *Diocletian and the Roman Recovery* (1985). An engagingly written portrayal of Diocletian as a masterful ruler who restored a faltering empire.

Sources

Once again, as mentioned in our earlier section on Greek culture, *The Norton Book of Classical Literature,* edited by B. Knox (1993), is a fundamental source on the writings of classical authors and poets. Other good anthologies include N. Lewis and M. Rinehold, *Roman Civilization* (1990 ed., 2 vols.), the best comprehensive collection of sources in English; B. Davenport, ed., *The Portable Roman Reader* (2003); and J. Shelton, ed., *As the Romans Did* (1998). An excellent collection of translated sources on women's history is *Women's Life in Greece and Rome,* edited by M. Lefkowitz and M. Fant (1982).

Virgil's *Aeneid* is best approached through A. Mandelbaum's admirable verse translation (1981, with striking illustrations by B. Moser). There are numerous editions of the works of Cicero, Livy, Sallust, Josephus, Petronius, Ovid, Catullus, Seneca, Horace, Plutarch, Tacitus, Suetonius, and other important Roman writers, many of which are available in Penguin Classics editions or in volumes in the Loeb Classical Library.

For early Christianity, the New Testament is the ideal source. Modern paperback editions of the four Gospels and the Acts of the Apostles are readily available. Of the several editions of Saint Augustine's *Confessions,* I suggest H. Chadwick's translation (1991) with references and index; for Augustine's *City of God,* I recommend H. Bettenson's translation (Penguin Classics, 1984). On Clovis and the early Franks, see Gregory of Tours, *History of the Franks,* translated by L. Thorpe (1974).

Glossary

A

Academy Philosophical school founded by Plato.

acropolis "High town" in Greek; usually a fortified citadel of a Greek polis.

Adrianople Battle in A.D. 378 at which the Visigoths killed Roman Emperor Valens and two-thirds of the Roman army.

Aeneas Refugee from Troy; hero of Virgil's *Aeneid*; Dido's beloved and founder of Lavinium in Italy.

Aeschylus (c. 525–456 B.C.) Athenian tragic poet, author of the *Oresteia* (458 B.C.).

ager publicus "Public land" of Rome, acquired by conquest or from rebellious allies of Rome; owned by the Roman state and leased out to its citizens.

agoge Public military and educational system for male citizens of Sparta.

Ahuramazda "Wise lord"; most important god of the Persians during the early empire.

Akkad Area of southern Mesopotamia between modern Baghdad and Nippur.

Alaric Gothic leader, c. A.D. 395–410; sacked Rome on 24 August A.D. 410.

Alexander III (356–323 B.C.) King of Macedon, conqueror of the Persian Empire.

Ambrose (c. A.D. 340–397); Christian writer, orator, and Bishop of Milan; classically educated; excommunicated Roman emperor Theodosius I in A.D. 390.

Amun-Re The "hidden" Egyptian creator god, combined with Re, the sun god.

Anaximander Early-sixth-century-B.C. natural philosopher from Miletus in Ionia.

anthropomorphic Having the form and personality of a human.

Antoninus Pius Roman emperor, A.D. 138–161; part of his family was from Nîmes in southern France; Rome's nine-hundredth anniversary (A.D. 148) was celebrated during his peaceful reign.

Anu Sumerian sky god.

Aphrodite Greek goddess of seduction and procreation.

apoikia (*apoikiai*, pl.) Greek polis established abroad by another polis (*metropolis*), such as Cyrene (modern Shahat in Libya), founded by Thera c. 630 B.C.

Apollo Greek god of healing, prophecy, music, and poetry.

Arcadius Emperor of the Eastern Roman Empire, A.D. 383–408.

arche "Rule" in Greek.

Archilochus Mid-seventh-century-B.C. Greek lyric poet from the island of Paros.

Archimedes (c. 287–211 B.C.) Mathematician and inventor from Syracuse.

archontes Leaders or rulers of early Greek city-states; nine chief magistrates were elected in Athens during the fifth and fourth centuries B.C.

Arianism Christian heresy of the fourth century A.D.; named after the Alexandrian presbyter Arius (c. A.D. 260–336), who held that the Son (Jesus) or the Word was distinct in essence from the Father (God).

Aristarchus Third-century-B.C. astronomer from the island of Samos; author of the heliocentric theory.

Aristophanes (c. 450–386 B.C.) Athenian comic poet; author of *The Clouds* and *Lysistrata*.

Aristotle (384–322 B.C.) Polymath and universal scholar from Stagira in the Chalcidice; founder of the Lyceum.

ataraxia Impassiveness; an attitude of philosophical calm in the face of trials and temptations, advocated by Epicurus (c. 341–270 B.C.).

Athena Greek goddess of crafts and warfare.

Attila King of the Huns, c. A.D. 435–453; invaded the Balkan provinces of the Roman Empire and sacked Italian cities.

Augustine (A.D. 354–430) Late-antique Christian rhetorician, orator, Neoplatonist philosopher, bishop, and saint, from Thagaste (Algeria).

autochthones "Born from the land"; a claim of indigenous origins made by citizens of Greek poleis, including Athenians.

B

basileus Title found in Linear B (Greek) texts from the mid-second millennium B.C., meaning "leader"; later meant "noble" and finally "king" in classical Greek.

belles lettres Writings, including essays and criticism, belonging to a literary tradition.

bishops Spiritual leaders of the first Christian communities and the Church.

Boethius (c. A.D. 480–524) Made consul and *magister officiorum* by Theoderic; wrote *De consolatione philosophiae* (On the Consolation of Philosophy) in prison; executed in A.D. 524.

boule Council in Greek city-states; prepared the agenda or business for the Assembly (*ekklesia*).

Brutus Supporter of Pompey who was later forgiven by Caesar; leader of the assassination of Caesar in 44 B.C.; committed suicide in 42 B.C.

C

Caligula Roman emperor, A.D. 37–41; alienated the senate and army; was murdered in Rome with his wife and daughter.

Callicrates Fifth-century-B.C. Athenian architect; worked with Ictinus on the design of the Parthenon (Temple of Athena Polias) on the Athenian Acropolis.

Cassiodorus (c. A.D. 490–585). Secretary and legal advisor of Theoderic; retired to the monastery of Vivarium, where he supervised translations and the copying of literary manuscripts for the rest of his life.

Cassius Supporter of Pompey who was later forgiven by Caesar; took part in the assassination of Caesar in 44 B.C.; committed suicide in 42 B.C.

Çatal Hüyük Neolithic village in Turkey.

Catiline Corrupt and politically frustrated Roman patrician who revolted against Rome; killed in 62 B.C.

Cato the Elder (234–149 B.C.) Roman soldier; censor, and writer; argued for the destruction of Carthage (*"Carthago delenda est"*).

Catullus (84–54 B.C.) Late Roman republican lyric poet; wrote poems about the ill-fated love of Lesbia (Clodia) and about contemporary Roman politicians, including Julius Caesar.

Centuriate Assembly See *comitia centuriata.*

Chaeronea City-state in northwest Boeotia, near which in 338 B.C. Philip II of Macedon, Alexander, and the Macedonians defeated the Greek city-states.

chora A place or space in classical Greek; the territory or agricultural hinterland of a polis.

Cicero Rome's greatest orator; consul of 63 B.C.; destroyed the conspiracy of Catiline; murdered by Mark Antony's agents in 43 B.C.

Cleisthenes Athenian aristocrat and politician; founder of Athenian democracy c. 508 B.C.

Cleopatra Egyptian queen; lover of Julius Caesar and wife of Mark Antony; committed suicide in 30 B.C.; last of the Ptolemaic rulers of Egypt.

Clovis Germanic king, A.D. 481–511; carved out a Frankish kingdom in Gaul; champion of orthodox Christianity (against Arianism).

coloni Tenant farmers; often tied to the land by official registration during the later Roman Empire.

comitia centuriata Centuriate Assembly of Rome, a timocratically based assembly that elected higher Roman magistrates, including consuls; declared war and peace, enacted laws, and served as a court of appeal.

comitia tributa populi Tribal Assembly of the Roman citizen body, including plebeians and patricians; elected quaestors, curule aediles, and military tribunes and enacted legislation.

Commodus Roman emperor, A.D. 180–192; son and successor of Marcus Aurelius; devoted to gladiatorial games; strangled; his memory was damned.

concilium plebis Council of the Plebs, an assembly of Rome's poorer citizens that elected tribunes of the plebs and aediles and enacted plebiscites (*plebiscita*).

Constantine Roman emperor (Augustus), A.D. 312–337; favored Christians and Christianity; founded Constantinople (Istanbul) on the site of Byzantium (324); was baptized when near death.

consul (*consules*, pl.) Title of two annual chief magistrates of Rome, elected in the *comitia centuriata*, whose powers were military command (*imperium*) and the right to summon the senate and the people.

cosmopolis The idea of a world-polis to which all humanity belongs.

Council of the Plebs See *concilium plebis.*

Crassus Richest man in Rome during the late Republic; victor over Spartacus; died fighting the Parthians in 53 B.C.

Cro-Magnon man *Homo sapiens sapiens;* lived in Europe c. 40,000 years ago.

cuneiform Wedge-shaped writing of the ancient Sumerians.

Cynics "Doglike" in Greek; followers of Diogenes (c. 403–321 B.C.), who lived according to nature.

Cypselus (657–627 B.C.) Tyrant of Corinth.

Cyrus II "The Great," reigned 559–530 B.C.; founder of the Persian Empire.

D

daimonion "Little spirit" in Greek; a personal, protecting spirit, such as the one heard by Socrates, during the classical period.

Darius I "The Great," reigned 521–486 B.C.; ruler of the Persian Empire at its height.

David King of Israel, c. 1000–960 B.C.; slayer of the Philistine giant Goliath.

Delian League Alliance of approximately 330 Greek poleis, formed in 478–477 B.C. to defend Greece against Persia.

deme Local district in the Greek world, usually a village; by extension, the people inhabiting the district.

Demeter Greek goddess of crops and vegetation.

Democritus mid-fifth-century-B.C. philosopher of materialism from Abdera in Thrace.

dictator Roman republican magistracy; nominated by a Roman magistrate following authorization by the Senate; appointed to command armies or perform a set task; office originally limited to a six-month tenure.

Diocletian Third-century-A.D. Roman emperor from Dalmatia; proclaimed Augustus (emperor) at Nicomedia in August A.D. 284; established Tetrarchy in A.D. 293.

Dionysus Greek god of wine and intoxication.

dithyrambs Choral songs sung to honor the god Dionysus, perhaps dating to seventh century B.C. in Greece.

E

Ebla "City of the White Stones," in Syria.

ekklesia Assembly of adult male citizens in Greek city-states.

Enlil Sumerian storm god.

emporion (*emporia*, pl.) Archaic-period Greek trading post such as Naucratis in the Nile Delta (founded by the Milesians) or Al Mina at the mouth of Orontes River in Syria.

ephors Five annually elected magistrates of Sparta.

Epicureans Followers of Epicurus (c. 341–270 B.C.) who sought happiness through the avoidance of disturbance.

Eratosthenes (c. 285–194 B.C.) Literary critic, chronographer, mathematician, philosopher, poet, and mapmaker from Cyrene; head of the Library at Alexandria.

ethnos A number of people living together; a tribe or tribally based society in Greece.

Etruria Region northwest of Rome where Etruscans lived (corresponding roughly to modern Tuscany).

Etruscans Either eastern (e.g., Asia Minor) or indigenous people who lived northwest of Rome in Etruria.

Euclid (c. 325–250 B.C.) Greek mathematician who wrote thirteen books (*Elements*) on the theory of numbers; organized plane and solid geometry into a systematic body of knowledge.

eunomia "Well ordered" in Greek; living according to a well-ordered constitution in Greek political theory, such as (allegedly) at Sparta.

Euripides (c. 485–406 B.C.) Athenian tragic poet; author of the *Medea* and the *Bacchae*.

G

Gaius Gracchus Tribune of Rome; murdered in 121 B.C. during a riot instigated by senators.

Galen (A.D. 131–201) Physician, philosopher, and medical writer from Pergamum in Asia Minor; influenced theory and practice of medicine into twentieth century.

Gaugamela Battle site near Irbil in modern Iraq where Alexander and the Macedonians decisively defeated the Persian army led by Darius III in 331 B.C.

ge The earth or tilled ground in classical Greek.

genius Attendant or tutelary spirit of a person, family, or place in Rome.

Gerousia Council of elders in Greek city-states.

Gnosticism Early Roman imperial (esp. second century A.D.) religious movement emphasizing cosmic dualism and the connection between humanity and divinity; influenced by Jewish apocalyptic thought and perhaps Platonic dialogues.

Gregory of Tours (c. A.D. 538–594) Frankish bishop of Tours and historian; his *History of the Franks* (*Historia Fancorum*) is a major source for late-antique history of Gaul.

H

Hadrian Roman emperor, A.D. 117–138; of Spanish ancestry; one of the "five good emperors"; a philhellene; abandoned Trajan's eastern conquests.

Hammurabi Amorite king of Babylon, c. 1792–1750 B.C.; promulgated law code.

Hattusa Capital of the Hittite empire; *Bogazköy* in present-day Turkey.

Hellenic Descendant of Hellen, the son or brother of Deucalion; came to mean "Greek."

helot *Heilotai* in Greek; Laconians and Messenians collectively enslaved by Sparta.

henotheism Belief in the supremacy of one god without denying the existence of other deities.

Herodotus Fifth-century-B.C. Greek historian from Halicarnassus in Asia Minor; wrote the history of war(s) between the Persians and the Greeks during the early fifth century B.C.

Hesiod Late eighth-century-B.C. Greek poet from Boeotia; author of *Works and Days* and *Theogony*.

hetairai "Female companions" in Greek; paid courtesans, selected for their beauty; often well educated.

Hipparchus Second-century-B.C. astronomer from Nicaea; constructed theories to explain the motions of the moon and the sun based upon observation.

Hippocrates (c. 469–399 B.C.) Physician from the island of Cos.

Holy Trinity Christian idea of a single divinity with three aspects: "the Father," the "Son," and "the Holy Ghost."

Homer Eighth-century-B.C. blind poet from the island of Chios or Smyrna in Ionia; author of the *Iliad* and the *Odyssey*.

Homo habilis "Skillful man," the earliest toolmaker.

homoioi Approximately 8,000 male citizen "equals" or "similars" of Sparta during the fifth century B.C.

Homo sapiens "The man who knows"; emerged some 75,000 years ago.

Honorius Emperor of the Western Roman Empire, A.D. 395–423; moved his court to Ravenna in northern Italy; failed to protect Rome from Alaric, who sacked Rome in 410.

hoplon Wooden or leather circular shield of the archaic and classical era of Greek infantry; the name "hoplites" (Greek *hoplitai*) derives from "hoplon."

Horace (65–8 B.C.) Roman lyric poet; sponsored by Maecenas, a friend and agent of Octavian Augustus.

humanoid Ancestor of the human race; remains date to c. 5 million years ago.

Huns Nomadic Mongolian peoples; drove the Goths into the

Roman Empire; invaded the Balkan provinces of the Roman Empire; sacked Italian cities during the fifth century A.D.

Hyksos "King-shepherds"; rulers in Lower Egypt c. 1648–1550 B.C.

I

Ictinus Fifth-century-B.C. architect and designer of the Parthenon on the Athenian Acropolis.

Inanna Sumerian earth goddess.

Indo-European Language family from which ancient Greek, Latin, and Hittite (Nesite), as well as modern Romance (Italian, French, etc.) and Germanic (German, English, etc.) languages descended.

Isis Egyptian goddess of fertile earth; sister and wife of Osiris.

Itj-towy "The Residence" in Memphis, Egypt.

ius gentium "Law of nations"; originally, Roman private law as it applied to both Roman citizens and non-Roman citizens.

ius naturale "Natural law"; Roman law applying to all nations and peoples, as opposed to civil laws, which applied only to the citizens of individual nations.

J

Jarmo Neolithic village in Iraq.

Jericho Neolithic village in Palestine; the oldest permanent settlement.

Jerome (c. A.D. 347–420) Late-antique, classically educated biblical scholar; produced a translation of the Hebrew Bible and a revision of the Gospels from Hebrew and Greek into Latin; his translation became the basis for the "Vulgate" medieval Latin Bible.

Josephus (born c. A.D. 37) Jewish priest, military leader, and writer of the Roman imperial era; took part in the great Jewish Revolt against Roman rule (A.D. 66–73); later wrote a history of the revolt and a massive account of Jewish antiquities.

Julian the Apostate Roman emperor A.D. 361–363; attempted to revive traditional, polytheistic cults.

Julius Caesar Roman general and politician who became dictator for life; murdered on 15 March 44 B.C. by senators.

Juno One of the chief goddesses of Rome; wife of Jupiter and goddess of marriage.

Jupiter King and sovereign of the Roman gods.

Justinian Emperor of the Eastern Roman Empire, A.D. 527–565; responsible for the codification of all imperial constitutions (*Codex Iustinianus*).

K

Kadesh Indecisive battle in Syria between Egyptians and Hittites in 1274 B.C.

Kanesh Modern Kültepe in Turkey; Hittite city where Nesite was spoken.

Knossos Center of Minoan civilization; palatial site on Crete, excavated by Sir Arthur Evans.

L

latifundia Large estates in Italy and eventually the provinces of the Roman Empire, composed of aggregated properties, usually worked by slaves.

Latins Peoples living in about twenty city-states within Latium, including Rome.

Latium fertile agricultural district in central Italy bounded to the northeast by the Rivers Tiber and Anio and to the east by the Apennine Mountains and the Monti Lepini.

leges (*lex,* sing.) Laws or statutes passed by an authorized assembly of Roman people.

Leo I Pope, A.D. 440–461; persuaded Attila, king of the Huns, to withdraw from Italy in A.D. 451.

lex talionis Law of retributive justice, found in the code of Hammurabi.

Linear A Undeciphered Minoan syllabary.

Linear B Syllabary found on clay tablets on Crete and Greek mainland, includeing Mycenae and Pylos; first written form of ancient Greek.

Lucian (born c. A.D. 120) Roman imperial-era satirist from Samosata (modern Samsat); wrote literary dialogues and attacks upon contemporary Sophists and religious charlatans.

Lyceum Philosophical school founded by Aristotle.

M

ma'at Egyptian word meaning "truth," "right behavior," or "correct balance."

Magna Graecia "Great Greece"; coastal area of Italy between Cumae and Tarentum and Sicily colonized by the Greeks.

Marathon Battle site in northeastern Attica where Athenians and Plataeans defeated the Persians in 490 B.C.

Marcus Aurelius Roman emperor, A.D. 161–180; philosopher-emperor who spent his reign fighting barbarian invaders of the empire; author of *Meditations.*

Mark Antony Roman general and right-hand man of Julius Caesar; triumvir; defeated by the forces of Octavian at Actium in 31 B.C.; committed suicide in 30 B.C.

Marius Roman consul of 107 B.C.; enlisted soldiers without property into a voluntary army to fight Jugurtha.

Mars Roman god of war and warriors.

Menes See **Narmer.**

Mesopotamia The land between the Tigris and the Euphrates rivers; roughly, modern Iraq.

metics Greek *metoikoi;* resident aliens in Athens who paid a special tax and had military obligations.

metropolis "Mother-polis" of a Greek colony; later, a larger polis.

Minerva Roman goddess of handicrafts; identified with Greek Athena.

Mithras Indo-Iranian god of the "compact" and the unconquered sun during the Roman Empire.

Moses In the Hebrew Bible, the leader of the Hebrews out of Egypt.

Museum "Home of the Muses" in Greek; a center of learning and the arts.

Mycenae Agamemnon's kingdom; site in Argolid in Greece excavated by Heinrich Schliemann.

N

Naram-Sin (c. 2260–2223 B.C.) Grandson of Sargon I of Akkad; conqueror of Ebla.

Narmer Legendary unifier of Upper and Lower Egypt; also known as Menes.

Near East Region that extends roughly from the Aegean coast of modern-day Turkey to Iran and from the coast of the Black Sea in northern Turkey south to the Red Sea and Egypt.

Neolithic era New Stone Age, beginning c. 8000 B.C., during which agriculture developed.

Neoplatonism Revival of Platonic philosophy during the third century A.D.; attempt to reconcile Platonic metaphysical ideas with the theology of polytheism.

Nero Roman emperor, A.D. 54–68; a philhellene, he was unpopular among senators and forced to commit suicide.

Nerva Roman emperor, A.D. 96–98; one of the "five good emperors"; last of the ethnically Italian emperors.

Nesite Indo-European language spoken in Kanesh in Asia Minor during the second millennium B.C.; language of Hittites.

Nicaea Iznik in modern Turkey; site of the first ecumenical Church Council in A.D. 325, where the Nicene Creed was sanctioned by Emperor Constantine.

nomarchs Greek term for the governors of districts in Egypt during the Hellenistic period (after 323 B.C.).

nomes Administrative districts of Egypt during the period of Greek domination (after 323 B.C.).

O

Octavian Augustus Grandnephew and adoptive son of Julius Caesar; became the first Roman emperor after the defeat of Antony at Actium in 31 B.C.

Odovacar Ruler of Italy, c. A.D. 476–493; deposed Romulus Augustulus, the last western Roman emperor.

Origen (A.D. 185–254) Roman imperial-era theologian and textual critic from Alexandria.

Orpheus Son of Apollo and Muse; singer and husband of Eurydice; descended to Hades to bring back Eurydice after she died from a snakebite.

Osiris Egyptian royal mortuary god; brother and husband of Isis.

ostracism Banishment of one citizen from Athens for ten years by vote during fifth century B.C.

Ostrogoths "East Goths"; created the Gothic kingdom in Italy during the late fifth century A.D.

Ovid (43 B.C.–A.D. 17); Roman elegiac poet banished to Tomis on the Black Sea by Augustus for a poem and an indiscretion.

P

Paleolithic era Old Stone Age, dating from c. 1.5 million years ago to c. 20,000 B.C.

panem et circenses "Bread and circuses" (chariot races, games, and food) provided free to Roman people, to keep Rome's poor preoccupied and depoliticized.

patricians Privileged class of Roman citizens belonging to related families or clans.

Pax Romana "Roman Peace"; ushered in by the creation of the Principate under Augustus; lasts until the mid-third century A.D.

Periander (627–587 B.C.) Tyrant of Corinth; son of the tyrant Cypselus.

Pericles (c. 495–429 B.C.) Athenian general, orator, and imperialist.

perioikoi "Those who live around"; free noncitizens in some Greek city-states, notably Sparta, where they served in the army but did not have full citizen rights.

phalanx Greek hoplite warriors fighting in lines.

pharaoh Ruler of the "great house," or *per'ao* in Egyptian, from which the term "pharaoh" derives.

Pheidon Early-seventh-century-B.C. tyrant of Argos.

Phidias Fifth-century-B.C. Athenian sculptor of the chryselephantine (gold and irory) statue of Athena Parthenos in the Temple of Athena Polias (Parthenon) on the Athenian Acropolis.

Philip II King of Macedon, 359–336 B.C.; father of Alexander the Great.

Philo Judaeus First-century-A.D. Jewish philosopher and writer living in Alexandria; led a Jewish embassy to Emperor Gaius in A.D. 39 to protest anti-Jewish violence.

Pisistratus Tyrant of Athens during the sixth century B.C.

Plataea City-state in southern Boeotia near where the Greek army destroyed the Persian invading army in 479 B.C.

Plato (c. 429–347 B.C.) Athenian philosopher; founder of the Academy.

plebeians The mass of poorer Roman citizens who, during the early Republic, probably were excluded from the highest magistracies, the Senate, and priesthoods.

plebiscita Plebiscites; resolutions of the Roman plebeian tribal assembly that were binding on the Roman citizen body after 287 B.C.

plebs See plebeians.

Pliny the Younger (c. A.D. 61–112) Roman imperial senator, consul, governor, and letter writer; friend of the emperor Trajan.

Plotinus (A.D. 205–270) Neoplatonist philosopher from Lycopolis in Egypt.

Plutarch (A.D. 46–120) Greek writer of the early Roman imperial period, from Chaeronea; author of *Parallel Lives*, containing twenty-three paired biographies of famous Greeks and Romans.

Poenus Punic; Latin word for "Carthaginian."

polis City-state of ancient Greece.

Pompey "The Great" Roman general and politician; fought Caesar during the Roman civil wars; murdered in Egypt in 48 B.C.

pontifex maximus Supreme priest of the most important of Rome's four priestly colleges, the *pontifices*; in charge of the state cult, various games, festivals, and sacrifices.

Pontius Pilate Roman prefect of Judaea, A.D. 26–36; possibly presided over the "trial" of Jesus.

proletarii Proletarians; citizens of Rome with little or no property to contribute to the Roman state; ordinarily not subject to military service.

princeps "First citizen" or "leading citizen" in Rome; taken as unofficial title by Augustus to suggest Republican roots and the civilian nature of his constitutional position.

prostates Unofficial chief or leader in a Greek city-state; not an elected position.

provincia the sphere of jurisdiction of a Roman magistrate.

Ptah God of the city of Memphis in Egypt.

Ptolemy Second-century-A.D. astronomer and geographer working in Alexandria; proposed a geocentric model of the universe.

Pythagoras Mid-sixth-century-B.C. philosopher from the island of Samos; introduced the doctrine of transmigration of souls into Greek philosophy.

R

Re Egyptian sun god.

Romulus Augustulus Last emperor of the Western Roman Empire, A.D. 475–476.

S

Salamis Bay between Attica and the island of Salamis, where Greeks decisively defeated the Persian navy in September of 480 B.C.

Sabines People who lived in the area northeast of Rome along the eastern side of the Tiber River to the Apennine Mountains.

Saint Paul Early-first-century-A.D. Greek/Roman/Jewish citizen of Tarsus in Asia Minor; Christian apostle to the gentile communities of the Roman Empire.

Sappho Greek lyric poetess of the mid- to late seventh century B.C. from the island of Lesbos.

Sargon I Akkadian ruler, c. 2340–2284 B.C.; unified Akkad and Sumer.

Sassanid Iranian dynasty from A.D. 224–651; carved out an empire from Syria to India and from Spain to Persian Gulf.

saturikon "Satyrlike play" in Greek; dance drama of satyrs from which tragedy developed.

Saul First king of Israel, c. 1020 B.C.

senatus consultum Nonbinding advisory decree or resolution of the Roman Senate; addressed to Roman magistrates.

Seneca First-century-A.D. Roman orator, statesman, diplomat, financier, writer, and philosopher; tutor of Nero; forced to commit suicide in A.D. 65.

Septimius Severus Roman emperor, A.D. 193–211; of Punic ancestry; raised three new legions; increased pay for soldiers; died at Eburacum (York, England).

Skeptics Followers of Pyrrhon of Elis (c. 365–275 B.C.) who denied the possibility of any real knowledge.

Socrates (c. 469–399 B.C.) Athenian philosopher; forced to drink hemlock by Athens.

Solomon King of Israel, c. 960–922 B.C.; builder of the first temple in Jerusalem.

Solon Athenian poet and lawgiver, c. 594 B.C.

Sophocles (c. 496–406 B.C.) Athenian tragic poet; author of *Antigone* and *Oedipus Tyrannus*.

Spartacus Thracian, ex-Roman auxiliary soldier and slave; led major revolt of slaves against Rome from 73 B.C.

Stilicho Regent and general, c. A.D. 395–408, for the western Roman Emperor Honorius; murdered in a coup in A.D. 408.

Stoicism Philosophy of the followers of Zeno of Citium (335–263 B.C.), who taught in the Painted Stoa in Athens and emphasized the supreme importance of virtue.

Suetonius (c. A.D. 70–130) Roman imperial biographer of men of letters and Roman "Caesars" from Julius Caesar to Domitian.

Sulla Roman patrician, military commander, and politician; became dictator in 82 B.C.

syncretism Combining or reconciling different ideas or conceptions into one, especially with respect to different conceptions of divinities.

synoikismos Unification of a number of smaller communities in the Greek world, usually poleis, into one larger polis.

syssitia Public messes or dining establishments of groups of fifteen Spartan citizens (during the classical period) to which each Spartan citizen contributed produce from his publicly assigned agricultural lots (*kleroi*).

T

Tacitus (c. A.D. 56–118) Roman imperial consul, governor, and historian of the early Roman Empire.

Tepe Yahya Neolithic village in Iran.

Tetrarchy "Fourth part of an *arche* (rule)"; term used by modern scholars to describe the system of government established by Diocletian in A.D. 293.

Thales Early-sixth-century-B.C. natural philosopher from Miletus in Ionia.

Themistocles (c. 524–459 B.C.) Athenian politician and general; hero of the Greek resistance to the Persian invasion of Greece.

Theodoric Arian-born Gothic king, A.D. 493–526; created the Ostrogothic kingdom including Italy, southern Gaul, and Spain.

Theodosius I Roman emperor, A.D. 379–395; strict Nicene; banned teachings of Arius; in A.D. 391 closed temples and banned polytheist worship.

Thermopylae Narrow pass in northern Greece where the Spartan King Leonidas and 300 Spartans were wiped out by the invading Persian army of Xerxes in August of 480 B.C.

tholoi Circular tombs or sites of religious rituals during Minoan and Mycenaean eras (c. 2000–1200 B.C.); other circular buildings, including memorials, later called *tholoi*.

Tiberius Gracchus Tribune of Rome; murdered in a riot instigated by senators in 133 B.C.

Trajan Roman emperor, A.D. 98–117, from Italica in Spain; one of the five "good emperors"; conqueror of Dacia (Romania); led Roman armies to Persian Gulf.

Tribal Assembly See *comitia tributa populi.*

tribunes See *tribuni plebis.*

tribuni plebis Tribunes of *plebs*, originally two and later ten, elected representatives of plebeians; defended plebeians and their property; declared sacrosanct and inviolate by plebeians; possessed the right of veto against acts of the Roman magistrate, laws, elections, and advisory opinions of the Senate.

Trittyes "Thirds" in Greek; clusters of neighboring demes in Attica combined into larger population centers by Cleisthenes; one *trittys* (sing.) from each of the three regions of Attica (coast, plain, and city) was then assigned to ten tribes created in 508 B.C.

Triumvirate, First Unofficial and later description of the coalition of 60 B.C. formed by Caesar, Pompey, and Crassus.

Triumvirate, Second Legally established coalition of Mark Antony, Lepidus, and Octavian, dated from 43 B.C. to 1 January 32 B.C., for sake of "constituting" the Republic.

Troy Hisarlik in modern Turkey; site of the Trojan War described by Homer in the *Iliad*.

Twelve Tables The first written compilation of Roman statutory law; published in the mid-fifth century B.C.

tyrannos Lydian word borrowed by the Greeks to designate unconstitutional rulers such as Pheidon of Argos or Periander of Corinth.

U

uraeus Cobra ornament on the crown of Egyptian pharaohs; identified with the goddess Wadjet and with the eye of the sun god Re.

Uruk Mesopotamian city dated to c. 3500 B.C.; picture writing was first developed here.

usus A form of common-law marriage in Rome, available to couples who lived together without interruption for at least a year.

V

Valens Emperor of the Eastern Roman Empire, c. A.D. 364–378; baptized Arian; allowed Arian Visigoths to cross the Danube and enter the Roman Empire in A.D. 376; was defeated and killed by the Visigoths at Adrianople in A.D. 378.

Valentinian III Western Roman emperor, A.D. 425–455; responded ineffectively to Vandal attacks upon Italy.

Venus Roman goddess of persuasive seductions.

Virgil (70–19 B.C.) Roman epic poet; author of the *Aeneid*; Rome's greatest poet.

Visigoths Germanic people; came into the Roman Empire during the third and especially fourth centuries A.D., at the invitation of Emperor Valens (A.D. 328–378); eventually established the Visigothic kingdom in Gaul and Spain.

X

Xerxes King of Persia, 486–465 B.C.; led an unsuccessful invasion of Greece.

Z

Zarathustra See **Zoroaster**.

Zeus King of the Greek gods of Olympus.

Zoroaster (c. 630–553 B.C.) Persian prophet and religious leader; founder of Zoroastrianism. Also known as Zarathustra.

Index